The Book of Stallone

The Extraordinary Career of Sylvester Stallone

By Graham Clews

Copyright © 2025 by Graham Clews

All rights reserved. No part of this book may be used or reproduced by any means, graphic, electronic, or mechanical, including photocopying, recording, taping, or by any information storage retrieval system, without the written permission of the publisher except in the case of brief quotations embodied in critical articles and reviews.

eBook ISBN: 978-1-64667-049-9
Paperback ISBN: 978-1-64667-050-5
Hardback ISBN: 978-1-64667-051-2

For Katie and Emma

CONTENTS

INTRODUCTION 2

ROCKY (1976) 19

1978 - F.I.S.T. , PARADISE ALLEY 36

ROCKY II (1979) 44

1981 - NIGHTHAWKS, ESCAPE TO VICTORY 52

ROCKY III (1982) 61

FIRST BLOOD (1982) 70

1983 - 1984 - STAYING ALIVE, RHINESTONE 77

RAMBO: FIRST BLOOD PART 2 (1985) 86

ROCKY IV (1985) 93

1986 - 1987 COBRA, OVER THE TOP 103

RAMBO III - 1988 113

1989 - LOCK UP, TANGO AND CASH 120

ROCKY V (1990) 131

1991 - 1992 OSCAR, STOP! OR MY MOM WILL SHOOT ... 140

1993 - CLIFFHANGER, DEMOLITION MAN 150

1994 - 1995 - THE SPECIALIST,
    JUDGE DREDD, ASSASSINS 165

1996 - 1997 - DAYLIGHT, COP LAND 179

1998 - 2001 - ANTZ, GET CARTER, DRIVEN 187

2002 - 2003 - D-TOX (EYE SEE YOU), AVENGING ANGELO, SHADE, SPY KIDS 3D: GAME OVER 197

ROCKY BALBOA (2006) 206

RAMBO (2008) 216

2010 - 2013 - THE EXPENDABLES, ZOOKEEPER, THE EXPENDABLES 2, BULLET TO THE HEAD, ... 229

2013 - 2014 - ESCAPE PLAN, HOMEFRONT, GRUDGE MATCH, THE EXPENDABLES 3, REACH ME 241

CREED (2015) 255

2016 - 2018 - RATCHET AND CLANK, GUARDIANS OF THE GALAXY VOL 2, ANIMAL CRACKERS, ESCAPE PLAN 2: HADES 261

CREED II (2018) 267

RAMBO: LAST BLOOD (2019) 274

2018 - 2022 - BACKTRACE, ESCAPE PLAN: THE EXTRACTORS, THE SUICIDE SQUAD, SAMARITAN . 282

2023 - 2025 - CREED III, GUARDIANS OF THE GALAXY VOL 3, EXPEND4BLES, SLY, ARMOR, ALARUM, TULSA KING, THE FAMILY STALLONE 290

CONCLUSION 302

ABOUT THE AUTHOR 312

ROCKY BALBOA (2006) - WRITTEN BY SYLVESTER STALLONE

CUT TO INTERIOR. BACKSTAGE AT THE MANDALAY BAY HOTEL, LAS VEGAS AFTER THE PRE-FIGHT WEIGH-IN AND PRESS CONFERENCE. HEAVYWEIGHT WORLD CHAMPION MASON "THE LINE" DIXON ASKS TO SPEAK TO HIS OPPONENT, ROCKY, PRIVATELY…….

ROCKY BALBOA:
You know, a lot of people come to Vegas to lose. I didn't.

MASON DIXON:
It's already over.

ROCKY BALBOA:
Ain't nothin' over till it's over.

MASON DIXON:
What's that from? The '80s?

ROCKY BALBOA:
That's probably the '70s.

INTRODUCTION

Selling your pet dog to get enough money to eat and pay the rent that day is a fairly extreme point to reach in life. Sinking to that level of desperation is dramatic to say the least but anyone working in Hollywood would tell you that it would make for a decent plot point in a family movie screenplay with a heartwarming finale. How about if the birth of your child was complicated when the forceps being used during delivery accidentally severed a nerve causing a permanent paralysis on the left side of the baby's face? That could be spun out into a gritty script centering on a boy battling with stigma, then overcoming his insecurities and eventually becoming the poster boy for late twentieth century masculinity. Perhaps there's a comedy drama to be created which is set in the uncompromising 'Hell's Kitchen' neighbourhood of the New York City borough of Manhattan where two brothers grow up with an eccentric women's professional wrestling promoter as a mother and a hairdressing father with anger issues. Or most unrealistic of all, a frustrated writer and actor with no foot in the door of Hollywood, blackmails a major studio into allowing him to play the lead role in the movie he wrote about a blue-collar, Philadelphia native who gets a shot at boxing's world heavyweight title.

In the current age and overabundance of streaming platforms there have been a thousand worse premises that have been elongated into a ten-part season or a forgettable film. But, imagine going to Netflix, Apple TV or Disney Plus or one of the many others and during the pitch meeting you told them that all four scenarios above are part of the same narrative. They have the same lead character and there are plenty more twists and turns and bizarre incidents and side-stories to incorporate into the finished draft; there's the three marriages, the family tragedy, the arch rival, the soft porn, the restaurant business, the art and the perpetual comebacks. The Oscars won and the Oscars lost, the sequels, the body building, the writing and directing, the accidental action hero, the vast pay cheques, the roles that almost were and the roles that should never have been. And along the way he became the biggest movie star on the planet. More than half a century of unparalleled silver screen success which then branched into TV, wouldn't fit into a miniseries or a feature film. Maybe only in a book.

No actor's career, no actor's life has ever been comparable to Sylvester Stallone's. From his troubled birth on July 6th 1946 up until his 30th year, he was just one of thousands of stumbling artistic souls looking for an outlet. Painting, writing, acting…anything would do, especially if it would pay for dinner. He'd already survived childhood in regular foster care and coped with bitterly divorcing parents. At five, his immigrant father moved the family to Washington where Frank Stallone Sr. opened a beauty parlor chain after attending hairdressing school in New York and learning the trade that would put a roof over his kid's heads. Brother Frank was born three years after Sylvester but parental stability was to be short lived. Frank Sr. and astrologer Jaqueline Labofish had married for love but their clash of wills boiled over repeatedly. The pair worked hard to build a home but long hours and fiery fights meant the two boys often got shipped out to boarding houses and kept at arm's length. While his reputation as a hairdresser grew, Frank Sr. also held stifled dreams of acting and writing but his desire to perform largely stayed dormant aside from amateur fare and his writing consisted of wholly unpublished works. (His only professional acting credit turned out to be a 1992 episode of US TV show *The Fifth Corner* which only aired three episodes before being cancelled and his unnamed timekeeper role in *Rocky*. He published one novel in 2010 called *Stewart Lane*).

When the acrimonious divorce began he lived with his father in Maryland but his already tumultuous upbringing was affecting his ability to study and engage in education and he attended 13 different schools in 12 years. Jaqueline married Anthony Filti two years after divorcing Frank Sr. and Sylvester went to live with his mother and new step-father in Philadelphia where he was admitted into a high school that was calibrated for troubled youths. He scraped through graduation but quickly felt the need to escape and explore and enrolled in the American College of Switzerland. In the town of Leysin he earned some cash by selling hamburgers on campus and as a dorm bouncer and gym instructor. As the Vietnam War raged in South East Asia, Stallone discovered he enjoyed building his body and the attention of female students that came with it. On a whim, he auditioned for a role in an amateur staging of the Arthur Miller play *Death of a Salesman* and to his bemusement he was offered a part. He found he loved the craft, the process of acting, the interpreting of the dialogue and raw human emotion involved. Despite the low-fi production having only completed a few performances, he was casually approached by a visiting Harvard professor at the end of the show. The stranger singled him out to tell him he should pursue acting as a passion and a career. He had been considering the arts as an avenue since he loved painting, writing and reading but hadn't focused on anything up to that point. But crucially, as a younger child, he and his brother Frank had escaped the reality of their peculiar upbringing inside a cinema. They would watch everything that the spare change in their pockets would allow and quite often they would use nefarious means to sneak in undetected. Gazing up at that huge window into other worlds, Stallone was transfixed by what he saw and in particular, he responded to the strong male figures represented on the silver screen. James Cagney, John Wayne and Kirk Douglas became favourites but more than anyone else, he was enraptured by Steve Reeves. The Montana-born former body builder became an actor after military service and his uncommonly muscular physique saw him cast in fantasy epics. 1958's *Hercules* was Stallone's gateway into movie fandom and heroic idolisation and many of Reeves action scenes contain plenty of the DNA of Stallone's biggest physical performances on screen. His love of cinema grew as he grew and by the time he had the chance to explore the medium himself at college, he pursued it doggedly. He dove into drama and writing and instigated workshops and performance spaces whenever the creative opportunities arose. He returned to the U.S. to the University of Miami to officially study drama but despite not graduating, he'd found his passion and so the New York acting scene became his life.

Early on in his twenties, he ditched the stage name Mike Stallone and started using Sylvester E. Stallone when he occasionally found some acting jobs, mostly unpaid. His real middle name of Gardenzio didn't get a chance. He found love in the big apple while he forged a career path and he and his new girlfriend Sasha Czack moved into a tiny, one room apartment that should have been closed down by health inspectors. Sasha was also an aspiring actor and took on waitressing jobs to help keep a damp roof over their heads. Stallone himself took jobs as a zoo cleaner and theatre usher and when acting work still wasn't forthcoming he developed his love of writing. But with no major upturn in their fortunes, he couldn't say no to a $200 paycheck to be in a softcore porn flick called *Party at Kitty and Studs*. He would later claim that it was either take that job or rob someone on the streets, such was the low ebb that the pair found themselves at. The film was low-rent, unerotic drivel and only became notorious when Stallone became a star, it would otherwise be completely forgotten. But it was a job on screen as an actor and it extended his stubborn willingness to keep trying to break into the industry. His attempt to be an extra on the new film being made around town called *The Godfather* went nowhere but there were some modest moments to spark more dreams of hope. Playing a subway hoodlum in Woody Allens' *Bananas* was one. A blink and you'll miss his background appearance in the Barbara Streisand vehicle *What's Up, Doc* was another. Spot him if you can in *Klute* and also *Prisoner of Second Avenue* where Jack Lemmon confuses Stallone's unnamed character as a pickpocket. While none of these jobs were particularly inspiring or well compensated, he was gaining valuable experience of the industry and in particular, the nuances and hierarchy of working on film sets.

1974 presented a step in the right direction but he was a long way from climbing the most famous steps in movie history. He bagged one of the the main roles of Stanley in the 50's set comedy drama *Lords of Flatbush* where he met and became lifelong friends with fellow cast member Henry Winkler. The film plays as a curious time-capsule of post-war Americana, almost like watching *Grease* but without any music and choreography and it was part of a wave of 1950's nostalgia that swept mid-seventies America. The leather jackets, the oiled-back hair and the James Dean/Marlon Brando infected youth are all present and correct and there's a welcome flicker of hope and love woven into the slight story. Set in an area of

Brooklyn in New York known as Flatbush, Stallone played Stanley Rosiello who was part of a four-person, edge-of-adulthood gang filled out by Winkler, Perry King and Paul Mace. But in rehearsals, one of the four was a young actor named Richard Gere. The charismatic and intense 23-year old was well accustomed to the era the film was set in as he'd made a name for himself playing the lead role of Danny Zuko in the original 1973 Broadway smash-hit staging of *Grease*. And while he had secured this film role via his undeniable acting talent, Gere and Stallone clashed instantly. Stallone understood Gere's desire to remain in character throughout but felt he was a little too stringent in his approach. Things came to head during a break for lunch where the pair found themselves eating in the back of a Toyota. Despite a clear warning from his co-star, Gere bit into his chicken sandwich and dripped mustard on Stallone's leg. The response was an elbow to the head and Gere found himself pushed out of the stationary vehicle. Directing pair Martin Davidson and Stephen F. Verona decided not to embark on the time-sensitive, sparsely-funded filming schedule with this antagonism among the key cast and gave Gere his marching orders and he was replaced with Perry King at a few days' notice. (It's why you'll never see the pair in a film or even in the same room together to this day). Its low budget of under $400 thousand dollars was raised by private investors and borrowing heavily from friends and family of the filmmakers and scenes were reshot when those investors voiced concerns about plot-points and the original downbeat ending where the gang have all but been divided. The wedding party finale was hastily arranged and filmed and coupled with two stand-out scenes in the closing 20 minutes of the film (Stallone's Stanley reluctantly buys an engagement ring for girlfriend Frannie played by Maria Smith and also Stanley's monologue about fostering his imagination) it would be easy to think Stallone was the first name on the call sheet despite King receiving top billing. *Lords of Flatbush* more than recouped its budget with a box office haul of close to $4 million dollars and a potential sequel called *Flatbush Abroad* (where Stallone's Stanley and bride Frannie would travel to Europe) was planned by Columbia Pictures but never got past the idea stage. *Lords of Flatbush* is a peculiar film to watch in the 21st century as its narrative is loose to say the least and it plays more like a mood piece or a Pinterest page for 50's rebellion. Only in the final third does a semblance of plot really develop but then that is abandoned as the end credits are imminent. Watching a pre-fame Stallone does make a viewing worthwhile and there are hints at what was to come but ultimately however, it didn't catapult Stallone into the Hollywood elite.

Lords of Flatbush was released in 1974 at a time when Stallone's Italian American heritage was already well represented in the cinema; Al Pacino was on a hot run of *Scarecrow, Serpico* and *The Godfather Part II* and Robert De Niro had broken through with *Mean Streets* and that same, second installment of *The Godfather*. The upside was that it was his first major film role and it had been a reasonable hit but Stallone had to watch as his career remained in neutral while Winkler followed *Lords of Flatbush* with the first episode of a new sitcom. Also set in the 1950's and also involving a leather jacket, the show called *Happy Days* would propel Winkler to iconic levels of global fame as the uber-cool, finger-clicking Arthur Fonzarelli, better known the world over as The Fonz. Perry King came close to global fame himself within 18 months as he was one of the last handful of actors being considered for the part of Han Solo in *Star Wars*. When the film role went to Harrison Ford, King did still get to be Solo in the radio adaptation of *Star Wars* and its subsequent audio sequels. And in a curious portent of the future, in the scene where Stallone's Stanley is berating Kings' character Chico for not having an open mind, Stanley jokingly refers to him as legendary boxer "Rocky Marciano".

But soon enough, Stallone had to resign himself to watching from the sidelines again and getting more supporting roles that utilised his broad physique in films such as *Farewell, My Lovely* and *Capone*. That was until he was given another shot at a sizable part in the violent, action satire *Death Race 2000* which became a cult favourite. Produced by famed low-budget, cheap-thrill, tongue-in-cheek legend Roger Corman and directed by Paul Bartel, *Death Race 2000* is set in a dystopian future where mass entertainment is provided by a televised coast to coast car race in which points are scored by killing innocent pedestrians along the way; women score 10 points more than men, teens are 40 points, children under twelve score 70 and anyone over 75 years of age is a 100 point bonus. Stallone gets to play the unstable villain Joe "The Machine Gun" Viterbo opposite the mercurial David Carradine. The Los Angeles born actor was enjoying huge fame as the star of TV's *Kung Fu* as the half-Chinese Shaolin monk who gets embroiled in weekly, episodic action. The series became iconic for birthing the moniker "Grasshopper" as a term of reference for any mentor figure for generations to come. In *Death Race 2000*, the wafer-thin Carradine plays the anti-hero Frankenstein who is clad in leather from head to toe, including mask, for the majority of the movie and his slight figure is exacerbated further in his scenes directly opposite Stallone. The pair have a fist fight midway through the film and the viewer must take a huge leap of faith to believe Carradine's fragile frame could overcome and beat the future Rambo. Working wonders considering the $500 thousand dollar budget, *Death Race 2000* achieves the shock value it aimed for and there's plenty of acutely observed satire in the same vein as Steven King's *The Running Man* that would be published in 1982 and turned into an early Arnie starrer in 1987. Stallone himself lets loose with a brash, comedic bad-guy turn that just stops short of cartoon-like despite the obvious inspiration from the long-running 60's animated series *Wacky Races*. It grossed $5 million dollars at the box office but, like *Lords of Flatbush,* it didn't prompt a torrent of offers and he had to accept one-episode TV roles again, on the likes of *Police Story* and *Kojak*.

But then on the 24th of March 1975, with $106 to his name, he needed a break from the drudgery and used some priceless cash on a ticket to watch a boxing match broadcast live onto the screen in a local movie theatre. Not just any fight, but the world heavyweight title fight between Muhammed Ali and Chuck Wepner in Ohio. The bout was won by Ali, but it was notable for a couple of other things; it included the rare sight of the legendary "Greatest of All Time" being knocked down and the unfancied and unfancy Wepner standing toe-to-toe with Ali for the full fifteen bruising, bloody rounds. It sparked something in the increasingly frustrated actor. He went straight back to his leaky apartment and started writing. He blocked out the windows with old newspapers, he didn't eat and he ignored time while focused creativity poured out of him and onto the page. Three days later and with his 30th birthday around the corner, he had created "the best friend I ever had".

It's one of the greatest watershed moments in Hollywood history and what followed next is legendary. He was about to break free from his existence as one of thousands of struggling actors looking for their break in New York. He was soon to be a star and then a superstar of the silver screen and his overnight rise to prominence would coincide with a shift in the dynamics of Hollywood and the movie business. The same year that *Death Race 2000* had been a quiet underground hit, 1975's *Jaws* had changed the entire game as Steven Spielberg's three-men-in-a-boat story set new benchmarks for what studio bosses could now hope for in terms of income. Its $260 million dollar worldwide gross in its original release smashed every record and from then on it was the requirement of all movies to be not just big, but huge. A hit was now nothing to do with critics and awards, it was about generating vast sums of profit. In 1977, the dollar signs in the movie executives' eyes grew even bigger as they watched millions roll in for *Star Wars* and *Close Encounters of the Third Kind*. With *Superman* about to fly along with the *Star Wars* sequels and *Raiders of the Lost Ark* and *ET* approaching too, the latter years of the 70's and into the 80's were a world away from the downbeat, real world dramas that had occupied cinema goers in the preceding years.

Stallone was indeed the right person in the right place at the right time. He created one cinematic beast in his desperate hour but he then developed another when he needed one most: a war veteran with coping issues. And while he enjoyed hits and sequels with other properties such as *The Expendables* and *Escape Plan*, if you ask an average movie fan to name two Stallone characters, we all know which they will be. Rocky and Rambo represent a very unique double act. Try to think of another cinematic presence that has two iconic, yet wildly different characters. The biggest movie stars commonly have one role or one type of character that they are indelibly linked to whether they like it or not. For example, take Stallone's former business partners in the restaurant chain Planet Hollywood. Bruce Willis's long career may have begun in comedy in TV's *Moonlighting* and involved landmark films such as *Pulp Fiction* and *The Sixth Sense* but he is and forever will be John McClane in the *Die Hard* franchise. Stallone's one-time mortal enemy turned close friend Arnold Schwarzenegger starred in some of the biggest grossing movies of the 90's such as *Total Recall* and *True Lies* but he could never and will never shake the image of *The Terminator*. Christopher Reeve is the immortal *Superman*. Robert Downey Jr became *Iron Man* and everything else was forgotten. Michael J Fox really only went *Back to the Future* three times and Will Smith's greatest hits are when he plays Will Smith. The more lauded type of actor such as Daniel Day Lewis, Robert DeNiro, Al Pacino, Meryl Streep and Dustin Hoffman are known for their body of work rather than one, specific career-defining part. They have all been in extraordinary projects and been rightly showered with awards but if the question of naming their best character pops up, a long winded discussion will ensue.

How about Keanu Reeves or Tom Cruise? Mr Reeves delivered iconography by the truck load in *The Matrix* and did it again with *John Wick*. But both his lead characters are in action films where the fighting styles are as significant as the plot and both have an affinity for the colour black when they go clothes shopping. Tom Cruise almost single-handedly resuscitated a struggling movie industry as the Covid pandemic finally relented with *Top Gun: Maverick* and his *Mission: Impossible* franchise, but as brilliant as his output is they are still Tom Cruise movies where his extraordinary watchability and dedication to his craft makes the need for him to play anyone but himself irrelevant.

Perhaps only Harrison Ford shares the Stallone two-card trick. He's Han Solo and he's also Indiana Jones. Both left an irreplaceable mark on the silver screen and both come under the heading 'iconic'. But drill a bit deeper and really, the two characters share many of the same traits. His space smuggler rogue and his archeologist adventurer both openly show fear of specific things, they both can get sidetracked by a beautiful woman and they both end up fighting to do the right thing with more than a hint of reluctance thrown in. (Stallone does share one bit of history with Ford, as they are the only two actors to have starred in box office number one films over six consecutive decades)

Maybe the more modern cinematic star isn't going to throw up a Rocky and Rambo facsimile after all then, so how about classic Hollywood? John Wayne, who is often cited as Stallone's predecessor in terms of cinematic presence, only ever played John Wayne. Stars were pigeon-holed to an even greater extent in the so-called Golden Age of Movies. Gene Kelly and Fred Astaire were never going to be offered the chance to play a drug-addicted gambler. Shirley Temple's career ended when she had the audacity to not be a child any more. When James Cagney turned his hand to being a gangster, he could kiss goodbye to those years of training in musical theatre and early roles and as a song and dance man.

Robert Redford, Paul Newman, Burt Reynolds, Clint Eastwood..the list continues. They found what worked as an onscreen persona but the moment they tried to deviate from what audiences and studios expected from them, they came crashing back down to earth until they succumbed to type.

But Rocky and Rambo, they are polar opposite characters. Where one is considerate and often has verbal diarrhoea, the other is angry and monosyllabic. Rocky loves to love while Rambo wants to hide away with his personal demons. From 1976, people shouted

"Rocky!" at Stallone across the street, instead of his real name as he was so identifiable as the soft-hearted big hitter. In his first six films that followed 1976's *Rocky*, he hardly carried a weapon on screen at all and was not destined for action hero status. He packed a gun as standard in the cop thriller *Nighthawks* and briefly in both *Escape to Victory* and at the end of *F.I.S.T.* but he was an actors' actor, trying different roles in different genres. He was an in-demand performer who was building up a CV of varying films in which he could explore characters. His Oscar nomination for *Rocky* carried some licence for him to experiment with his choices but then he made *First Blood* and his career path became something very different. From then on (with few exceptions) for many years he created, crafted and perfected the new phenomenon of the Action Hero. But watching any of the Rambo films, it's impossible to see any of Rocky in there. Even with his most recognizable of face's, the two characters are two totally different human beings. The way he stands, the way he walks, the way he stares, the way he communicates, the way he intimidates - Rambo is as far from Rocky as a male actor could get. Yet inexplicably and uniquely, audiences accepted it. They accepted and embraced an actor as intensely for that role as they did for his breakout character.

Both characters are now by-words for real life situations or events. Many journalists remain loyal to using the 'rags to riches *Rocky* story' as an intro to an upbeat sporting tale or alternatively, news reports of a mass shooting will more often than not unfortunately include the phrase '*Rambo*-like'. Boxing as a sport wholeheartedly embraced Stallone and the *Rocky* myth and many boxers themselves cite those movies as their inspiration to get in the ring rather than actual real-world fighters. And in terms of box-office in the sport, agents and promoters are always trying to find a 'real life

Rocky' knowing that the similarities with the fictional character will bring in the fans, the media and the cash. Simultaneously, anyone who gets a little over aggressive in a social situation, dresses in combat-type clothing or is carrying a weapon, will at some point be temporarily nicknamed 'Rambo' by friends and enemies alike. Stories of extraordinary feats of courage and bravery in a warzone can often include the phrase "and then he went all Rambo". Every new instalment of Rocky or Rambo was released when Stallone felt he had a new story to tell or his career longevity was precarious. He returned to his two unbreakable masks when his personal life or the real world (or both) instigated inspiration to extend their stories. Twice in his career, he provided new Rocky and new Rambo in the same year. He dominated 1982 with *Rocky III* and *First Blood* and then did it again (to even bigger box office returns) in 1985 with *Rambo: First Blood Part 2* and *Rocky IV*.

So, it's with that incredible one-two punch of *Rocky* and *Rambo* that I have anchored this book with individual chapters for each film in those series. As they are the lynchpin of his remarkable and lengthy resume it would feel remiss not to extend those films special, solo treatment. But fear not, we will look at every movie in the Stallone filmography, many of which I class as my favourites outside of R and R. The likes of *Cliffhanger, Demolition Man, Tango and Cash, Lock Up, Daylight, Bullet To The Head* and yes even *Oscar*, come out favourably with this author. We were sucked in by brand-Stallone enough to go and see the none-more-eighties *Cobra* and *Over the Top* but how do they fare in the cold light of day around 40 years later? Is *Stop, Or My Mom Will Shoot* a misunderstood gem or is it as horrific a misstep as Stallone himself freely suggests? We will dive into what some critics consider his best performance in a non-*Rocky* film, *Cop Land,* where he more than holds his own against those gilded types of Robert DeNiro, Ray Liotta and Harvey Keitel. We will look at his more recent movie fare and the questionable direct-to-streaming choices he has been making in the 2020's. His dipping of his muscular big toe into the world of superheroes with DC (*The Suicide Squad*) and Marvel (*Guardians of the Galaxy Vol. 2*) and his own, almost caped crusader (*Samaritan*). And speaking of streaming services, we can't and shouldn't ignore the success of Stallone's first real forays into the world of television with the enjoyably outrageous *Tulsa King* and his inevitable addition to the reality TV market with *The Family Stallone*.

My original aim in writing this book was for it to be the book that I wanted to read. It's not the first book about him and won't be the last and everything that follows is readily available information. Some of the titbits of production you may already be aware of but I hope there are many more that raise your eyebrow and make you chuckle on the beach, on your sofa or wherever you find yourself now. I want it to feel definitive and comprehensive but it's more than likely I have missed some things that a Stallone-devotee would consider crucial information or vital background and in those cases I can only apologise and hope you read on in the spirit that this was intended. This is an appreciation and thank you to my favourite movie star that tries to bring together all the scattered information, facts and figures and inside stories that fairly represent his first 50 years as a legend. The high highs and the low lows that really began in 1976 and are still going strong now. The next time you intentionally or unintentionally find yourself watching one of his films, maybe you'll remember something about the production, the release and the impact of it to the world and to Stallone himself. This book has tried to be the one-stop shop for everything Stallone so it's part encyclopedia, part backstage gossip and part review of his entire back catalogue to date but neither one of those aspects should outweigh the other.

What should also be noted is that in the course of writing, I have watched every single movie again in the harsh reality of the mid-2020's. Obviously some of the choices and attitudes seen on screen in his films, especially pre the turn of the century, could be problematic to the more sensitive, modern day viewer. More positive and inclusive perspectives on race, gender and sexuality are all developed further as we move through the decades. But it's also about changing creative styles. The 90-minute blockbuster that was such a staple of the multiplex's in the 1980's has made way for popcorn movies that tap-out around the 3 hour mark in the present day. The long-form, 10-episode seasons on the streaming platforms have affected movies too and filmmakers now feel a pressure to have longer running times in a bid to create a prestige buzz around their efforts. As a result, when you watch films from before 2000 they can feel quick and almost rushed. Some can feel simplistic with their visuals and cinematography and character development is sometimes jarringly abrupt. (Conversely, a lot of modern films could learn lessons from the brevity of effective storytelling before 20th Century Fox became 21st Century Fox.) I've tried to take this all into account and any criticisms I make should mostly be viewed as unrelated to when I watched the film most recently.

One thing though, I don't refer to him as 'Sly' throughout this book. It seems like that's something you are allowed to do upon meeting him and/or befriending him. It means that if a future re-issue of this book comes out where every 'Stallone' has been replaced with a 'Sly', you know I've died and gone to heaven.

So, sit back and prepare to go the distance with the wildest movie career of them all. The hits and the flops, the so-called career killers and the comeback classics. Let's run up those steps (68 of them, fact fans) with Bill Conti ringing in our ears and lay waste to a few hundred extra's in a jungle or desert somewhere.

And heading back to the middle of the 1970's, after the bit parts, the false starts, the knockbacks, the hunger and the desperation, we begin with that before-and-after moment cinema history that he willed into existence by himself. The low budget movie about a small-time debt collector in Philadelphia who also does some boxing and quite likes the shy girl that works in the local pet shop…..

ROCKY (1976)

HIS WHOLE LIFE WAS A MILLION-TO-ONE SHOT

Starring - Sylvester Stallone, Talia Shire, Burt Young, Carl Weathers, Burgess Meredith
Written by - Sylvester Stallone
Original Score by - Bill Conti
Directed by - John G. Avildsen

The story behind the story of *Rocky* is mythical for a reason because it just shouldn't and just doesn't happen this way. No-one who has zero influence in the industry has ever managed to convince a major studio to resist adding a bankable leading man to the script they want to produce and instead to allow an untested, unfamiliar, unconventional actor take the main part that has over a million dollars of production resting on them. Let alone the same man who wrote the screenplay and has already been offered life-changing sums to hand over the script and leave them to it.

As principal photography began on *Rocky* in the first weeks of 1976, the ultimately uplifting tale was certainly going to go against the grain. As filming would progress, cinemas were presenting a series of very un-uplifting stories. A depressing view of contemporary 70's life was being reflected in *Marathon Man, All The President's Men, Network* and *Taxi Driver*. Conspiracy and deception were everywhere and governments and big business couldn't be trusted. Lone figures who attempted to fight the system were usually expelling their dying breath as the end credits rolled or at the very least, they were having to accept the world order and that there was nothing they could do to change the status quo.

So the fact that United Artists accepted the blackmail from Stallone to star in a movie that had a positive, life-affirming ending is both surprising and reassuring. At the time, Stallone was being represented by Film Artists Management Enterprises (FAME) who had bagged him the *Lords of Flatbush* and *Death Race 2000* gigs and when they read the script that had taken just three days to sculpt, they saw the potential immediately. It was a simple tale of a down on his luck Philadelphian who has fallen for the shyest girl in town and is handed the offer of the lifetime; a one-time shot at the World Heavyweight Championship. Winning the fight wasn't an objective but winning some self-respect after 30-odd years of scraping a living, meant everything. The plot wasn't wholly original but the screenplay by S. Stallone was. It infused intense realism with aspiration. All the characters had flaws and three dimensions and they each had journeys to go on. The central figure of Robert "Rocky" Balboa was the most flawed of them all. In the opening scenes he would be seen to lose control in a backstreet boxing match and play mob-enforcer to a dock worker who owed cash. His quiet attempts at humanity would often remain unresolved and on occasion, cause him emotional damage. A scene that remained virtually untouched from the original draft plays out at 2 and a half minutes in the finished film. Walking through those cold, tightly packed streets, Rocky spots a young girl called Marie. He knows her brother and suggests he walks her home rather than let her hang around the liquor store with guys twice her age. On their trek to her home, Rocky offers life-advice of a relatable nature, suggesting his own mistakes can be avoided and choosing better friends might be a good place to start. Finally arriving at her family's front door, little Marie (played by Jodi Letizia in the movie) departs into the house with the parting shot of "Screw you, creepo!". Rocky is dejected, hurt and rightly feeling a little betrayed. Its scenes like those that made *Rocky* stand-out as a screenplay and those who read it, felt the lure towards the ultimately joyous finale.

His pitch meeting with producers Irwin Winkler and Robert Chartoff had been going ok as they had shown some interest in a period comedy-drama script he had written about three brothers trying to make a living in post-war New York (eventually made as *Paradise Alley*) but as he got up to leave, he was asked if he had anything else. Fiercely protective of his *Rocky* story but sensing he needed to pique their interest further, he said yes, he did have another script to show them. He pulled out his drafted screenplay from his bag and dropped it on their desk. Winkler responded favourably to the brief summarisation that Stallone offered and when he had finished reading the full script, Winkler instinctively knew it was something special. They called Stallone back to their office and instantly offered to buy the film from him. Like Stallone's agents had also felt originally, the producers saw the potential as a star vehicle for one of the many established male leads of the time; Burt Reynolds, Robert Redford, James Caan, Ryan O'Neil were all mooted (and initially contacted). But the emotional bond Stallone had with this story made things very different as he had written it with himself in mind as the lead. Frustrated with trying to fit himself into other people's projects, he reasoned that if he wanted the perfect role, he had to create it himself. Further meetings ensued and a bidding battle began with Chartoff and Winkler upping their offers to have full control over *Rocky* while Stallone and his FAME agents, Craig T. Rumar and Larry Kubik, stood firm and insisted only he could embody that lead role and only he could deliver the performance he had written.

The producers and studio United Artists continued their search for their leading man while the heated negotiations continued, finally offering a staggering $300,000 for Stallone to sell them the script and walk away. But as Stallone persisted, they eventually started to imagine the writer as the fighter. Stallone's enthusiasm and self-confidence was infectious and after numerous follow-up meetings that then became unofficial and then official auditions and then screen tests and promises, Chartoff and Winkler's hands were finally offered on a deal for Sylvester Stallone to star in *Rocky*. But any agreement came with a wealth of caveats and provisions, including the budget which was to be kept to an almost cripplingly low sum of just over $1 million dollars. For comparison, Clint Eastwood's third film as no-nonsense cop Dirty Harry, *The Enforcer*, had a $9 million dollar price tag in the same year. There were other guarantees made as well which included the producers having the right to look at the dailies and the rushes whenever they wanted and if the studio bosses were not happy with Stallone's interpretation of the character, they would immediately replace him with one of their established and available choices and re-film what had been done so far. They offered Stallone a flat fee of $35,000 dollars to cover his writing and acting plus a percentage of the profits should the film eventually scrape more than its budget back. With that take it or leave offer on the table, Stallone took it.

With *Rocky* now greenlit and its star precariously in place, casting got underway in earnest. One of the significant figures in the film would be the character of Adrian Pennino and her chemistry with Stallone would be key to the success or failure of the emotional core. Auditions were held with producers Winkler and Chartoff, director John G Avildsen (who had previously helmed *Joe* in 1970 and *Save the Tiger* with Jack Lemmon in 1973) and Stallone himself all in attendance. Dozens of young actresses read the lines opposite Stallone and Carrie Snodgress came closest to the image in the writer's mind. Snodgress had won acclaim and an Academy Award nomination for her performance in the comedy drama *Diary of a Mad Housewife* in 1970 and her audition was deemed superior to Susan Sarandon, Kathy Bates and Cher, who all also came to try out for the part. But the slimline budget meant that Snodgress was offered a slimline salary and she turned it down almost immediately. After she rejected the meagre counter offers and walked away from the film, it was back to square one again as *Rocky* without Adrian wasn't an option. Talia Rose Coppola grew up in Queens, New York and was already well known as the increasingly hard-edged sister of Michael Corleone (Al Pacino) in *The Godfather* and *The Godfather Part II*. Despite being the sister of the director Francis Ford Coppola she had gotten the role in *The Godfather* almost without him knowing and there was friction early on in the shoot when the siblings began filming. But soon matters were smoothed over and her work on *The Godfather Part II* earned her a Best Supporting Actress Oscar nomination. But it also caught the eye of Sylvester Stallone who asked her to come and audition despite her short hair and glasses appearance being the opposite of how he had pictured Adrian. Talia Coppola was now Talia Shire after marrying composer David Shire and it was her new husband that encouraged her to go to the audition after hearing himself that the production was despairing of finding its leading lady. When she arrived at the meeting, she found the director and producers sitting behind a table but the leading man was jogging around the room to warm up for the scene. As soon as the pair locked eyes and began to read lines, it was clear that they had found Rocky's true love and she was offered the role. Another native of Queens was cast as the drunk, abusive brother of Adrian and best friend of Rocky's, Paulie Peninno. Former U.S. Marine Burt Young was gaining traction as a unique character actor in *Chinatown* and *The Gambler* and as a former boxer as well, he knew the world they were creating. But while Young wouldn't be required to perform any boxing in *Rocky*, the search for heavyweight champion Apollo Creed became exhausting. The part written was imbued with the spirit of Muhammed Ali but after witnessing more than a hundred auditions, the filmmakers were now loosening their parameters of what they would accept. That was until Carl Weathers walked into the room at 10pm one night. The 6ft 2 inch former professional footballer had only started pursuing acting seriously the year before after retiring from the NFL. His stature and charisma was never in question from the moment he stepped into view but auditions are the proving ground. He was introduced to the writer and the pair began to run the lines in front of the producers and director. After a few minutes of the audition, Weathers stopped proceedings and claimed he could do a better performance with a real actor opposite him, rather than just the movie's writer. At this point, Stallone revealed himself to not only be the writer but the star also and while a moment of awkwardness ensued, they knew they had found Apollo Creed. Burgess Meredith's film career had begun in 1935, before any of his *Rocky* co-stars were born, with an uncredited role in Noel Cowards' *The Scoundrel* but he garnered early acclaim for his performance in the 1939 version of the classic *Of Mice and Men*. After hundreds of film jobs he gained household recognition on TV by playing The Penguin in the camp and colourful 60's series *Batman*. But in 1976 he still had to audition for most of his potential film work and it was no different on *Rocky*. The filmmakers had asked to see famed acting teacher Lee Strasburg but didn't feel his audition was gruff enough. Lee J Cobb was also on their radar, having achieved TV fame as the star of western series *The Virginian* and prominent roles in all-time classics *On The Waterfront* and *12 Angry Men*. Cobb came to the audition room but refused to read lines, saying his career was his audition and the producers sensed trouble ahead. But when Meredith walked in, his infectious energy coupled with his pitch-perfect line-reading sealed his offer to play trainer Mickey Goldsmith.

The origin story of Rocky Balboa took inspiration from the Ali v Wepner title fight, but nothing more. Whether you believe *Rocky* is a love story that also has some boxing in it, or it's a boxing film with a romance attached at the sides is largely irrelevant as the viewer takes from the film whatever they want to. What Stallone took from Wepner's stubborn display in the ring against the greatest fighter of them all was resilience. It's a word that is never spoken in the screenplay, but it defines the character throughout the original film and the next seven times he appeared on the big screen.

Rocky tells the story of a sympathetic debt collector struggling to make headway in his world and juggling working on behalf of a local loan shark with his untapped talent in the boxing rings of Philadelphia. Even though he boxes by night they are small, backstreet bouts with small, backstreet winnings. Seemingly, the only light in his life is the painfully shy girl who works in the pet shop opposite the gym he goes to. Rocky's conversations with Adrian (Talia Shire) are awkward and involve no eye contact and little else but waffle from the smitten Rocky. At the gym run by snarling Mickey (Burgess Meredith), Rocky trains and occasionally helps out with menial tasks. He can't afford gym membership but he tries to earn his spot with labor on request. As the romance between Rocky and Adrian begins to blossom, albeit painfully slowly and despite the interference of Adrian's brother and Rocky's best friend, Paulie (Burt Young), a once in a lifetime opportunity presents itself. The reigning heavyweight champion of the world Apollo Creed (Carl Weathers) is in danger of not fighting any time soon as his expected next opponent has had to pull out. Looking for inspiration in a who's who book of local fighters, he stumbles across the nickname 'The Italian Stallion'. Instantly seeing some marketing potential with the fight set for Thanksgiving Day, he instructs his people to get whoever the Italian Stallion is to sign a fight contract. Creed insists he will give the crowd a good show before knocking the amateur out, as and when he pleases. Rocky initially says no, immediately sensing the potential to be humiliated on TV in front of millions. Reluctantly though, the promise of a monetary windfall and the support of now-girlfriend Adrian sees him change his mind and he accepts the fight. He trains half-heartedly alone and without much direction until one evening when Mickey approaches him at his fleapit apartment, to ask if he can train him properly. This is where Stallone unleashes a scene of such intensity, it must have been the clip that ensured he was nominated for an Oscar. Rocky rejects the old man, reasoning that Mickey has never helped him before but now there's some money floating around, he's suddenly interested. As a deflated Mickey shuffles out of the apartment, Rocky lets everything out. With the line between character and actor blurred, Stallone/Rocky vents by yelling and slamming his fist into the bathroom door and screaming his despair about how his life stinks, his apartment stinks and how he doesn't need anyone. And then in a first sign that all is not lost, a brief silence is followed by the sight of Rocky running out of his apartment to catch the dejected Mickey, make amends and shake hands on a training partnership.

It's here that the gritty, chilly 70's movie ends and we get something unusually buoyant for the times. Up to this point Bill Conti's score has been mostly mournful piano and lonely cello's but now we are going to train and audiences around the country felt their heartbeats increase as a fanfare that is now as familiar as anything ever used in film, started up. Rocky runs through the train yard, through the park, along the docks and through the busy market place (the orange that was thrown to him by a trader was completely unplanned as the market workers had no idea why an unfamiliar guy was being filmed running) Rocky sweats and runs faster and the brassy music builds. Official permits were often difficult and expensive to attain so cast and crew would have to jump out of the van, set up the shot, film it and jump back in and drive off before authorities caught them. Eventually, Rocky rounds a corner and ahead of him now are the vast stone steps leading up to the Philadelphia Art Museum. Earlier in the film, he'd abandoned the steps ascent due a stitch and lack of belief but now with Adrian in his heart and Mickey in his corner, he bounces up to the summit as *Gonna Fly Now* hits its crescendo. More than the performances, the writing, the optimism, the final fight and the romantic epilogue, it's this scene that afforded Stallone a career in the cinema.

William Conti was born in Rhode Island and graduated from the Louisiana State University School of Music before earning a masters degree with honours from the acclaimed Juilliard School of Music. Aside from coordinating Italian pop music recordings he also found lucrative work ghost writing the scores for spaghetti westerns. The *Rocky* producers had already approached established composers (including Talia Shire's husband, David) but their unappealing offer was a flat salary of only $25,000 dollars and the composer had to pay for his own musicians, studio costs and the recording tape itself. There was the possibility of a dividend payout if the movie was a hit, but that was unlikely so when they eventually approached Conti, he had to accept the financial risk. The actual *Gonna Fly Now* track was in fact a cobbled together product of director and composer interaction. Avildsen asked Conti to write some music for a 30 second training montage, but then the director kept calling him back and asking for it to be another 30 seconds longer and then another 30 seconds because the training footage he was filming was too good to edit down to just half a minute. With costs so tight, Conti booked the Hollywood recording studio for just three hours and he and the 39 musicians, including six trumpet players, managed to get the entire 30 minute score on tape before the studio kicked them out. When time came to record *Gonna Fly Now* itself, Conti realised he had written choral lyrics but he had no singers. He phoned his wife who worked at local radio station KHJ and asked her to bring over any colleagues who could hold a tune. In their lunch break, Conti's wife Shelby and four work friends taxied over to the studio and sang his seemingly random words: *Trying hard now. It's so hard now. Trying hard now. Getting strong now. Won't be long now. Getting strong now. Gonna fly now. Flying high now. Gonna fly, fly.* Following the recording, Conti thanked the makeshift group and apologised for not being able to pay them anything. They all then went back to work as normal, assuming it would never see the light of day.

Aside from that music, the sequence would also hugely benefit visually thanks to new technology. The tight budget meant that hiring a helicopter to film Rocky's run from the air was out of the question, but Avildsen still wanted the audience to feel the momentum of the moment. Strapping the camera to the van was going to achieve plenty of the desired sensation but it relied on flat roads and even paths. Going up the steps was intended to be the big climax of the montage, but it was assumed that it could only be captured by stationary cameras positioned at the bottom, halfway and the top and the flowing movement of the sequence up to that point would have to be sacrificed to see Rocky reach the summit of the cement, metaphorical mountain. But not too far away inventor Garret Brown had designed and built a new system that he was testing in New Jersey called the Steadicam. His invention kept a camera lens free from shaking and wobbling even when moving at a rapid pace. The system involved a balanced harness that compensated for jarring movements leaving the filmed footage looking smooth and graceful. Brown had been employed a few weeks earlier on Hal Ashby's movie *Bound for Glory* but Avilsden heard about Garret's design and asked him to test it further on *Rocky*. If the footage didn't come out well, they wouldn't use it and they would stick with the traditional filming methods they were employing anyway. Garret made one rehearsal run up the steps and gave Avildsen the thumbs up and minutes later, he was following Stallone up the same steps and the results were startling and pure cinematic gold. Watching Rocky's triumphant run up those steps with Bill Conti reaching his climax remains one of the defining moments in film history and it's no surprise that Stallone recreated this moment in one form or another in every subsequent *Rocky* story.

After the euphoria of the training sequence, the big fight between Creed and Balboa is a choreographed dance of a most violent nature. Stallone and Weathers trained and rehearsed for months to reproduce every punch, jab and reaction that was now written in detail into the script. Boxing movies previously (and inexplicably, still most boxing movies afterwards) didn't bother to define each precise movement and the onscreen results were consistently underwhelming. Actors were told to "throw a few shots here" and "swipe at each other over there" which deflated any intended intensity. For *Rocky*, it wasn't going to be left to chance and the writer and director were determined that every punch had to mean something emotionally. The two actors needed to know exactly what strike was coming next, to react to it realistically and allow the director to get the best possible angle on the action. The exhaustive weeks of rehearsal between Weathers and Stallone meant that when they got to the empty, 8,000 seat Los Angeles Grand Olympic Auditorium (standing in for Philadelphia) they had muscle memory of every stage of the fight. The pair worked on the choreography for weeks in a Santa Monica gym with Avildsen filming much of the rehearsals so everyone involved could forensically decide what would look better on screen. In the vast auditorium itself, they filmed each round three times; once with cameras outside the ring, once with cameras inside the ropes and once again with Garret Brown and his Steadicam circling them. To try and give a sense of a packed-out arena, Avildsen relied on plenty of Hollywood sleight of hand. Art director James Spencer had most of the venue lights turned off except for those illuminating the ring and hung Christmas lighting halfway up the empty seating to give the illusion of depth. He also had crew members walk in front of the open entrance ways to the seating to make it seem as though a sell-out crowd was constantly moving. The sparse number of extras plus every available crew member (and family member) was moved around the arena to sit wherever the camera was pointing at the time. Stallone's estranged father is the uncredited bell ringer. The original ending filmed had Rocky surviving all 15 rounds and still on his feet but Apollo winning by judges decision. Apollo was then held aloft by his adoring fans while Rocky and Adrian would quietly exit hand in hand through the parking lot. That image is the one used on the now famous poster campaign but it never saw the inside of a cinema screen. Two months after filming the fight and that ending, Avildsen and Stallone called crew members back and recreated the furore in the ring after the final bell. Feeling as though their original ending was too long and labored, they now had Adrian struggling to eventually reach Rocky inside the ring with chaos all around, the pair confessing their love for each other there and then and their embrace providing the freeze-frame that the movie ends on. The filmmakers agreed that this moment was the pinnacle of Rocky's humble life and the film should end right there with them.

The original parking lot ending was unfortunately lost in a fire so the iconic poster is the only evidence of its existence.

Despite only commencing production in January of 1976, the finished movie was released in cinemas in New York on 21st of November that same year with Los Angeles showing the film from December the 1st. The night before the movie opened in New York, Stallone and brother Frank went to visit the Paramount Theatre where the word ROCKY was now displayed above the entrance. It was coincidentally the movie theatre where he had earned minimum wage as an usher only a few years before. Sensing the enormity of the occasion, Frank told his brother that the next day would either be the best of his life or the worst. If *Rocky* did decent business, he would have a career and income but if it tanked, he would never get another shot like it ever again. The preview screenings had not gone well and Stallone was convinced he was going to be humiliated on opening night. But as the movie began, the audience's murmuring quickly silenced and everyone was transfixed and absorbed by what unfolded in front of them. Some spontaneous applause broke out during the 'Gonna Fly Now' sequence and then during the first round of the fight itself, people began cheering and shouting at the screen. The cinema became a sports venue and the crowd were responding to the film as if they were watching a real, title fight. Over the next few days, similar stories were being recounted at every screening and soon newspapers and TV stations were reporting on the extraordinary reactions to this little, low budget movie.

Around the same time, studios were expecting big returns from other releases such as *Carrie* co-starring a young John Travolta, the train-based comedy with Gene Wilder and Richard Pryor called

Silver Streak, Peter Sellers' latest Inspector Clouseau effort *Pink Panther Strikes Again* and a new big budget *King Kong* with Jeff Bridges (who had also been suggested as a possible Rocky Balboa). But on release, *Rocky* instantly knocked them all out. It grossed $5 million dollars on its opening weekend and went on to earn $117 million in North America which is roughly half a billion dollars in today's money. It finished its initial worldwide run on $225 million, making it the highest grossing film of 1976 and the second highest of 1977 behind only *Star Wars - A New Hope.* For Stallone personally, his $35,000 dollar paycheck paled into insignificance as he eventually made $2.5 million thanks to the profit-share deal in his contract.

Hindsight, five *Rocky* sequels and the *Creed* series later perhaps makes it hard to fully assess the movie on its own merits. Budget restraints on this level would never affect a *Rocky* film again which actually makes the finished product even more remarkable. Rocky's charming first date with Adrian was meant to be at a packed out ice-rink, but with no money to pay the hundreds of extras needed it was decided to film it late at night, in an empty venue and it's one of the standout scenes. The scene also includes a line that was a copy and paste straight from Stallone's own life: "I was told I wasn't born with much of a brain, so I better start using my body," was passive aggressive advice he'd received from his father, years before. But inviting his father to participate in the filming of *Rocky* built a few bridges between the pair and they would bond further over Stallone's inherited love of playing polo. Brother Frank was also drafted in as a street singer that Rocky has a passing friendship with. His acapella song *Take You Back* from the film was on the soundtrack too and became an unofficial, second anthem for the *Rocky* movie series.

The film's overnight success was the stuff of dreams and *Rocky*'s message of a nobody getting a shot at being a somebody was far too similar to Stallone's personal journey for the media to ignore it. Every interview he gave focussed on the struggle to get the film made and his casting as Rocky. It was an irresistible rags to riches story that saw him start 1976 as an inconsequential creative and end the year as the most talked about human in the industry. He had been overlooked, cast aside and dismissed beforehand but suddenly, $220 million dollars later, he was the biggest name in his field.

The film received 9 Oscar nominations and on March 28th 1977 Stallone found himself essentially invited to the Land of Oz. The 49th Academy Awards were presented by a combination of Richard Pryor, Ellen Burstyn, Jane Fonda and Warren Beatty and just as the Oscars remain to this day, there is a gaping chasm between what wins awards and what is popular. Undeniably impressive as they are, *All The President's Men* and *Network* have fairly niche appeal but they won the four acting awards between them (*Network*'s Peter Finch and Faye Dunaway for Best Actor and Actress and Beatrice Straight won Best Supporting Actress for the same film while Jason Robarts won Best Supporting Actor for *All The President's Men*) The pair of films also bagged the writing awards and Jerry Goldsmith won the Best Music Original Score for *The Omen*, while Conti wasn't even nominated and *Gonna Fly Now* lost to Streisand's *Evergreen* from *A Star is Born* in the Best Song category. Bill Conti's Oscar snub for *Gonna Fly Now* didn't stop it going to the top of the Billboard charts and a disco version soon followed and he would be asked to score every subsequent sequel except one (*Rocky IV*). Coincidentally, Conti was employed to conduct the orchestra for this Academy Awards show and in rehearsals for the TV extravaganza, he lifted his baton to run through the song

Evergreen that was to be performed on the night by Barbara Streisand, only for her to pause and turn to Conti and inform him that she listened to *Gonna Fly Now* every morning to get herself up for the day ahead.

While the evening didn't seem to be going as the *Rocky* contingent hoped, Stallone did get a nice moment on the stage when he presented the Best Supporting Actress award and surprise guest Muhammed Ali popped out to briefly spar with him. But the evening would have a fitting *Rocky*-like climax as the film rightfully won Richard Halsey and Scott Conrad the award for Best Editing and then the movie took the championship belts too; it picked up the Academy Awards for Best Director for Avildsen and the big one, the Academy Award for Best Picture beating out the aforementioned *Network* and *All The President's Men* plus *Bound for Glory* and *Taxi Driver*. While Stallone may have been disappointed to not pick up the statuette for his writing or his acting (De Niro didn't win for *Taxi Driver* either) it was an evening that vindicated all the hard work, the negotiations, the worry and the bruises.

But the legacy of *Rocky* turned out to be far more than most Oscar winners. Stallone turned this character into a place of refuge in his career. When other projects didn't turn out the way he hoped, he could always further the story of the Italian Stallion and he would have complete control over all aspects of it. This original film created something that was entirely unpredictable and would last through the next four decades. Inevitably, a follow-up to this heavyweight hit was soon going to be requested by the studio. But as it transpired, it was a follow-up that was much needed by its creator.

1978 - F.I.S.T. , PARADISE ALLEY

When your first film turns out to be a box office goliath, the repercussions will naturally be a mix of positive and negative. The positive is of course the money, the relief, the accolades and the new opportunities that are presented to you but the downside is you now have to produce the difficult second album. Previously, you were flying under the radar and if things didn't work out, no one was watching anyway. With the unprecedented success of *Rocky* it meant that EVERYONE in the industry was now watching Sylvester Stallone. *Paradise Alley* on paper would have looked a decent option as Stallone's first post-*Rocky* project. It was in fact a pre-*Rocky* project as it was a screenplay he had written and presented to various studios before he had thought about the Philly boxer. He wrote the original story as a novel and then turned it into a feature film script. Meetings were hard to come by and unfruitful until Universal Pictures optioned his idea. It was languishing in development hell until *Rocky* hit big and Universal Pictures realised they had a sports drama set in a ring with Rocky himself, right under their noses.

The plot revolves around the three Carboni brothers in 1940's New York, the same 'Hell's Kitchen' backstreets that Stallone knew so well and in fact, he had originally called the script *Hell's Kitchen* (other potential titles included *Pepper Alley* and *Italian Stallion)*. One of the brothers, Victor, is a gentle giant while the other two are a fast-talking hustler Cosmo (Stallone) and a World War 2 veteran Lenny who discovers a taste for money when Victor starts to show an aptitude for professional wrestling. The potential of the comedy drama would have had producers rubbing their hands with glee as Stallone would also make his directorial debut and Bill Conti was among the *Rocky* alumni coming aboard. The period story would attempt a mix of family drama and comedic high-jinx with a Rocky-esque finale and so $6 million dollars was handed over to Stallone to get it made. The script had been sold to Force Ten productions and their producers John F. Roach and Ronald A. Suppa before *Rocky* was made and it was originally set in the world of boxing too. Before *Rocky* was on the horizon, Stallone and Force Ten had offered the script of *Paradise Alley* to United Artists and Chartoff-Winkler Productions. Post-*Rocky* mania, Force Ten sued UA and Chartoff Winkler arguing that the similarities between *Paradise Alley* and *Rocky* were too great and they wanted extra compensation for, as they saw it, essentially giving UA and Chartoff-Winkler the idea to support *Rocky*. Changing *Paradise Alley* from a boxing story to a wrestling story had been one of the outcomes of Chartoff-Winkler passing on the *Paradise Alley* script and instead pursuing Stallone's *Rocky* idea. Stallone went to Universal Pictures with the *Paradise Alley* screenplay after *Rocky* had landed and Universal agreed to pay-off the Force Ten producers and the legal action was also settled out of court two years later. John F. Roach and Ronald A. Suppa remained as credited producers on *Paradise Alley* but were largely left out of the day to day production. Stallone took on most of the producer responsibility role (although it went uncredited) alongside Universal vice-president Peter Saphier and the pair managed to complete the 50–day shoot in early 1978, three days ahead of schedule.

New York born actor Armand Assante had met Stallone when he worked on *Lords of Flatbush* although his role ended up on the cutting room floor but he'd gained some level of fame on TV on two NBC soap operas; *How to Survive a Marriage* and *The Doctors*. The *Paradise Alley* producers had briefly envisioned the film as the onscreen pairing of Stallone and Al Pacino but Assante's talent and obvious resemblance to Pacino, secured him his first major film role. 6 ft 5 inch Texan Lee Canalito's physicality bagged him the part of the third brother Victor with the stunning Anne Archer providing the requisite femme-fatale vibes. Although he played the role of the mobsters' heavy Frankie The Thumper, Terry Funk was a key addition to the cast. By 1978, he was already considered one of the most influential pro-wrestlers in the United States and his expertise in the industry saw him receive a wrestling choreography solo credit on *Paradise Alley* as he helped Stallone tailor the in-ring action to best suit the cameras. Funk would reunite with Stallone nine years later on *Over The Top*.

But in actual fact, Stallone already had his *Rocky* follow-up in the can. In April of 1978, just as *Paradise Alley* was in the throes of post-production, *F.I.S.T* was released nationwide. Directed by Norman Jewison, the United Artists production cast Stallone as Johnny Kovak, a factory worker turned union leader whose story bares more than a little resemblance to the real life figure of Jimmy Hoffa, the real life President of the International Brotherhood of Teamsters who was allegedly assassinated by the Mafia in 1975. (Al Pacino played Jimmy Hoffa himself alongside Robert De Niro and Joe Pesci in the 2019 epic *The Irishman*) Originally written by Joe Eszterhas (who would go on to pen huge commercial hits such as *Basic Instinct, Jagged Edge and Flashdance*) the script was then given to Stallone to try and streamline the immense 400 page treatment. The sprawling epic would begin in the 1930's and go up until the death of the lead character in the 60's. *F.I.S.T.* was originally written by

Eszterhas with Jack Nicholson in mind in the lead but it soon found its way to Stallone who sensed an awards-baiting epic. (Nicholson would go on to play Jimmy Hoffa in the very standard biopic *Hoffa*, in 1992). It meant that Stallone's double-headed follow up to *Rocky* would be a duo of period pieces. But taken as a pair, they are very different beasts. *Paradise Alley* was meant as an aspirational tale with plenty of laughs and drama along the way. *F.I.S.T.* was treating itself very seriously however and was expected to showcase the acting chops of its star who would be onscreen against proven talent such as Rod Steiger and Peter Boyle. Steiger would only appear in the final third of the film but he was happy to do the director a favour after Norman Jewison had directed him to the Best Actor Oscar in the racially charged classic *In The Heat of the NIght* in 1968. Also in the cast was Kevin Conroy who must have gotten to know Stallone very well in 1977 and 1978 as he was in both *Paradise Alley* and *F.I.S.T.* And he probably didn't have to worry too much about wardrobe as he essentially played the same role in both. His archetypal gangster became more comedic in *Paradise Alley* than in *F.I.S.T.* but neither part was a stretch for the New York native. Additionally, but in a smaller role, was Connecticut-born, former US Marine Brian Dennehy. Dennehy was an acclaimed stage actor who was just starting his film career. With hindsight, it's always fun to watch actors before major moments in their careers have happened. Little did he or Stallone know at the time but four years later both their lives would change forever when they battled each other in *First Blood*.

Stallone was to receive half a million dollars for his work, officially divided up as $350 thousand for his acting and $150 thousand for his writing skills. Most of the shooting was completed in Dubuque, Iowa as it still had the tough, working class look of the 1930's that the first half of the film required. *F.I.S.T.* clearly had ambition at its heart and it was desperate to be seen as a prestige movie. It had a lot of plot and a sizable time-line to cram into its life-story narrative. It involved large set pieces such as worker strike action and congressional hearings and Stallone's Kovak would visibly age as the film moved through its eventual two and a half hours' running time.

F.I.S.T arrived in cinemas in April of 1978, with *Paradise Alley* appearing in November of that year. In terms of box office returns, *F.I.S.T* was to be considered a hit as it conjured up over $20 million dollars in the US, on its $8 million dollar budget. It ended the year as number 28 in the 1978 Box Office standings, sandwiched between the *Wizard of Oz* spin off, *The Wiz* and grizzled war pic *The Boys From Brazil*. Number one that year was *Grease*.

Although it received mostly positive reviews at the time, it's seen more of a curiosity nowadays, if it's seen at all. It starts off as a fairly standard but well-made biopic of a union leader and Stallone is more than charismatic in his role. But as the story moves into corruption, mafia links and public hearings the narrative becomes a bit more jumbled, hasty and uneven. You get the feeling that there's a lot that has been left out and perhaps its aspiration to be a part of the next Academy Awards night outweighed its effectiveness. (*F.I.S.T.* was totally ignored in the following awards season although Stallone did present the Best Actor Oscar to Richard Dreyfuss for *The Goodbye Girl* at the 50th Academy Awards in 1978, two weeks before *F.I.S.T.* was released).

Stallone and Jewison clearly thought hard about the transformation of his character from ambitious young spokesperson to jaded leader of men in the finale. The ageing make-up is unconvincing when he is opposite actors who are actually the age that his character is supposed to be and he also puts on weight and lowers his voice into a curious rasp to indicate a man in middle age. It's a decent, competent biopic but the film just lacks a sparkle, a bit of extra flair and originality.

It's a similar sensation when watching *Paradise Alley*. You can't help but shake the feeling that stuff is missing or could have been tweaked somehow. Unlike *F.I.S.T,* *Paradise Alley* ended up as a swift 109 minutes and Stallone later insisted that Universal Pictures had cut out the heart and soul of his film and had removed close to 40 scenes against his wishes. But if the editing was so ruthless, then why did they leave in Stallone singing the title song over the opening credits? That really should have been the first thing to go. *Too Close to Paradise* was written by Carole Bayer Sager, Bruce Roberts and Bill Conti and while Stallone can undoubtedly hold a tune, it sounds like someone is playing it at the wrong speed. Maybe it was for cost reasons that the writer, director and lead actor also recorded the theme song but surely he could have got his singing brother Frank to step in at least. Frank Stallone Jr was around the production anyway as his brother gave him the non-speaking part of nightclub singer and his *Angel Voice / Please Be Someone To Me* would appear on the soundtrack album. Big band jazz would become a staple of the Frank Stallone musical output and he would go on to record several studio albums in the genre including *Day In Day Out* with The Billy May Orchestra in 1991 and *Close Your Eyes* with The Sammy Nesco Big Band two years later. But, we will return to S. Stallone's singing when we reach *Rhinestone* in a few years time. Bill Conti's *Paradise Alley* score is traditional jazz and bluesy motifs with some of his orchestral cues sounding almost identical to some of the slower melodies he used in *Rocky*. As a first stab at directing though, this had some impressive aspects to it and had the film not been ripped apart in the editing room as Stallone insists, you have to wonder if there was a more coherent movie that he thought he had made. The negatives of *Paradise Alley* are unavoidable though; Stallone's Cosmo character becomes a bit grating with his incessant, rapid-fire delivery and the character development of Armand Assante's Lenny from despondent war veteran to money-crazed wrestling manager is sudden and unconvincing. A couple of scenes in an early subplot involving a monkey would nowadays have the animal rights groups up in arms. Also, the end of the movie is slightly incoherent and rushed but conversely, Stallone showed flair in the director's chair and combined with his cinematographer Lazlo Kovaks to great effect with the montage of rain-soaked action in the wrestling ring in the climatic match-up.

Ultimately, *Paradise Alley* was not considered a success however, scraping in $8 million dollars on its $7 million budget. And neither *Paradise Alley* or *F.I.S.T.* have gone down as classics and neither is really remembered at all. Although it was a blow at the time, it was surely a steep learning curve for Stallone. From this point onwards, he only ever appeared in two projects that were not set in either present day or the future (*Escape to Victory* and *Oscar*)

While these two productions did not damage the fledgling Stallone brand irrevocably, it did start what would become a repeating cycle. Critics would be quick to pounce on the box office returns of any movie that wasn't a Balboa flick as an indication that Stallone was a one-trick actor and was destined to be forgotten sooner rather than later. Neither *Paradise Alley* or *F.I.S.T.* were necessarily risky projects for Stallone and it must be remembered that his movie career was very much at the newborn stage at this point so he was probably overwhelmed to be offered anything at that time anyway. The offers and discussions for both films would have been happening before and during production on *Rocky*, so he had no reason to think he would ever be presented with two leading roles in major productions ever again.

But as things stood at the end of 1978, Stallone was now a known name in the business, but his ability to generate profits for a studio already appeared inconsistent. A movie studio is a business like any other, where profit margins are the be all and end all. Creativity is fine, awards are great and a positive audience reaction is welcome but nobody is running a charity. Stallone needed to show that he was a conduit to more cash and if United Artists was to invest something in the region of another $7 million dollars in him, he had to turn that into a healthy profit. So without much hesitation on United Artists or Stallone's part, a continuation of the Oscar-winning boxer's journey was ordered next on the agenda.

ROCKY II (1979)

THE MOST ELECTRIFYING REMATCH IN MOTION PICTURE HISTORY

Starring - Sylvester Stallone, Talia Shire, Burt Young, Carl Weathers, Burgess Meredith
Written by - Sylvester Stallone
Original Score by - Bill Conti
Directed by - Sylvester Stallone

Sequels are nothing new and although it feels like current movie studio's are petrified to try anything original, not much has changed really. Characters that proved popular in one movie would be called on again and again until the receipts showed that audiences had had enough. And even that would only mean a pause and a rethink before an inevitable, attempted reboot. All through cinematic history, repeating what worked before has been a mantra that served the most successful producers, studios and stars well. From Charlie Chaplin's Tramp character, The Keystone Cops, The Marx Brothers, through multiple Tarzan stories, Sherlock Holmes, Pink Panther, James Bond and Mission: Impossible adventures, doing something again has never been off the table in Hollywood. *Star Wars* will continue to mine their galaxy far, far away as long as there's a screen and a possibility of profit. Marvel's extraordinary rise since 2008's *Iron Man* has been predicated on familiarity with the characters and extending their shelf life.

And in 1979, it was no different. *Jaws 2* had unsurprisingly been a hit the year before, as had the sequels *The Omen 2* and *Revenge of the Pink Panther* and readying for release in this year were two sequels of sorts: existing properties that were trying to turn small profits on TV into big winnings on the silver screen: *Star Trek - The Motion Picture* and *The Muppet Movie*. Not to mention the 11th film in the Bond series, *Moonraker.*

As soon as *Rocky* became an instant global phenomenon, United Artists approached Stallone about a second film. Stallone had already started penning ideas before the first movie was finished and he outlined the plot for *Rocky 2: Redemption* as he planned to call it (*Rocky Returns* was also in the running as the title). Learning a lesson from his negotiations to star in the first film, he pulled the same trick again to get into the directors chair. Producers Winkler and Chartoff naturally were inclined more towards getting John G Avilsden to direct again, since he'd won the Oscar for it and if it ain't broke....

But Avilsden was busy on another movie and this one was again about working class life in a tough, U.S. city but instead of boxing, there was dancing. Avilsden had chosen to helm *Saturday Night Fever*, so Stallone put himself forward again, but again the producers hesitated. Stallone's directorial debut *Paradise Alley* had sunk without a trace, so they were reluctant to give him the chance to blow up this potential gold mine. But after much discussion and reassurance they accepted that despite the poor box office performance of *Paradise Alley*, his direction had shown both flair and capability. They acknowledged that no-one could know the *Rocky* characters and that world better than the original creator and he was granted his wish. Soon after, the rest of the returning cast was re-employed and a budget of $7 million dollars (compared to the first film's $1 million) was set.

As with the previous film and all the subsequent *Rocky* films, Stallone's life was the inspiration for the story arc. That's why Rocky's second outing on the big screen looks at what happens after you get that million to one shot. After 30 years of hoping and struggling, how do you cope when you finally get the moment you had dreamt about and can you really ever leave your old life behind? Simply put, for Stallone and Rocky, is rags to riches really all it's cracked up to be?

An angry Apollo Creed (Carl Weathers) feels unsatisfied. The fight with the nobody from Philadelphia was supposed to be a walkover. But the extraordinary staying power of his opponent meant he now felt he had to get him back in the ring and prove it was just a lucky night for Balboa the first time around. For Rocky though, he had his life how he wanted it. Him and Adrian got married and little Rocky was already on the way. His new found celebrity status meant he was trying to do TV commercials and earn money in any way he could, legally, outside of the ring. But with Creed talking to the media via TV news and radio to taunt Rocky back into the ring, could he resist? The love of his life was adamant that watching him get beaten to a pulp again, was not going to go down well at home. His new marriage was put under strain as everyone except Adrian was telling him to fight Creed again. But his loyalty beyond anything else was to Adrian and his unborn baby. The stress of it all causes Adrian to go into early labour and Rocky disengages from all other aspects of life to be next to his wife as she lay in a coma. When she wakes up, Rocky meets his son (played by newborn Seargeoh Stallone, the second son of Sylvester Stallone and Sasha Czack) and Adrian has had a change of heart. She now wants him to win. Cue the music, cue the montage and then eventually (arguably) the greatest boxing match ever committed to celluloid. In the 15th round, the fighters both hit the canvas and eventually Rocky staggers to his feet, just before the end of the 10-second count and is the new heavyweight champion of the world.

I say arguably the greatest boxing match ever committed to celluloid but I will forever be in a state of flux over this. For this author, it comes down to either this one or *Rocky IV* because the *Rocky II* fight is extraordinary. With that bigger budget, the fight can have an arena full of actual people rather than clever lighting and shifting a dozen extras into the camera's line of sight with each new set-up shot (as was the case on *Rocky*). That in turn means there can be wider shots of the battle as it wears on. The reactions of the crowd to the titanic struggle adds to the intensity of 'Superfight 2' as it's called in the movie. That bigger budget had also led to planning the final fight in The Colosseum in Rome, to reflect Rocky's Italian heritage, but it was soon back on US soil with the Los Angeles Sports Arena pretending to be the Philadelphia Spectrum.

In total, the match-up runs for 20 minutes which is more than twice the length of the first bout in *Rocky*. Bill Conti guides us through the majority of the fight with his track *Conquest* that includes both fighters having periods of success, slow motion punches hitting their target and that recurrent, brassy fanfare that so perfectly captured the gladiatorial atmosphere. In the last few seconds of the final round, both fighters are running on empty. Weathers' physicality as Apollo Creed here is hugely underestimated. His mind and soul have left that ring, but he is still swinging because so is his opponent. And as Rocky catches Creed's jaw once again, the pair are sent flying to the canvas. The editing to maximise the tension as both fighters struggle to get to their feet in time, is a lesson in the art-form from [Danford B. Greene](), Stanford C Allen and Janice Hampon, who are all credited as editors. And by the time Rocky beats the clock, we are on our feet with him and the release of emotion is exceptional. Stallone and Weathers trained for 10 weeks at a specially constructed boxing ring in the Metro-Goldwyn-Mayer studio facility in California. Helping the pair fuse real-world boxing with film-fighting to greater effect than in the first film was trainer Al Silvani. The Californian, part-time stunt performer worked with them every day and used all his experience of training the likes of Floyd Patterson, Rocky Graziano and the *Raging Bull* himself, Jake LaMotta. Silvani is seen in the original *Rocky* as Mickey's cutman during the final fight. Another plot point that was actually a movie making solution was switching Rocky from a southpaw (left-handed boxer who leads with their right hand) to a traditional right-hander.

Stallone suffered an almost catastrophic tear to his right pectoralis muscle when he was attempting to lift more than 100kg, which meant that he couldn't swing his left arm as required. The boxing style switch added an extra dimension to 'Superfight 2' whilst allowing the leading man to be able to fight back properly against Apollo.

Rocky II is seen by many as an extension of the first film more than any other in the series. From this point on, the Balboa stories move more with the times, in terms of production values, filmmaking trends, commercial opportunities and slick editing. But *Rocky* and *Rocky II* can be seen as two halves of the same fable. The second film follows on just minutes from the first film's ending. The new Bill Conti track *Redemption* (which is the only remnant from Stallone's original full title of this film) plays over the opening credits as Rocky's ambulance speeds through the Philadelphia night to hospital after the climactic bout in *Rocky*. Unlike other sequels that would try to distance themselves from the previous film for fear of alienating an audience who may not have seen it, Stallone and Co. assume you watched *Rocky* and loved it. The second feature is totally reliant on the first film for its motivation. But it's also better. Not just because the budget is there but because now everyone on screen is more comfortable with their characters. Talia Shire has moved her character on. She still has the shy tendencies but with the love of her man, Adrian now feels the personal strength to stand up for what she believes in. Case in point, she refuses to accept Paulie's (Burt Young) belief that letting Rocky fight Apollo again is best for everyone. Weathers is improved too. In the first film he is more than slightly modelled on the public persona of Muhammed Ali. In this film, he is bitter and angry. He isn't the grinning, confident self-PR machine he was. He just wants to beat Rocky and beat him definitively. Burt Young himself gets to be more of a friend to Rocky rather than the drunk, abusive, spanner-in-the-works that he was in the first movie.

Also improving on the first film, is 'the run'. When a scene becomes instantly iconic and the music to that scene also permeates the public consciousness, how are you supposed to follow it up? Do you try to do something different and hope the fans don't mind? Or do you give the people what they want? Stallone is always striving to give the people what they want and in terms of 'the run', he gives it to the audience again but with both barrels. As soon as Adrian wakes from her coma and jointly meets her new son with Rocky, she tells her husband to "win, win". Cue what turns out to be the first of two training montages. This first one has every exertion except running. It re-uses the score that Bill Conti used for the final fight in *Rocky* called *Going The Distance*. It involves punch bags, skipping, weights and catching chickens and pumps the audience up for the big bout. But that's not all. Just as the cinema going public is wondering where is *Gonna Fly Now*? They get that too. Conti re-recorded the tune with a slightly fuller sound and Stallone repeated his famous run but added hundreds of kids chasing Rocky as he goes for his jaunt around Philadelphia. A call was sent out to local schools, and kids who wanted to be a part of filming should be ready on a brisk Tuesday morning in town. 800 turned up and it required Stallone and his crew to employ more cameras than they had planned, to get as many of them in shot, running a few feet behind Rocky. The sequence stays just the right side of cheesy and provides a wonderful final burst of punch-the-air optimism as the final showdown approaches. Some years later, the publication *Philly Mag* wrote a tongue-in-cheek article that claimed the running scenes in both *Rocky* and *Rocky II* geographically covered more than 30 miles of Philadelphia and in actual fact, it would have taken Rocky Balboa more than four hours to run through each location shown during the sequences.

Rocky II opened to $6 million dollars in its opening weekend, beating its predecessor by a million. It did not match the overall total of the first film though and ended its worldwide run on just over $200 million dollars, $25 million less than *Rocky*. But it was still deemed a huge success and ended up 3rd in the 1979 North American Box Office totals. Ahead of *Star Trek - The Motion Picture, Apocalypse Now, Moonraker* and *Alien* and only behind *The Amityville Horror* and *Kramer vs Kramer*.

For Stallone and United Artists, it vindicated their decision to allow Stallone to direct and to have complete control over the project. Oscar ignored the film however, handing out the majority of their awards that year to the repercussions of the Vietnam War with *The Deer Hunter* and *Coming Home*. Stallone was still a few years away from his version of a Vietnam War veteran but there were murmurs of discontent despite the financial success of *Rocky II*. At this stage of his career, Stallone had now made four big studio pictures and only two of them had made a significant impact and that had been with the same character repeated. Film offers that were being presented to him were for wrestlers, football stars and other athletic type figures. The fear of typecasting was very real so he needed to have some success with something that didn't involve strapping on boxing gloves or his personal goal of being a respected actor may already be in jeopardy.

1981 - NIGHTHAWKS, ESCAPE TO VICTORY

For his second, double-try at finding success outside of *Rocky*, Stallone chose to accept roles in two films that sat in two genres he would have been hopeful about; cop thriller and war adventure. *Nighthawks* and *Escape to Victory* both followed a long tradition that had served leading men pretty well by putting them in circumstances that were familiar to audiences and surrounding them with quality co-stars who would all try to elevate the project into being more than the sum of its generic parts. The cop film had received a shot in the arm in the 70's with both *Dirty Harry* and *The French Connection* pushing the envelope when they both hit cinemas in 1971 and the dirty-cop-busting of *Serpico* with Al Pacino would add again to the changing public image of law enforcement in 1973. The thrilling and influential car chase that was the centerpiece of *The French Connection* was enhanced by the lead character of Detective Jimmy 'Popeye' Doyle (Gene Hackman) whose motivations were murky to say the least. The response to the film was impressive both financially (it was the third most successful film of the year) and critically (it won five Academy Awards including Best Picture). *The French Connection II* arrived in 1975 but wasn't a hit like its predecessor, finishing the year as the 24th biggest film at the U.S. box office. Regardless, Twentieth Century Fox pressed ahead and commissioned another script for a potential third film which was written by David Shaber and would have teamed Hackman's anti-hero detective with a new character that was to be offered to Richard Pryor. When the star showed reluctance to portray Popeye Doyle again, the screenplay was sold to Universal Studios and Shaber retooled his work and gave it the new name of *The Attack*. The plot was quite unusual for the time as it had two New York cops joining a new, elite squad tasked with stopping a pair of terrorists from setting off bombs in their city. In his first film, distinctive Dutch actor Rutger Hauer was offered the main villain role of Heymar 'Wulfgar' Reinhardt. Hauer had already made waves in Dutch TV and film but this was to be his first role in an American production. The Shaber script echoed the 1973 thriller *The Day of the Jackal* that saw French British actor Michael Lonsdale trying to track and stop an assassin. That hit film relied heavily on the magnetism of The Jackal himself as portrayed chillingly by Edward Fox and *The Attack* would have a better chance of being successful if it too could boast a captivating bad guy that would be an equal to the heroes. The Dutchman's lack of Hollywood experience actually helped the movie as for the first half an hour of the film he would be in prosthetics to change the shape of his nose and chin and he would sport a different hair style and colour. When his character undergoes plastic surgery to change his identity, we then get to see his now familiar piercing stare and overwhelming charisma. Hauer was already close to being cast as Roy Batty in *Blade Runner* as production on *Nighthawks* reached the end and *Blade Runner* director Ridley Scott confirmed that it was Hauer's work in Dutch film that got him the role of a lifetime and his compelling turn in *Nighthawks* only cemented the decision to cast him in the sci-fi classic the next year.

Stallone's character of Detective Sergeant Deke DaSilva was partnered to DS Matthew Fox and Billy Dee Williams was given that part as he was still riding high on the massive career-boost of appearing as Lando Calrissian in *Star Wars: Episode V - The Empire Strikes Back*. American actress Lindsay Wagner had recently finished her star-making turn on TV as *The Bionic Woman* and was trying to break into film and she was cast as DaSilva's ex-wife. The title of the film then went through several alterations; first it became just *Attack* and that changed to *Hawks* and then finally *Nighthawks* was settled on. Persis Khambatta and Nigel Davenport filled out the other main characters and principal photography began in the first month of 1980 under director Gary Nelson. Nelson had plenty of experience in TV but his film work so far had been mainly family fare with *Freaky Friday* and *The Black Hole*, both for Disney. After just one week, Nelson was fired and novice Bruce Malmuth was told to get from Los Angeles to the location in New York. Malmuth had only one film directing credit prior to being offered the gig on *Nighthawks,* but his work on comedy anthology movie *Fore Play* was alongside John G Avildsen, so it was the *Rocky* director who had instigated Malmuth as replacement director on *Nighthawks*. While Malmuth was still in the air, production continued with filming of the subway chase sequence and Stallone sat in the director's chair for the day. When word got out that the star had taken over in the meantime, the Directors Guild of America fined the production for breaking their code of conduct. Studio bosses were also getting feedback that their main actor was clashing with Hauer when they were on set together, with Stallone concerned that Hauer was overshadowing his work on screen. To add to the baptism of fire for Hauer on his first major film, his mother and his best friend both passed away after filming had commenced. He flew back to the Netherlands for both of their funerals but was back on set again each time, as soon as was humanly possible. Reports leaked of clashes between Stallone and

Hauer on-set although in the intervening years, both denied personal issues and blamed the difficulty of the shoot for any workplace tensions. Hauer got a sharp lesson in making American action films as he was severely burnt when a blood squib (a little bag of fake blood hidden inside an actor's clothing that is burst open on-demand to simulate a gunshot injury) went off early. He also suffered a debilitating back injury when the cable that pulled him backwards (again simulating the impact of a gunshot) was yanked too hard.

Once filming wrapped, the editing process began and immediately ran into more issues. The level of violence that the script and the production called for was worrying both the studio and the distributors. Universal Studios was told by the Motion Picture Association of America (MPAA) that unless they removed a lot of the more disturbing content, they would only allow the film to be released with an 'X' certificate. This adult-only rating would severely damage the chances of the film being a hit as it would exclude the younger age group who made up the larger majority of cinemagoers, so they told the director to cut out a lot more of the most intense moments. They re-issued the new version to the MPAA but again, they were told that their film would be classed as 'X'. This time Stallone himself went into the editing room and was increasingly frustrated at the demands of the MPAA. He ended up with two versions of the film, one that focused more on the cops and the other that leaned more towards the terrorists. Stallone convinced Universal that the version with less Hauer was the better version although test screenings had suggested the opposite. Regardless of the screen time of either actor, the final cut that was granted an 'R' rating was considered by everyone involved as a very watered-down version of the film they all thought they had made.

Nighthawks represents a watershed period in movie history and unwittingly indicated both the old and the new. The new was the novel plotline of terrorism in New York. It was virtually unthinkable in 1980 and the depiction of that type of indiscriminate, large-scale violence in the United States' most famous city was part of the reason the sensitive censors were so adamant about edits. Stallone's character could be seen as 'Cobra, The Early Years' and with his full beard, coiffed hair and contemporary clothing, he was officially stepping into male sex symbol territory for the first time. But the film also has a 70's cop thriller vibe that it only barely shakes off in the second half of the movie. Before the New York detectives become obsessed with catching the terrorist group, they are basically a big-screen *Starsky and Hutch*. The TV drama that ran from 1975 to 1979 made legends of its stars David Soul and Paul Michael Glaser but, coupled with the *Dirty Harry* ideology, cop movies found themselves bound by convention. Keith Emerson (of Emerson, Lake and Palmer prog rock supergroup fame) was given the opportunity to score the film but he was clearly given the brief of "make it sound like Lalo Shifrin and every other 70's police drama". It's a cool soundtrack but indistinguishable from others at the time. That being said, *Nighthawks* is an effective thriller even with its cliches and melodrama and as it was Stallone's first starring role in a non-*Rocky* film set in the present day, he more than proves his credentials as a leading man.

Upon release, *Nighthawks* saw Stallone receive some of his best non-Rocky reviews and the $5 million dollar budget was recouped with a worldwide gross nudging $20 million dollars, but in the U.S. it didn't break the top fifty of the top earners of 1981. Its profit margin was encouraging but, yet again, the industry talk was that

Stallone was destined to be remembered as that actor who played that boxer a few times.

Number one in 1981 was *Raiders of the Lost Ark* and Indy's first adventure wasn't going to be troubled by Stallone's other release of the year despite both taking place during World War II. *Escape to Victory* (released as *Victory* in the U.S.) is a boys-own adventure that has become a staple of Easter holiday TV viewing in the UK. It is also put into the terrestrial TV schedules whenever the England and Germany national football teams are about to meet in competition. For better or for worse, it is still considered the most enjoyable football/soccer movie ever made but it doesn't have much competition. The only serious attempt to bring the sport to the silver screen in a global way was the *Goal!* trilogy that began in 2005 with much fanfare and stunt casting. It didn't prove to be a big hit and *Goal 2: Living the Dream* was released two years later to noticeably less attention. By the time *Goal 3: Taking on the World* was completed in 2009, it was more of a contractual necessity and clearly the budget and the motivation was long gone. *Escape to Victory* ended up as an inoffensive film that the family could safely watch together but its origins were decidedly more upsetting. Squad members of the Ukrainian club FC Dynamo Kiev played a series of games against German soldiers during the early days of Nazi occupation, and won them all. The Ukrainian players were all later sent to prison camps by the Gestapo. The truth mixed with some poetic license and was put on screen in a 1962 Hungarian film called *Two Half Times In Hell* where Allied soldiers played against German soldiers, for their freedom. A 1979 Hollywood adaptation was announced with Clint Eastwood speculated for the lead and it was to be directed by Brian Hutton who had already made two, hit World War 2 pictures with Eastwood; *Where Eagles Dare* and

Kelly's Heroes. Eastwood never committed though and Hutton left the project but it soon found its way to the desk of the legendary filmmaker John Huston. Having made some of the greatest movies of all-time such as *The Maltese Falcon, The Treasure of the Sierra Madrid, The African Queen* and *The Man Who Would Be King*, his involvement immediately unlocked access to star names who wanted to experience working under his direction. Michael Caine and Max von Sydow signed on quickly and Stallone was offered the role of captured American soldier, Captain Robert Hatch.

The part as written was a bit of a departure for Stallone as he would be required to play a mixture of matinee idol and comic relief, incorporating the commonly held belief that Americans didn't understand the game at all. The other headline grabbing bit of casting was that much of the supporting cast would be current stars of the sport. Many players from England's Ipswich Town Football Club were to be involved as they were one of the most successful sides in Europe in the late seventies and other professional footballers including Argentina's Osvaldo Ardiles and former Manchester City star Mike Summerbee. But they would be outshone by England's 1966 World Cup winning captain Bobby Moore and the Brazilian superstar Pele who was then, and still is, considered the greatest the game has ever seen. Pele would receive an acting credit on the film and also an additional mention for designing some of the onscreen football, culminating in that extraordinary bicycle kick that Pele performed for real and was so good, Huston repeated it from various angles in the final, edited movie.

The updated plot saw Michael Caine's Captain John Colby agree to get a team together in their prisoner of war camp and get them ready to face a German team in a show of supposed sportsmanship. Once the match is agreed, the Allie's decide to use the game as an elaborate cover so that the men involved could escape. Stallone's bemused American POW needs to get out as well, as he needs to deliver important info to his military and so, he is reluctantly given the position of goalkeeper so he can be a part of the mass escape plan. It's then a combination of comic skits with Stallone's character trying to get to grips with the sport, watching the best footballers of their day make their acting debuts and driving the plot towards the climax and the big match. Locations in Ireland, Austria, Germany, England and Canada were all scouted but Budapest in Hungary was chosen as it still maintained a lot of the aesthetic of the era and was a convincing substitute for wartime Paris. Plus, the cost of production would be halved compared to the other possible locations. Shooting got underway in earnest in May of 1980 but was suspended in July due to a Screen Actors Guild (SAG) strike. With only a week of main filming left to go, Huston and the studio executives had to maintain a good relationship with the Hungarian government, as they consistently had to keep asking for extensions on their permits so they could leave the sets built and ready as they waited for the strike action to be over. The main POW camp set had taken two months to construct. In the end, producer Freddie Fields got special dispensation from SAG which allowed them to complete filming without any issues in early September. Bill Conti was hired to write the score that would riff on the well known style of crowd-pleasing war films such as the 1963 classic *The Great Escape* which greatly benefitted from Elmer Bernstein's unforgettable and whistle-able main theme. The *Rocky* connection didn't end with Conti's involvement as Huston spent time with Stallone discussing those extraordinary training scenes from the first two *Rocky*'s. And it must have been very flattering to Stallone that the montage during the final football match bears more than a passing resemblance to those sequences of his.

Despite the film being a fun adventure with plenty of entertainment value and despite a lot of publicity in the lead up to its cinematic release, *Escape to Victory* underperformed at the box office. With a budget of $12 million dollars it struggled domestically, making only $10 million of that money back. It's perhaps understandable as it was a film based around a sport that has notoriously struggled to make an impact in the United States. Globally it did better and eventually its total reached over $27 million dollars, but again it was a film with Sylvester Stallone that wasn't *Rocky* and had not resonated with audiences. *Rocky III* was greenlit long before *Escape to Victory* and *Nighthawks*, but it felt like it would be the last time he would be allowed to get away with elongating his career by boxing.

ROCKY III (1982)

THE GREATEST CHALLENGE

Starring - Sylvester Stallone, Talia Shire, Burt Young, Carl Weathers, Burgess Meredith, Mr T
Written by - Sylvester Stallone
Original Score by - Bill Conti
Directed by - Sylvester Stallone

This book is not about me, but allow me just this bit because this is where my story and my relationship to Sylvester Stallone got started. As an impressionable and already film-addicted 13 year old, I went on a family holiday to the tiny island of Jersey, which is in the English Channel and is a curious mix of its two larger, neighbouring countries of England and (the much closer) France. It was the first holiday that I was without my older brother Pete as he was off on his first, all boys summer extravaganza. It meant that I would get the biggest treat of all; a hotel room all of my own and that also meant a TV of my own that I could watch while in bed. It may seem unthinkable now, but in the mid-eighties most families had one TV set in their home. Additional TV's in other rooms and bedrooms was the domain of the likes of the recently deceased Elvis Presley and soon-to-be-shot J.R. Ewing. I remember that the BBC was showing a season of old James Cagney movies which I really liked but something much more seismic happened one night. In those days, hotels would often have a movie channel. Essentially it meant they would press play on a VHS of a big movie that was now on home video release and it would be piped into the TV's in every room. After dinner in the hotel restaurant with my parents, I went to my room to turn on my very own TV and see what awaited me. I skipped through the four channels (yep, only four channels and that included the recently started Channel 4) and then I decided to take a look at the hotel movie channel, not having registered what the movie was tonight. What burst out of the small screen was a frenetic fight in a boxing ring. There was expansive, brassy orchestral music, there was intense emotion being conveyed and there was B.A. Baracus from *The A-Team* being beaten up by a dark haired man with a sloping mouth. The slopey mouth guy knocked B.A. down and people watching just outside the ring seemed delighted. There was then another scene with the same guy and a different man, talking and walking towards another boxing ring but there was nobody else around. They climbed in the ring, talked more and despite seeming like they were friends they both went in for a punch at the same time. The action froze, the image morphed into an expressionist painting and a song I knew called *Eye of the Tiger* started playing over the end credits. I was exhilarated and more than a little confused. The next day I checked the hotels' information board to find that the same movie would be played on their channel at 10pm that night. I had my dinner in the evening, I feigned tiredness and got back upstairs well in time for the poor receptionist to click play at the right time again. I watched *Rocky III* and looking back, I guess my life had changed. If you have a healthy obsession or something you love to enjoy that's just for you, try to remember the moment you discovered it and were hooked. That was me, in my own hotel room in Jersey. I'd never seen anything like it. Of course I'd seen a lot of films and at the age of 13 my tastes were maturing and I was allowed to watch Bond films, war films and more adult-oriented stuff. But I'd never been affected like this by a movie before. The intensity of the fight scenes, the emotion conveyed so effectively, the editing to make sure the slower scenes are just long enough, the mesmerising leading man, the co-stars who all brought their own charisma to parts that none of them ever bettered in their careers. I didn't know it at the time but it was engineered to be the highest form of popcorn entertainment and I had watched it via VHS about 18 months after it had hit cinemas.

Now while a spotty, awkward teenager from Watford in England was just starting his journey with *Rocky* and the back catalogue, for the creator of that world, this was the moment he went from movie star to movie god. The insipid reaction to *Nighthawks* and *Escape to*

Victory meant that Sylvester Stallone was starting to think he may be running out of chances. If he was really a boxer, his record would stand at 6 fights but only 2 wins. *Rocky* and *Rocky II* had been knockouts but he was losing on points with the other four films he had fronted. Whether he liked it or not, the only way to elongate his standing in the movie business and the only way to guarantee he got more time to prove himself outside of the ring, was to get back in the ring. A recent merger between studios meant that this was to be the first film in the franchise not to be solely funded by United Artists. Metro Goldwyn Mayer had joined with the company to form MGM/UA Entertainment Co. But whatever the name of the backers, they wanted more *Rocky* on screen as soon as possible. In planning for the third film in the series, Stallone was overwhelmed with the worry that it had to somehow be different from the first two. It had to retain the elements that the public responded to but it had to move with the times a little. The first thing he addressed was himself. In the first two films, Rocky is a powerful athlete but he certainly couldn't be described as lithe. For this third entry, Stallone went on a strict and dangerous diet that he confessed years later consisted of "very small portions of oatmeal cookies made with brown rice and up to 25 cups of coffee a day with honey and a couple of scoops of tuna fish". His diet was so severe he said he forgot his phone number as he got his body fat down to an astonishing 4.8 percent. The results were impressive on screen but led to serious issues off it. In filming part of the training montage in a swimming pool he was rushed to hospital suffering from heart palpitations.

The plot was again going to mirror his real life and this Rocky story would address how becoming rich and successful will naturally mean you can lose your edge and forget your humble roots. After becoming heavyweight champion of the world in that dramatic climax to *Rocky II*, Balboa is now a star. He is on chat shows, has a dozen endorsement deals and he even has the ultimate accolade of being invited on *The Muppet Show*. After a bizarre charity exhibition event which pits boxer against wrestler (in the form of 80's wrestling superstar Hulk Hogan playing a version of himself called 'Thunderlips') he is then challenged for the title by the hungry, laser-focused contender Clubber Lang. Real life fighters Joe Frasier and Earnie Shavers were both considered (Shavers proved to be too aggressive when he and Stallone attempted sparring) until casting directors saw an NBC program called *America's Toughest Bouncers*. The mohawked winner of that show was soon tracked down, auditioned and cast and Mr T's career took off. (He was subsequently cast as B.A. Baracus in the action TV series *The A-Team* a year later and has been an icon ever since). Rocky's trainer Mickey doesn't want him to take up the challenge and soon confesses that he has been feeding Rocky easy fights since he won the title years before against Apollo Creed. Rocky feels he can beat Lang and after some lacklustre training (which features a fan kissing Rocky on the cheek who is actually Stallone's then wife, Sasha) he fights and is soon brutally beaten by Lang. In the build up to the fight, Mickey suffers a heart attack and then dies just as Rocky is losing his world championship title. After some soul searching his old foe Apollo Creed tracks Rocky down and tells him that he has lost his desire, he has lost his *"eye of the tiger"*. In fact, Apollo wants to train Rocky and win that belt back. The rest is as gloriously predictable as you want it to be but it's done with such pace, heart and energy that the previous two films could never keep up. In his ongoing desire to make it different from the first two *Rocky* films, Stallone changes the script of the final fight. In *Rocky* and *Rocky II*, the climatic bouts both go the full distance of 15 rounds, but here Rocky gets this done in half the time (literally as the final fight in *Rocky III* is nine and a half minutes compared to *Rocky II*'s twenty minute battle). His slimmed down physique allows him to be a much faster, impactful fighter and with Apollo, Adrian and Paulie all in his corner, he demolishes and beats Lang in a flurry of fists and self-motivation.

Stallone had toyed again with the idea of this final fight being located in The Colosseum in Rome (early drafts also had Rocky facing a Russian opponent) but that was again scrapped. Other possible fight venues were scouted at Caesars Palace in Las Vegas and New Zealand also got consideration. But in the end, the battle was put on screen via three different locations; with the Olympic Auditorium, the Olympic Gym and the Main Street Gym of downtown Los Angeles all seamlessly edited together. As with films one and two, Stallone and Mr T spent weeks choreographing and rehearsing every move of their two, on screen fights. The second bout accounted for fourteen pages of the *Rocky III* script and included detailed descriptions of 130 punches. During filming in early April of 1981, the 4,000 strong cast and crew had to leave the Los Angeles Sports Arena hastily when a bomb threat was reported to authorities. For the scenes set at the new Balboa mansion, Muhammad Ali's home in Hancock Park in Los Angeles was used for the exteriors. There were news reports that Stallone's mother Jaqueline was going to portray Rocky's mother in the film but the character was never in any draft of the screenplay.

There was also a typical example of bureaucracy battling popular opinion when it came to the Rocky statue. Commissioned by Sylvester Stallone and United Artists and created by Colorado-based sculptor A. Thomas Schomberg for the movie, it features heavily in the film as positioned at the top of the steps to the Philadelphia Art Museum. Post-filming it was suggested it should stay there since those steps and *Rocky* were two of the most famous things about the area and it now attracted thousands of new tourists every year who wanted to run up the steps themselves. An extraordinary public argument broke out between the Art Museum itself and the City's Art Commission with the commission insisting that a movie prop was not art and it should be removed. It was soon moved to infront of The Spectrum, the indoor sports arena nearby, before returning to the top of the steps in 1990 for the filming of *Rocky V*. It was then moved back to The Spectrum before shifting to the bottom of the famous steps yet again in 2006 where it remains today.

As for the wonderful epilogue to *Rocky III* that had been teased throughout the movie, it took more than a decade to clear up what happened after the credits rolled. Apollo keeps insisting that Rocky will owe him a favour once he has helped him regain his world title from Clubber Lang. It turns out the favour is strapping on the gloves and climbing in a ring, well away from the view of anyone else, to finally complete a third fight between the pair. The scene brilliantly encapsulates male friendship and male ego in tandem and ends with a freeze frame of the two fighters throwing their opening punches to the throes of *Eye of the Tiger*. That image then morphs into a vibrant, expressionist painting by Minnesota born LeRoy Nieman. Nieman was a friend and muse of fellow artist Stallone and was also given the small role of the ring announcer in *Rocky III* (and again in *Rocky IV* and *Rocky Balboa*). As for what happened after those opening punches were unleashed, it wasn't until *Creed* in 2015 that Rocky explained that Apollo had won that third, secret fight.

The film was a blockbuster and did much better numbers than both the first two installments. Its worldwide haul was a stunning $270 million dollars which was almost $100 million dollars better than the third placed film of the year, *Tootsie*. Number one in 1982 was *E.T. The Extra Terrestrial* which took a frankly stupid amount of money for the times of $797 million dollars. The critics were mixed in their assessment of the film though and it was only that hit song *Eye of the Tiger* by Chicago based rock band Survivor that received an Oscar nomination. But that unforgettable record failed to win any film-based awards despite being nominated at the BAFTAs and the Golden Globes as well. The Oscar for Best Original Song that year went to *Up Where We Belong* from *An Officer and A Gentleman* starring Richard Gere. Stallone had approached *Queen* to use their *Another One Bites the Dust* but when those discussions broke down, he had to quickly find an alternative and approached *Survivor* who were in danger of being dropped by their record label after two unsuccessful albums. Stallone asked for a rock sound with hard drums and dominant guitar that could accompany punches being thrown. The tune was first called *Survival* until the band read the script and saw Apollo Creeds' lines about regaining an "Eye of the Tiger". Time was of the essence however and they recorded a demo in Chicago on February the 1st and they promised to cut another demo if Stallone liked the song. But Stallone loved the tune and the original demo and that is why the *Eye of the Tiger* that is used in the movie sounds different to the released version. They did eventually get back in the studio and cut a fuller, cleaner take that was used on the soundtrack album and their own single and album releases. The track was number one in the U.S. Billboard charts for six weeks (and the UK number one for four weeks) and won Best

Rock Performance by Duo or Group with Vocal at the 25th Grammy Awards.

So, Stallone was a box office champion again and this third *Rocky* movie had proven to be more popular than the previous pair. Celebrity culture exploded as the 80's began which meant that as the biggest movie actor in the world, he was a much sought after commodity as a magazine cover star. His life mirrored that of Rocky Balboa's more than ever before and scrutiny over his career became forensic. Try as he might to persuade journalists and interviewers that he was happy with his all-conquering status, he was fully aware that a crisis was on the horizon. *Rocky III* had kept Sylvester Stallone at the forefront of the movie industry but he had to find an alternative to the boxing fables. He would certainly bring *Rocky* back for a fourth installment when the time was right but he was searching harder than ever for a character that wasn't *Rocky* and was well received by audiences and critics. He was now finally about to find him and while this next character shared Rocky's ability to fight, he couldn't have been more different.

FIRST BLOOD (1982)

THIS TIME HE'S FIGHTING FOR HIS LIFE

Starring - Sylvester Stallone, Richard Crenna, Brian Dennehy
Written by - Michael Kozoll, William Sackheim and Sylvester Stallone. From the book by David Morell.
Original Score - Jerry Goldsmith
Directed by - Ted Kotcheff

The legend behind getting *Rocky* to the screen and its subsequent success is of course a one-off, never been repeated tale. It made Stallone a star and afforded him the income he had never imagined before. But if you take in his entire filmography there's one film that could stake a claim to be just as, if not even more, important in his career. It's a film that meant he was no longer a one-trick pony and he could now be considered a bona-fide movie superstar who could potentially open any film and make it a hit. It required a completely new on screen presence from its lead actor and when you think that it was originally offered to Robert De Niro, Clint Eastwood, Paul Newman, James Caan and Robert Redford, the end result couldn't possibly have been predicted.

Canadian American author David Morell wrote his original novel about a troubled and homeless Vietnam war veteran known only by his surname of Rambo in 1972. The character was bullied into leaving a small town in Kentucky by the local sheriff, which would eventually push the former soldier over the edge as he was suffering from post-traumatic stress disorder from his experiences fighting in the Vietnam War as one of the elite Green Beret's. His former Vietnam commanding officer, Captain Samuel Trautman is called in to try and diffuse the escalating situation after Rambo escapes custody and flees to the surrounding area. Pursued by the Sheriff's half-interested and half-trained officers and also the part-timers of the National Guard, Rambo gives them all a swift lesson in elite combat. In the book, Rambo kills many of those pursuing him and after a dramatic standoff between him, Trautman and Sheriff Teasle, Rambo is killed.

Several attempts had been made to turn this violent tale into a movie script. Italian actor Tomas Milan read and enjoyed the book and wanted to make it as a movie, but he couldn't get Italian backing and he abandoned the idea, although he did adopt the character name Rambo for his 1975 film *Syndicate Sadists*. Author Morell sold the film rights to his book to Colombia Pictures in the same year he published it and those rights were then sold on to Warner Bros Pictures, but it remained in development hell. The fact that neither side in the story is clearly right or wrong made the concept seem too difficult to adapt. Eventually two fledgling producers bought the rights as they were looking to break into the industry with something significant. Hungarian Andrew G. Vajna and Lebanese American Mario Kassar were distributors who wanted to upgrade their business cards to 'Movie Producers'. Their new company Carolco Pictures acquired the rights from Warner Bros and they set about speaking to director Ted Kotcheff who had been a part of the failed attempts to develop *First Blood* into a movie in the 70's. Filled with renewed enthusiasm by Vajna and Kassar, Kotcheff sent the script to Sylvester Stallone who read it and accepted the role in the same weekend. Of course when you hired Stallone the actor you inevitably got Stallone the writer too and he quickly made the changes he felt were necessary. The script he'd been sent saw Rambo killing more than 15 people during the movie before dying himself at the end. It was something Stallone quickly identified as an issue and he campaigned to make the character more sympathetic so he wouldn't murder anyone and in fact the only death would be accidental. But, Rambo would still be killed by Colonel (not Captain anymore) Trautman at the end.

With Stallone onboard, casting then hired veteran actor Brian Dennehy (who had shared one scene with Stallone in *F.I.S.T.*) to embody Sheriff Teasle who balanced weary with edgy better than most at the time. Next, producers went in search of their Colonel Trautman and honed in on Hollywood legend Kirk Douglas.

Douglas agreed, which was an added bonus as he had been one of Stallone's cinematic idols as a kid and he had been trying to find a way to work with him for several years. But as rehearsals were about to turn into filming in November of 1981 in Fraser Valley in British Columbia, Stallone and Douglas found they had a difference of creative opinion. Stallone was advocating for letting John Rambo (now his full name) live at the end which would deny Douglas his big final moment in the film when he was to kill Rambo in what his character considered a humane act. Douglas had already expressed concern that he didn't have much screen time and that he didn't even enter the film until halfway through. It resulted in Douglas quitting the role a day into shooting. Rock Hudson was approached as a replacement but ill health meant he couldn't accept. With less than a day to make a decision on the role and travel to the location, jobbing actor Richard Crenna was hired and thrust in front of the cameras. That scene when he enters the tent to introduce himself to the local authorities was the day he had arrived on set. (As with so many things in the movie business, his last minute employment resulted in the most famous role of his career. He reprised Trautman in the first two sequels and also lampooned the character brilliantly in the 1993 spoof *Hot Shots! Part Deux*).

Although Stallone was well versed in putting his body on the line for the sake of a movie, this was another level. In filming his part of the stunt where Rambo leaps from a cliff face onto a tree, he suffered a painful back injury and broken ribs causing production to shut down for several weeks. In the scene where he runs into an old mine tunnel as the national guard fires machine guns at him, one of the special effects to imitate a bullet impacting around him was set-off slightly too early while Stallone's hand was on top of the mini-explosion. It resulted in him losing the tip of his finger but, like his painful fall into the tree, both the moments were used in the finished film.

Once filming finally ended, the first cut lasted three and a half hours and when Stallone watched it he asked his agent to buy the movie and burn it as he felt it was going to be the film that would kill his career. It was eventually trimmed down to 93 minutes and had two alternative endings. Stallone and Crenna did film an ending where Rambo dies but they also shot another version which would see him survive but only after an emotional breakdown in front of his former commanding officer. After remaining virtually silent throughout the film, this powerful ending saw Rambo deliver a rambling, dramatically-charged speech recounting some of the horrors he saw in Vietnam and how he felt like a stranger back in his home country now. Producers wanted to stick with the Rambo death ending but Stallone pleaded about the message that would send to all the veterans in the country. Stallone had spoken to dozens of former soldiers and used a lot of what he had been told in that speech and he said to the producers that if Rambo does die at the end, the film would be telling all those thousands of struggling veterans that death is their only way out of their mental anguish..

The scene is as powerful today as it was when audiences first saw it. And again, try and see an ounce of Rocky in that performance. There is none. Some of what Rambo is saying is virtually unintelligible but that makes it all the more raw and affecting. And after all the masochism of the movie up to that point, to see our protagonist pull his former commander in for a hug while he sobs uncontrollably, explains the veterans mindset better than any Oscar winner ever did. And let's not deny the reasons for not killing off Rambo also included the potential for sequels.

First Blood is one of the great movies on Stallone's CV and although it divided critics on release, it generated an impressive $127 million dollars and finished 6th on the 1982 global box office chart, faring better than *Poltergeist, Star Trek II: Wrath of Khan* and *48 Hrs* but behind the likes of *Gandhi, An Officer and a Gentleman* and his own *Rocky III*. Jerry Goldsmith provided the unique music score that only bursts into an heroic fanfare once in the entire movie, when Rambo drives his stolen army truck through the police blockade heading back into town. The choice to only go big on brassy music at that moment is a clear indication that the character of Rambo isn't meant to be a full-blooded American hero, it's much more complex than that (although the sequels would not leave any grey areas). The only death in the finished film is that of Officer Art Galt and that is cleverly handled by director Ted Kotcheff. Played in ideal fashion by actor Jack Starret, Officer Galt is the instigator for the bullying and harassment that Rambo suffers in the police station which then causes his Vietnam flashbacks which lead him to break out of custody. As the chase to recapture Rambo moves into the cold, rocky landscape Galt is now with a rifle in a helicopter and training his sights on Rambo who is taking shelter behind a tree. With bullets being sprayed around him, Rambo grabs a rock from the floor and hurls it in desperation at the helicopter. The rock impact causes the pilot to briefly lose control of the chopper and Galt falls to his death on the rocks below. Now Rambo didn't cause the death but his actions led to the death. It's what lesser critics failed to understand when they were already dubbing the character as a 'one-man killing machine'. The sequels take the character firmly into heroic territory but *First Blood* is a different animal to what followed. It actually does what all movies want to do, which is that it has a message while it also thoroughly entertains.

It also became historic as the first major Hollywood film to be widely released in cinemas in China and remained top of the charts for tickets sold for a foreign film in China up until 2018. But for Stallone personally it was finally the moment where the audience, the critics and the studios accepted that he had versatility, which is like gold-dust for a movie star. The success of *First Blood* meant that the inevitable approaches about a sequel were finally not just about boxing. And the sequels to this property would send Stallone into an even bigger stratosphere of fame. This new character that he could return to would transcend the movie industry and become a poster-boy, for better or for worse, for billions of men. A byword for supposed masculinity which would prove both a blessing and a curse. But after his most impressive year in his career so far, he was riding high and seemed unbeatable and unstoppable. So, and not for the first time as it would turn out, he decided to go against the grain and try something different again. And it proved that old adage that after every big success, there inevitably comes a fall.

1983 - 1984 - STAYING ALIVE, RHINESTONE

As with many points in the Stallone timeline, the career choices can sometimes feel a little strange. It's always worth reiterating however that scripts deals and actor agreements are often made months and years in advance and sometimes the detail in the contract signed can mean that it is easier (and cheaper) to plough ahead on a project than to pull the plug early. The arrival of a third Rocky movie was the only guarantee of some money coming into the studios via Sylvester Stallone in 1982. And even *Rocky III* could well have been the victim of the law of diminishing returns. A second sequel is often the last sequel as everyone involved has become bored, the box office returns have become a bit soul destroying and completing a 'trilogy' seems to be the only motivation. But if Balboa's latest fight was guaranteeing some financial success, the angry war vet story was by no means something to bet your house on. Maybe I'm being overly generous, but I like to think that the agreement to make both *Staying Alive* and *Rhinestone* was based on the status quo prior to the enormous success of both *Rocky III* and *First Blood*.

What was clear at this time though was that Stallone was a one-man movie making machine. Since his breakthrough film, he had had a credited or uncredited influence either as writer, producer or director (or singer) on every single film that he was attached to. It's not to say that other stars don't exert themselves over a production but Stallone clearly wanted to have his fingers in most of the production pie. But many of the most lauded screen actors have had their career highs under the guidance of a great director. Think Robert DeNiro and Martin Scorsese, Tom Hanks and Steven Spielberg, Samuel L Jackson and Quentin Tarantino. That special collaboration between performer and auteur that creates magic on screen. Bruce Willis' most profitable movie was not a *Die Hard* film, it was *The Sixth Sense* where he gave himself to visionary director M. Night Shyamalan (and again in *Unbreakable* and *Glass*). But throughout his career, Stallone never bet on anyone as much as he bet on himself. When he made *Cop Land* in 1997 under the direction of James Mangold, it was for a pretty untried director at the time. Of course Mangold went on to direct some hugely notable projects such as *Girl, Interrupted*, *Walk The Line, Logan, Indiana Jones and the Dial Of Destiny* and *A Complete Unknown*, but when he had Stallone to use he was still very green. From the mid-nineties onwards there were always stories in the trade press that Tarantino was talking to Stallone for his next film. Tarantino is a self-confessed Stallone fan but for whatever reason, it hasn't materialised up to this point. When you look through his entire filmography, Stallone has almost never entrusted himself to what could best be termed as a "celebrity director". He has never been in a film by Steven Spielberg, Martin Scorcese, George Lucas, Quentin Tarantino, Christopher Nolan, The Coen Brothers, David Lynch, Francis Ford Coppolla or James Cameron to name a few. There must have been conversations, perhaps even tentative agreements. There was a period when Stallone was to make *The Godfather Part III (*with John Travolta coincidentally*)* but that was on the understanding that Stallone would be directing, not that other guy that had done Parts I and II.

I don't have a conclusion to this sidebar and perhaps as his career cruises into the sunset, he may try it. But it does show a supreme confidence in his own abilities to be over every aspect of a movie and make it work. But what you wouldn't have predicted after the double whammy of *Rocky III* and *First Blood* is that he would then want to make John Travolta get the fever again and that he himself would duet with Dolly Parton. Yet, that is where we find ourselves now.

Saturday Night Fever and *Rocky* shared a lot of similarities. Although released a year apart, they both told aspirational tales of young, working class Italian Americans making their way in life and love in a tough urban environment. John Travolta's Tony Manero is by day a painter and decorator of sorts but he lives for the night and the weekends when he can show off his dance skills in the new city discotheques that were springing up around New York at the time. With supreme confidence, the flashy dance floor was his boxing ring. In 1977 the film was a smash hit and a cultural phenomenon, much like *Rocky* the previous year. It finished third overall, ahead of *Smokey and the Bandit* but behind *Close Encounters of the First Kind* and the unstoppable *Star Wars - A New Hope*. It boasted the same director as *Rocky*, John G Avilsden, and also like *Rocky*, a sequel was immediately discussed. *Saturday Night Fever* producers and writers Robert Stigwood and Normal Wexler had almost instantly set about writing a follow-up. But the pessimistic script for what was already called *Staying Alive* (after the hit song from the Bee Gees on the hugely successful soundtrack album) was something that Travolta wasn't keen on. He wanted his character to have some success and some positivity this time around. The project stalled for a few years while Travolta continued to have more hits with *Grease, Urban Cowboy* and *Blow Out*. Paramount

Pictures found renewed enthusiasm for *Staying Alive* when Travolta suggested that he wanted the sequel to have some of the energy and optimistic tone of the *Rocky* films. Against the odds, Paramount's studio boss, Michael Eisner managed to get Stallone to commit to directing. As everyone expected by this point, Stallone was also going to rewrite the script. With Travolta's blessing, Stallone moved the Tony Manero character on in terms of maturity and set the film chronologically six years after the end of *Saturday Night Fever*. Manero is now a struggling Broadway dancer, albeit with the same confidence and swagger. He has an on-off relationship with best friend Jackie (Cynthia Rhodes) but becomes enthralled by the superstar dancer Laura played by Finola Hughes. What follows is a pacy, Rocky-like build up to an opening night on Broadway, where Manero comes out of the shadows to steal the limelight in heroic fashion and thus, his future life in dance is assumed certain. Now while ultimately this is a vehicle for the wickedly talented John Travolta, this is through and through a film by Mr Sylvester Stallone. If you put red gloves on Manero and squint, you could sometimes think you are watching the outtakes and offcuts from *Rocky III*. You could even do a checklist to make sure. Handsome Italian-American is very at home in a big, American city? Tick. That same Italian American is in perfect physical shape? Tick. (The director put Travolta on an intense, five months training programme to develop his physique and he ended up losing 20 pounds, just over 9 kilograms, as a result and has never looked more impressive on screen). Musical montages that show the main character improving and preparing for a big finale to come? Tick. The main character produces physical excellence to achieve his goal at the end of a frantically paced, action climax? Tick. Does Frank Stallone appear on the soundtrack? Tick. (This actually provided brother Frank with a hit song. *Far From Over* is used over the opening credits and again during one of the rehearsal montages. Written by Frank Stallone and Vince DiCola, the unashamedly pumped-up slice of pop broke into the top 10 in the Billboard Hot 100 in 1983 and proved to be Frank's biggest hit). Whether the checklist is valid or not, you can't complain that Travolta's wish to make *Staying Alive* a lot more like *Rocky III*, didn't come true.

But if you can accept some of the absurdity of the film and go along for the shameless ride, its best moment probably comes in the epilogue. After his triumphant moment on the Broadway stage and his reconciliation with Jackie (who stuck by him despite Manero treating her like crap for most of the film) he tells her and the audience that the only thing he wants to do now is "strut". In sync with Travolta bursting open the backstage door, the Bee Gees titular song kicks in and we are treated to a good minute or so of a grinning, chiseled Travolta walking as only he can, along to that baseline and those unforgettable falsettos.

The film opened on the 15th of July 1983 and was actually a box office hit. Its $12 million dollar opening weekend was, at the time, the biggest opening weekend for a musical ever. It went on to gross $127 million worldwide in the year that was dominated by *Star Wars Episode 6 - Return of the Jedi* . Overall though it made less than *Saturday Night Fever* and the franchise came to a crashing halt. Perhaps the reason there was no third movie in this series was not so much about the money but more about the critics. They savaged the film, repeatedly insisting it was just a *Rocky* in disguise (which is hard to argue against). In 2006, Entertainment Tonight still named it the Worst Sequel Ever and Travolta has never really talked about it since. For Stallone, he never directed a film he wasn't in, ever again (although he does appear in an early moment in *Staying Alive*. As Travolta strides along a busy sidewalk, he bumps shoulders with a fur-coated, sunglasses-wearing man of similar dimensions. The guy turns around briefly as they continue walking in opposite directions while everyone was asking their cinema partner if they saw what they think they saw).

In fact Stallone put pen to paper on a film he wasn't in only twice more in his career. Both times it was for typical Jason Statham fare. He wrote *Homefront* in 2013 and then wrote again for his *Expendables* co-star in 2025 for the film *A Working Man*. Both are movies that he would have starred in himself had they gone into production years before.

So with this financial success but critical mauling, enter stage left…Dolly Parton. As movie pitch meetings go, it must have been awe-inspiring. "So, you know that 1975 song *Rhinestone Cowboy*, well nearly a decade later we will centre a fish out of water comedy around that title but with Rambo." It's a simplistic summary but it holds water. The story as written by Phil Alden Robinson was always intended to be a vehicle for country music legend Dolly Parton. After proving her cinematic pull with *9 to 5* and *The Best Little Whorehouse in Texas*, this *My Fair Lady*-type of script saw a New York cab driver become embroiled in a bet between Parton's established singing-star character Jake Farris and her agent / nightclub manager Freddie Ugo (Rob Liebman). Jake bets Freddie that she could turn anyone into a singing sensation. Freddie takes the bet and insists he picks the subject. Up screeches a taxi cab with our male lead Nick Martinelli at the wheel. After much 'hilarity', Jake manages to whip Nick into shape as a country singer and the two perform a crowd-pleasing show in a New York redneck bar called 'Rhinestone' to end the movie.

So far so good and everyone was looking forward to Parton re-teaming with her *The Best Little Whorehouse in Texas* co-star Burt Reynolds in what was predicted to be a nice little money spinner for all concerned. But as is often the case in showbiz, people in suits intervened. Both Parton and Stallone were clients of the same talent agency, Creative Artists Agency (CAA). Their manager Mike Ovitz was immediately decisive in saying that if 20th Century Fox wanted Dolly Parton for *Rhinestone*, then they had to take Stallone for the Nick Martinelli role. It's hard to believe that Stallone had no say in this and it's hard to believe that he hadn't wanted to try his hand at an out and out comedy. But to throw yourself into a comedy with singing was brave to say the least. Reportedly, although never confirmed, Stallone had to turn down *Romancing The Stone* to do *Rhinestone* and it's not a secret that he was well into discussion and rewrites to star in *Beverly Hills Cop* . When that fell through, the cowboy comedy was moved up in the schedule and Stallone was given $5 million dollars and a slice of the presumed profits as added incentive. Stallone set about altering (total rewriting) the Phil Alden Robinson script and they both received screen credit for the story. But the directing gig was a lot less transparent. Editor turned director Don Zimmerman was in charge for the first few weeks but then dismissed and in came Bob Clark, who had proven his comedy credentials with the juvenile hits *Porky's* and *Porky's II: The Next Day* . On set however it was increasingly reported that Stallone was actually directing. His rewrites had not gone down well with studio bosses or the original author and Phil Alden Robinson even considered having his name removed from the credits in disgust. But the CAA agency seemed to have the upper hand since they controlled both the movie's stars and they made sure the production rolled along despite many concerns over Stallone's comedic performance and the tone of the whole project.

Upon release, the concerns proved real. The huge $28 million dollar budget (of which Stallone got $5 million) was not recouped and the film only salvaged $21 million at the box office. The critics ravaged the film more than they had with *Staying Alive,* singling out Stallone for most of the damage done. And of course there was the singing. Unlike his theme song for *Paradise Alley,* his singing in this film is meant to be poor. It means you can forgive most of the efforts as merely comedic in the early stages of the movie. When it gets to the final, triumphant concert and duet with Parton, it's probably best to just fast forward. An actor who couldn't sing never tried to prove they could opposite Elvis Presley on screen, for a reason. To take on country music alongside one of the genres biggest names is asking for trouble. (By contrast and despite the failure of the movie, Dolly Parton got two top ten country singles out of the official soundtrack album: "Tennessee Homesick Blues" and "God Won't Get You"). But, this clear miscalculation also gives credence to the story that Stallone was in fact directing this film and therefore, he couldn't see the wood for the out of tune trees. If he was indeed on a self-indulgent ego trip during production, it would explain the apparent lack of any singing tuition prior to filming his musical performances. But singing aside, the performance is the issue. In the right circumstances, Stallone has now proven his comedic ability to most. In his current TV series *Tulsa King* he knocks his one-liners out of the park. His comedy timing in other films is spot on too, such as *Demolition Man, Bullet to the Head, Grudge Match* and his brief appearance in *Guardians of the Galaxy Vol. 2*. *Rocky* is often a witty character and Stallone sell's that stuff superbly. But here in *Rhinestone,* it's just too much. Some of his comedy work is fine, it's not all bad. A scene near the climax of the film where he battles with a stubborn apartment door will make anyone giggle. But the bad is really, really bad. If you were on set during production and you were a brave person you would have taken him aside and simply told him to not try so hard. Subtlety goes out the window and at times you have to wince at the amount of visible effort he seems to be putting in to hammer the joke home. The final script is also to blame as it wallows in every cliche possible and it relies on the actors to make more of the limp screenplay. Parton and Stallone have always insisted they had a lot of fun working together but their chemistry on screen fails to sizzle and even though it's only 111 minutes long *Rhinestone* still feels like it should have had an interval.

At the start of this chapter, I pondered the strangeness of the career choices in 1983 and 1984. Two very risky projects, neither of which were really in his comfort zone and neither of which turned out to be great. No one sets out to make a bad film of course but these two years with these two flops could have sunk many a career. So, why did he pursue both films when he had the chance to do eventual hits like *Romancing the Stone* and *Beverly Hills Cop?* Obviously, there was no way of knowing that Michael Douglas and Eddie Murphy would take over those projects and turn them into big, solid hits that would themselves spawn sequels. But maybe Stallone knew that in his back pocket he had 1985 ahead and his two iconic characters were about to have their biggest hits and he was about to have his biggest year as a movie star.

RAMBO: FIRST BLOOD PART 2 (1985)

NO MAN, NO LAW, NO WAR CAN STOP HIM

Starring - Sylvester Stallone, Richard Crenna, Charles Napier, Steven Berkoff
Written by - Kevin Jarre, James Cameron and Sylvester Stallone
Original Score by - Jerry Goldsmith
Directed by - George P. Cosmatos

When watching the first and second *Rocky* movies, there's clearly more budget on number two but the tone is in keeping with the original film. There are creative changes as the series wears on but it's really only *Rocky IV* that sticks out as being most unlike the others in the franchise. In following up *First Blood* however, almost everything that had made that film a hit was jettisoned. In its place came the ultimate star vehicle, the ultimate 80's action film and the wish-fulfillment of millions of disgruntled Americans.

Let's get the plot out of the way first and as all the best blockbusters should be, it's fairly easy to follow. After the events of *First Blood*, John Rambo is now serving his time in prison. His former Green Beret Commander, Colonel Samuel Trautman (Richard Crenna returning) comes to him with a deal. He has a mission to offer him to take photos to prove the remaining prisoner of war camps in Vietnam do not contain any American soldiers. Rather than cracking rocks for no apparent reason in jail, he agrees and is parachuted into where he fought the war a decade earlier. What he finds there is that there are in fact many American POWs plus the Vietnamese army is in cahoots with evil Russian military types. After reporting his findings back to base, he is told to leave the captured American soldiers behind and forget all about it. Rambo doesn't follow that order and he loses his shit and it doesn't end well for anyone except Rambo and the soldiers he has rescued.

In a nutshell that's it and if you think of the plot of *First Blood*, that was also just as easy to follow. So what's the big difference between the debut of the character of John Rambo and the second film with John Rambo? It's all in the execution.

A second film featuring the John Rambo character was understandably something Stallone was very keen to push forward. He had just had another big hit with *Rocky III* which proved to be the biggest of the trilogy, but outside of that character it was only *First Blood* that had connected with the public. Sequels to *Nighthawks, Escape to Victory, Paradise Alley* or *F.I.S.T.* were not an option but he and the studio certainly felt there was more story to tell with this monosyllabic former soldier. Screenwriter Kevin Jarre came up with the original outline and it wasn't too different from the final film. An up and coming writer and director called James Cameron was then employed to draft the screenplay and he would write that while he was also working on two other scripts called *The Terminator* and *Aliens*. Cameron's *First Blood II: The Mission* was then handed to Stallone who set about creating the final shooting script. In interviews since, Cameron has suggested that he came up with the action and set-pieces while Stallone injected the emotion and politics. Producers wanted Rambo to have a partner for this mission and John Travolta was put forward but Stallone and Cameron were adamant that he had to remain a lone-wolf character. In earlier drafts as well, there was a lot more build up before Rambo got in action-mode and again that was ripped out in favour of getting the pace of the film going as soon as possible. Greek Italian director George P Cosmatos was brought on board although his CV only boasted one high profile film: the war-flick *Escape to Athena* that starred Roger Moore, David Niven, Telly Savalas and Elliot Gould which had only been a modest hit more than 6 years before. Again, rumours quickly sprung up that in actual fact, the leading man was in charge of more than just the acting and writing.

Shooting in the summer of 1984 in Mexico and Thailand, the gruelling process was overshadowed by tragedy. While creating one of the movie's memorable set-pieces at a waterfall, special effects coordinator Clifford P. Wenger, Jr. accidentally lost his footing and fell to his death although some reports suggested he was caught up in a mis-timed explosion. As production resumed, the marketing machine in the United States started up a full year before the movie's release. A teaser trailer was put into theaters with some hastily shot body close ups and one zoom-in of Stallone's face with his trademark headband on. Nothing from the film was ready to use at that time. Posters appeared well in advance and tie-in toys were delivered to shops despite the film heading towards having an adult-only R-rating. Jerry Goldsmith returned to score the film and although he did use some cues from his first effort, much of this soundtrack was clearly more vitriolic and heroic. His main Rambo fanfare was to recur in the same way as that legendary Monty Norman theme surfaces whenever James Bond does something very 007-like.

Released in prime blockbuster scheduling territory on May 22nd 1985 it was big from the start. It broke a new record for opening on more than 2,000 screens in America on the same day (2,074). It made over $50 million in the U.S. alone and more than $300 million worldwide. It ended the year second in the U.S. Box Office charts behind *Back to the Future* and worldwide it was the same. But while *Back to the Future* was rightly applauded for being simply a brilliant film, *Rambo: First Blood Part 2* affected the psyche of the nation. Its unapologetic leaning towards the right wing, America-knows-best ideal chimed perfectly with the Ronald Reagan presidency. So much so that Reagan was caught on microphone in the Oval Office following a hostage crisis by saying, "After seeing 'Rambo' last night, I know what to do next time this happens."

The Cold War was still raging between America and the Soviet Union and the Presidency of the day must have been delighted to see Rambo tackle and defeat Russian soldiers as well as the Vietnamese military. Just as many Americans suspected (and hoped), behind the local militia in the movie lay snarling, hissable Russian villains led by British stage actor Steven Berkoff who had played another pantomime villain in *Beverly Hills Cop* the year before. It allowed for the film to maximise Rambo's efficiency in killing pretty much every bad guy that the U.S. electorate felt was a threat to them. But it wasn't just your average person on the street that responded to the film's unhidden coding. The military and especially Vietnam veterans publicly praised the underlying message, which was similar to the first movie but now without any ambiguity whatsoever. In *First Blood* it's up to the viewer to decide ultimately whether Rambo was justified or whether the Sheriff did try to do the right thing but it just got out of hand. Despite that burst of emotion in Stallone's final scene in *First Blood* and the sympathy you feel for him you can still debate the realities of the outcome. With the sequel however, there's one opinion and one opinion only. Vietnam veterans felt unwelcomed and unloved to say the least, when they came home from the conflict and no one had really addressed that properly and publicly until now. John Rambo's carnage was viewed as cathartic by many across America. It was revenge and it was completely acceptable. After the bloodletting and killing, Colonel Trautman asks Rambo what he wants from life now. He replies, "I want, what they want (points to the rescued POWs) and every other guy who came over here and spilled his guts and gave everything he had, wants. For our country to love us as much as we love it. That's what I want."

It's cheesy and Stallone delivers it wholeheartedly but it resonated and propelled the movie and in particular the character, to mythical status. The movie is now so well known that perhaps it's hard to take a step back and judge it on its own merits. It now comes as a package with the sequels, the legend of Rambo and the constant name-checking of the character by the media whenever they need a quick reference for armed male violence. As a film it zips along, just as the makers intended. Stallone's physique is fat-free and perfectly sculpted and he must have had someone constantly on hand to smother his torso in baby oil at all times. But it works and Stallone is totally compelling in what is HIS movie. Just as Indiana Jones has a jacket, a hat and a whip and 007 has a tuxedo and a Walther PPK gun, Rambo now had an iconic look. The shirt removed, the combat trousers and boots, the headband, the bow and arrow, the knife and other assorted weapons. He was now one of those rare movie characters that could be identified without hesitation purely by silhouette. And that also veered Rambo into the realms of a superhero. For all intents and purposes, the John Rambo we see in *Rambo: First Blood Part II* and again in *Rambo III* is a comic book character. He has to dress in his particular costume, he has to save the day and the realities of the extreme violence he inflicts and has inflicted on him have no relation to real life. He has a superheroes musical theme and the one guarantee is he will never, ever be killed.

The early 80's action efforts from Clint Eastwood and Burt Reynolds had been fine but any intense physical moments were completely left to a stuntman from a distance and when compared to this movie, they must have known their heroic role days were all but over. Now you had an action star who wanted the camera to show it was him as much as possible. A stunt double wasn't sent to the Philippines to wear similar clothes and jump off a few rocks, it was the star himself who was bruising and battering his own body to get the intensity they wanted on screen. Stallone certainly wasn't the first silver screen star to put his body on the line for the sake of the movie, but he took it to the next level. The *Rocky* films up to this point and *First Blood* had left him with enough aches, pains and battle scars to last a normal persons' lifetime, but now in *Rambo: First Blood Part II* he had taken it up another notch. Charlie Chaplin, Tom Mix, Buster Keaton and Jackie Chan are just some of the headliners who put themselves at risk for their art. But as the 1960s had moved into the 1970s most Hollywood movies had become more cerebral and method acting saw actors putting their mental well-being in harm's way, rather than their physical being. Now, with Sylvester Stallone at the forefront, mainstream movies were pushing for extreme realism again, when it came to action. Tom Cruise's *Mission: Impossible* antics owe a debt to Stallone's willingness and insistence to do as much as he could, himself. Besides, not many stuntmen could take their top off and convincingly pass for that extraordinary body.

The overwhelming success of his second stab (pun intended) at Rambo meant he would certainly be asked to reprise the character again. But in an unmatched, one-two punch at the box office, Stallone was stepping back into the ring and this time he wasn't taking on a champion, he wasn't taking on a brute from the slums, this time he was taking on an entire country.

ROCKY IV (1985)

*HE'S FACING THE ULTIMATE CHALLENGE.
AND FIGHTING FOR HIS LIFE*

Starring - Sylvester Stallone, Talia Shire, Burt Young, Carl Weathers, Doplh Lundgren, Brigitte Nielsen
Written by - Sylvester Stallone
Original Score by - Vince Di Cola
Directed by - Sylvester Stallone

Rocky IV has its detractors. Some more cerebral critics would say this is just a long MTV video and bears little if no resemblance to the three instalments that preceded it. Some would say that Stallone is playing 'Movie Star Sylvester Stallone' and the character that won him an Oscar nomination has been cast aside. They may even go on to criticise its simplistic depiction of U.S.- Russia relations and its use of cliched stereotypes and that its message at the end is both naive and heavy-handed. They would be right. But it's still the most unashamedly entertaining movie that he ever made. It took until 2019's *Avengers: Endgame* for this author to experience levels of cinema-screen frenzy to match the experience of watching *Rocky IV* in the mid-eighties. The unparalleled final fight was treated as real by the packed-out cinema and Rocky's victory brought cheers, clapping and plenty of popcorn in the air.

The seeds of moving the Balboa story away from street-level realism and towards mass entertainment were sowed in *Rocky III*. The gritty capturing of tough lives lived on the streets of Philadelphia had been replaced with mostly attractive, physical specimens in designer clothes. *Rocky* and *Rocky II*'s long, dialogue heavy scenes were now shorter, punchier and ended with some form of soap-opera-esque stare into the distance. Bill Conti's score was no longer the only music on the soundtrack album as Survivor's hit song became the main sonic-soundscape for *Rocky III*. Intentionally avoiding a backward step, Stallone wrote and designed *Rocky IV* to be a crowd-pleasing blockbuster and that is exactly what it was. But, as in the tradition of the best big-screen successes, it was one of the hardest films he ever made and it nearly cost him his life.

Early drafts of the script for *Rocky IV* had Mr. T reprising his role as Clubber Lang from *Rocky III* but that was quickly discarded as Stallone wanted to move the story away from what had come before.

Rocky's 1 to 3 had all linked together in some way and they had featured Rocky fighting both Apollo Creed and Clubber Lang twice over the course of the trilogy. Once to lose to his opponent and then a rematch to win. But now he felt he wanted the audience to not require too much knowledge of the first three films so that *Rocky IV* could stand alone if necessary. The Cold War was very much at the forefront of America's minds in the early eighties, and many Hollywood films were putting Russians front and centre as their bad guys. *Red Dawn, War Games* and *Firefox* were among dozens that used the political climate as their in-built antagonist. Clearly it was on Stallone's mind too as he helped James Cameron shape *Rambo: First Blood Part II* into an America versus the Soviets showdown. For *Rocky IV* he conceived of a brutish Russian fighter that seemed impossible to beat. Originally he envisaged him as a mountainous, hairy animalistic-type that was worlds away from the skilled fighters Balboa had faced before. As he continued to flesh-out the basic premise he knew that casting of his opponent would be crucial to the success or failure of the movie. He and his casting agent Amanda Mackey trawled through more than 8,000 male actor resumes. Stallone's friend and filmmaker John Herzveld then met 26-year old Swedish model turned actor Dolph Lundgren and everything clicked into place. Lundgren had been a keen proponent of martial arts since he was 14 and won European Championships in Karate in 1980 and 1981 all while graduating with a Masters Degree in Chemical Engineering from the University of Sydney. While his athletic ability wasn't in doubt, it was when Herzveld put the young actor's head-shot in front of Stallone that it all changed. Gone was the neanderthal Russian challenge to Rocky and now he was imagined as the ultimate athlete. An opponent that had been trained with ultra-modern equipment and with the most extreme methods to be a fighting machine designed to humiliate any American who dared to stand in the ring opposite him. While Lundgren was a keen actor he hadn't had much experience up to that point. His first big-screen appearance had been a non-speaking role as a bodyguard in the last Roger Moore led James Bond film, *A View To A Kill*. It was a job he had acquired thanks to his on-off relationship with the force of nature that was the model and actress Grace Jones, who was also in that 007 adventure. Once cast, it was Lundgren's suggestion that to make his character even more intimidating, he should hardly speak. It worked for *Rambo* after all. In the finished film, Lundgren had to learn just nine lines of dialogue but that did include two all-time classics: "I will break you," and "If he dies, he dies." Danish actress Brigitte Nielsen was a late addition to the cast and took many of the lines that were originally spoken by Drago's trainer Nikolai Koloff (played by American actor Michael Pataki). Nielsen played Ludmilla, the wife of Drago, and it was perhaps the fact she was dating and about to marry Stallone at the time, that helped her secure the part.

The finished draft saw a very self-contained Rocky story where what had come before was largely irrelevant and it didn't necessarily leave doors open at the end either. It was a perfect product where you didn't need to have seen previous *Rocky*'s for this film to work. Stallone had intended *Rocky III* to be the closing chapter of a trilogy and after beating Clubber Lang at the end, he would peacefully die next to Adrian in the taxi leaving the fight venue. Ever increasing box office returns would soon erase that ending. Now a super-rich, super-happy heavyweight champion of the world, Rocky Balboa lives with his wife Adrian (Talia Shire returning) and their young son Rocky Junior (Rocky Krakoff, but born as Angelo Bruno Krakoff) in their huge mansion. Best pal Apollo Creed (Carl Weathers, looking in arguably better shape than Rocky) has seen that a Russian soldier and boxer Ivan Drago (Lundgren) has arrived in the US and is looking to challenge Balboa to an exhibition bout. Creed wants to face him himself and show he still has one more fight in him and reluctantly Balboa agrees to be in his corner for the show-fight in Las Vegas. Things turn tragic when Drago kills Creed in the ring and in the aftermath, Balboa says he wants revenge and will fight Drago, in Moscow, on Christmas Day.

Principal photography began on the 18th of March 1985 in Jackson Hole, Wyoming which was standing in for the snowy wastelands of Russia where Rocky prepares for the fight. Temperatures were reaching minus 10 as a helicopter filmed Stallone running up an 11,000 foot mountain as part of one of the two training montages. The final fight was also filmed early in the schedule at the Agrodome in Vancouver, British Columbia. The facility was chosen as it had a modern-look in keeping with the idea that Moscow was putting itself on show for this boxing match. Recognising that he had to push the envelope further with the fight scenes in *Rocky IV* it was decided that for close-ups, particular angles and to increase the intensity, Stallone and Lundgren would have to actually hit each other. The slow-motion punches that you see in the film are real punches albeit slowed down slightly by the actors, for accuracy. But, one real punch to Stallone's chest caused real problems. Immediately falling backwards, Stallone felt his breathing suddenly become labored and his vision became blurry. Lundgren had struck him so hard that his breastbone had squashed his heart which in turn had caused his heart to swell. His blood pressure increased to over 260 as that evening wore on and he was evacuated to hospital. He was flown to Saint John's Regional Medical Centre in Santa Monica in California and kept in intensive care for four days.

Fortunately, the vast majority of filming for the climactic fight had been done so the production was able to resume within two weeks. Next on the filming schedule was the fateful fight between Apollo Creed and Drago for which the actual MGM Grand Hotel in Las Vegas was used. Soul singing legend James Brown had been asked to provide music for the soundtrack album but that was soon upgraded to asking him to be in the film, performing the song himself as part of an elaborate pre-fight, pro-America show orchestrated by the showman that was Apollo Creed. Brown had trouble lip syncing to the backing track during filming so eventually Stallone let him sing it live although it is the recorded version that is used in the film. When later released as a single, *Living in America* became James Brown's first top ten single in more than a decade but it was also his last.

Filming of the Creed vs Drago fight also produced a battle between Weathers and Lundgren. More than once, Weathers stormed off the set complaining that Lundgren was going at him too hard and someone was going to get hurt. Stallone would find Weathers and diffuse the situation so filming could resume. The remaining interior and exterior scenes were filmed last at MGM/UA's Culver City Studios and other locations around Los Angeles and the film wrapped in mid-July. Stallone and his two editors, John W Wheeler and Don Zimmerman then had just over four months to cut the film before its intended Christmas release. The climatic bout of the film had been set at Christmas so the release date was impossible to move.

Rocky IV ended up being the only film in the *Rocky* franchise that wasn't scored by Bill Conti. The veteran composer was already committed to *The Karate Kid Part II,* so again Stallone saw it as an opportunity to forge new ground in the series. Composer and arranger Vince DiCola had worked with Frank Stallone to create *Far From Over* and a few other tracks on the soundtrack for *Staying Alive* and it was enough to convince Stallone to approach him for his first, film-scoring assignment. Inclined towards electronic pop and rock, DiCola and his synthesiser produced tracks that could not have been further from the familiar *Rocky* sound. Although a slow version of *Gonna Fly Now* appeared on the *Rocky IV* soundtrack album released, the iconic music was notably absent from the film itself and is only heard briefly near the end of one of the training montages. The only compositions from his score that were on the official soundtrack recording were titled *War* and *Training Montage*, but both versions were very different from the ones used in the movie. (The discrepancy was finally atoned for with a complete score for *Rocky IV* being released in 2010). But aside from those two tracks, the rest of the album was designed to be a hit record. The eighties had seen movie scores go from rare, elitist collectors items to multi-million selling chart-toppers. The soundtrack albums for films such as *Flashdance, Grease, Saturday Night Fever, Beverly Hills Cop, The Big Chill* and *Purple Rain* were considered as important financially as the movie itself. *Rocky IV* jumped on the bandwagon with Stallone requesting new songs from many of the biggest pop artists of the day. *Go West* gave him *One Way Street*, *Touch* offered *The Sweetest Victory*, Robert Tepper gave him the powerful *No Easy Way Out* while *Survivor* had another hit thanks to *Rocky*, in the form of *Burning Heart*. Kenny Loggins and Gladys Knight duetted *Double or Nothing* to go on the album along with James Brown's flag-waving hit. And Stallone was offered another choice of two songs that were going to be either for a *Rocky* or a *Karate Kid* film. Peter Cetera's *Glory of*

Love was eventually passed-on by Stallone in favour of John Cafferty's *Hearts on Fire* which he used twice in the movie. There is so much music in the film (and the influence of the launch of MTV in 1981 is so prevalent) that 39 percent of the total 91 minute running time is taken up with music montages.

When the finished movie was released it produced a clear divide between critics and audiences. Critics were scathing in their assessment but many missed the message in-built into the finale. Pages of newspaper print was dedicated to how anti-Russian and pro-America the film was (aligning it to the politics of *Rambo: First Blood Part II*) while completely failing to take in what Stallone attempted in the final ten minutes. It may have been cheesy and slightly clumsily executed, but in the last few rounds of the big fight the Russian crowd recognise the courage of the little American in the ring and start to chant his name instead of Drago's. After Rocky's victory speech where he pleads "If I can change and you can change, everybody can change," the highest ranking Russian official in the arena stands to applaud the sentiment and is grudgingly followed by his underlings. (The Soviet premier portrayed was very intentionally modelled on the recently risen to power Mikhail Gorbachev who was seen as moderate and willing to mend ties with the West. He was played by British actor David Lloyd Austin who went on to repeat the trick in *The Naked Gun*.)

But while the critics refused to have a good time, audiences lapped it up. It went straight to number one in the US box office and stayed there for six weeks. Domestically it gulped up $127 million dollars and globally it crossed the $300 million dollar mark. It remains the highest grossing *Rocky* film and finished third in the worldwide chart for 1985, just behind *Rambo: First Blood Part II* and *Back to the Future.* To this day it remains third on his career-box office list and that's only behind *Guardians of the Galaxy Vol. 2* and *The Expendables 2* which were released in a different century where ticket prices had more than quadrupled.

During the pandemic in 2020, Stallone went back into an editing suite and produced a 35th anniversary re-edit of the film that he retitled - *Rocky IV: Rocky vs Drago.* This new version was a couple of minutes longer but quite different in tone in many ways. Scenes that are more sympathetic to Drago are in, other scenes are extended slightly and some of Bill Conti's previous *Rocky* work sits alongside the DiCola score. Gone is the bizarre sub-plot for Paulie (Burt Young) involving a six-foot talking robot. Created and named *Sico* by International Robotics in 1982, Stallone saw it at a party and squeezed it into his film as a gift that is given to Paulie on his birthday. The robot toured many electronics exhibitions in the 1980's and his appearance in *Rocky IV* meant it actually became a member of the Screen Actors Guild. But, for the re-release the robot plot was completely removed. More subtle changes were made that perhaps only hardcore fans would notice but in general the new version went down favourably with critics as well as audiences this time.

The impact and legacy of *Rocky IV* was such that the reboot of the franchise felt it couldn't ignore it. *Creed II* in 2018 built its entire plot around the repercussions of the events of *Rocky IV* and Dolph Lundgren reprised his role as Ivan Drago, now full of bitterness after decades of living with the loss to Rocky. Brigitte Nielsen also briefly returned as Ludmillia but *Creed II* never captures the thrill and pure entertainment value of *Rocky IV.*

Overall, 1985 was the peak of Sylvester Stallone's success. His two films that year had made over half a billion dollars and he was the most recognisable face in cinema, if not planet earth. If he couldn't get critics to go along for the ride with him, cinema-goers had definitely given him their complete approval. And he was set to marry again. Nielsen had made an impression both on and off the *Rocky IV* set, so Stallone made sure he would work onscreen with her again in his very next film as he attempted to try and follow up what had been, his most triumphant year.

1986 - 1987 COBRA, OVER THE TOP

By the mid-eighties, star power was so prevalent that movies would be greenlit on the basis of who the lead performer was alone. Story, motivation, genre, dialogue, effects, music, promotion and budget would all come after the fact of getting that bankable commodity to commit to a (or any) project. Movie executives were now professional at stroking the ego of their chosen actor to the point that they would give over almost total creative control to the star, as long as they signed-on to be in a film for them. Rightly or wrongly, they believed that the mere surname of some actors was enough to guarantee a return on their investment and the finished product was almost an afterthought. The whim of the star was pandered to and critical good judgement was being overlooked so that theoretical boxes could be ticked in order to guarantee maximum profit. Stallone was cemented as the biggest movie star in the world and was at the top of every studio's wishlist when it came to crafting a new film. He had two blockbuster franchises and was comfortable in his role as Hollywood's favourite money-making tough guy. The attempts to broaden his back catalogue with comedy and directing had fallen flat and the salaries he was now being offered to show his muscles or pick up a gun on screen made trying something new redundant. But Hollywood and the movie business moves fast and as soon as you think you have it all figured out, it leaves you for dust. Audiences can quickly tire of a formula and the studios were usually the last ones to find out.

From the start of 1985 to the end of 1986, cinema went through another metamorphosis. Family audiences embraced *Back to the Future* and *The Goonies* and teenagers started to move away from films with lead actors who were much older than them and responded more to stories that reflected their lives such as *The Breakfast Club*, *Pretty in Pink* and *Ferris Bueller's Day Off*. *Cobra* opened the week after *Top Gun*. It was also the year of *Crocodile Dundee*, *Aliens*, *Star Trek IV: The Voyage Home* and *Highlander*, none of which featured an heroic lead character who was muscle-bound. Not to mention the fact that anything to do with the Vietnam War was now a serious business after the multi-Oscar winning *Platoon*.

Cobra sits as a bit of an oddity in Stallone's filmography as it was a box office hit but it didn't lead to a sequel and is widely regarded as fairly unsuccessful. It began life as a 1974 thriller novel by Paula Gosling called *A Running Duck*. It follows a young woman who finds she is being targeted by a hitman and when former Vietnam veteran sniper Lieutenant Malchek is assigned to protect her, they fall in love. The book was retitled *Fair Game* and found its way to the offices of Cannon Films, which was a relatively new player in Hollywood and run by two larger than life characters, Menahem Golan and Yoram Globus. Cannon Films had already had moderate success with low-budget action starring Chuck Norris and Charles Bronson but after watching the success of *Rambo: First Blood Part II* they wanted to up their game. They approached Warner Bros. to jointly fund two movies that would star Stallone (they would end up as *Cobra* and *Over the Top*). When Golan and Globus went to offer the deal to Stallone he was wooed by the creative licence he would be given and the chance to right what he saw as, a wrong. Two years earlier, Stallone was prepared to star in *Beverly Hills Cop* and he had virtually rewritten the entire screenplay he had been offered, removing most of the comedy and adding very expensive action sequences. When he eventually walked away from that film (and Eddie Murphy stepped in) he was left with a number of scenes and ideas that he had concocted that were in danger of never seeing the light of a cinema screen. The *Fair Game* story instantly appealed to Stallone as he felt he could re-tool much of the script he had worked on and adapt it to this new project, so he set to work and 'Stallone-d' his next film.

Part of the appeal of this project was also his desire to do something reminiscent of the hugely influential *Dirty Harry* series. The four films up to then had all been hits and the box office returns had increased with each installment. The original *Dirty Harry* in 1971 had introduced Clint Eastwood as a unique cop hero at the time. His shoot-first, ask-questions-later style of policing was very different from what audiences were used to and its impact was still being felt. The main character from *Fair Game* now became Marion 'Cobra' Cobretti and Stallone's wish was to produce a film that would push the boundaries of violence on screen and add elements of horror to the action-tropes he knew so well. Lieutenant Cobretti now worked in the so-called 'Zombie-squad' of the Los Angeles Police Department, doing the dirty work that other cops wouldn't do. When a satanic cult fails to kill one of its targets, leaving a living witness, Cobretti becomes protector and detective until the bloody end. While the plot wasn't exactly groundbreaking, it was to be about the style, the mood and the execution. In the end, if you are ever asked to summarise the excess of 1980's action films, *Cobra* would be a good selection.

Stallone's director from *Rambo: First Blood Part II* was hired to repeat the trick again but George P Cosmatos was widely regarded as a semi-ghost-director on *Cobra*, with Stallone doing the job without the onscreen official credit. Casting of the main bad guy, The Night Slasher, took longer than expected and it took seven auditions before Brian Thompson convinced the filmmakers that he was right for the part of lead-psycho. Despite the actor's formidable appearance (and undeniable physical similarities to Arnold Schwarzenegger, which must have been noted at the time) it was felt he was just too nice in the auditions. But as soon as they did a screen test with him, he was offered the role on the spot. And there was more than just the behind the scenes influence of *Dirty Harry*, as two members of that original cast found roles on *Cobra*. Reni Santoni was hired as Cobra's partner Sergeant Tony Gonzales who would provide some welcome, lighter moments in the film. And Andrew Robinson went from being the main bad guy that Eastwood was chasing in *Dirty Harry* (and was on the receiving end of the legendary "Do you feel lucky, Punk?" speech) to the by-the-book Detective Monte who hates everything that Marion Cobretti stands for. Star power was also evident as Stallone's new wife Brigitte Nielsen was cast as the model and damsel in distress, Ingrid Knudsen. After appearing together in *Rocky IV*, they had recently married and they were said to be besotted with each other all the way through the filming of *Cobra*. (They divorced in 1987 and the only time they were in the same film again was in 2018's *Creed II*, although they didn't share a scene in person).

Filming began in October of 1985 and ran through to the beginning of 1986. The film was to be set in Seattle but Stallone changed it to California with a budget of $25 million dollars. Attention was paid to craft a new, iconic look for the lead character that could be as recognisable to audiences as Rocky and Rambo but the desire to make Cobretti the coolest cop on screen in the 1980's has since led to this film becoming something of a cult classic. Although seemingly on an average police salary by the looks of his apartment, Marion Cobretti still drives a custom 1950 Mercury and he has fitted it with a nitro speed-boost switch (which is only used once in the film to minimal effect). The studio built two more replicas for the various stunt work required, but the original (which Stallone owned) was used for all the close-ups and dialogue scenes. In many moments in the film, the decision was made to have Cobretti with a toothpick hanging out of his mouth and sunglasses that never seem to come off. An early scene that certainly led to its cult status sees our hero returning to his apartment after a morning of shooting a bad guy in a supermarket. He is reading a newspaper but for some reason, puts it in a portable barbeque outside his front door. Once inside, he decides to use a pair of scissors to cut off a small piece of leftover pizza, for his dinner while he watches the news on TV. All this is done with sunglasses still firmly on his face. Speaking of his gun, it's hardly a police issue weapon as it's a custom Colt Gold Cup National Match 1911 and in a staggering piece of self-branding, Cobretti has had the marble handle made with a cobra snake's head printed on it. The performance of Stallone in the lead role demonstrates how uncertain everyone was when making the film. He speaks in a strange, low rasp that must have given him a sore throat every day but the tone throughout veers wildly from traditional cop thriller to squeamish horror and even buddy comedy. Some of the genuine highlights are the interactions between Stallone and Reni Santori as his partner, where improvised dialogue adds some much needed reality to the outlandish mood. Nielsen herself does a very creditable job in what is a thankless task.

Despite *Aliens* being released in the same year with Sigourney Weavers' lead character setting a new benchmark, female roles in action-orientated movies were normally one-dimensional. Mrs Stallone is required to shriek and scream and run and fall at regular intervals, but she does it with full commitment and really helps to sell some of the more terrifying scenes.

When filming was complete, the original cut of the movie was well over two and a quarter hours and almost immediately when it was submitted to the MPAA for approval, the filmmakers were told that it would be given the dreaded 'X' certificate in its current form. Some of the bloody gore and lingering shots of mutilated bodies were immediately called into question. James R Symons and Don Zimmerman joined Stallone in the editing room and started to snip out the most upsetting scenes. As the premier approached, Cannon Films and Warner Bros. suddenly panicked and told Stallone to make more severe cuts and bring the film in at under 90 minutes. *Top Gun* was released the week before and was already a huge hit so Stallone only had a few days to make the film much more accessible to a wider audience and sacrifice his own vision for an ultra-violent, adult thriller. Hungarian composer Sylvester Levy had only just been hired to create the score. His previous credits had been as arranger on Al Pacino's *Scarface* and he had composed the theme and score for TV's *Airwolf*, but nothing on this scale. John Caffery, Robert Tepper, Miami Sound Machine and Bill Medley all supplied tracks for the soundtrack album but it never caught fire like the *Rocky IV* soundtrack had a year earlier.

Cobra made just over $49 million dollars in the United States, which was over $130 million less than *Top Gun*. Globally however, the film did really well and finished its run with a total of $160 million dollars. One of the original story outlines, when it was still called *Fair Game,* was adapted into another movie nearly ten years later starring William Baldwin and Cindy Crawford but it failed to ignite either stars' film careers.

Cobra is certainly an uneven film, where you can feel the tug of war between the star, the producers, the distributors and the MPAA. One of the main action sequences is a car chase midway through the movie, which is a real highlight and very effectively staged but the final confrontation with the bad guy is a let down. The end sequence tries to copy the sequences in all *Rambo* films where he would pick off teams of attackers in various, stealthy methods. It all leads to an inevitable showdown with The Night Slasher, but that is mostly banal dialogue and zero ingenuity and in the end it feels like an extended episode of TV shows like *The Equaliser* or *Miami Vice*, but with a huge budget and a mega-movie star in the middle of it. Despite the financial success overseas, planned sequels for another big franchise for Stallone were quickly shelved as everyone soon lost faith in the character's longevity. Today the film is treated with a combination of retro derision and nostalgia and it is much the same for his next movie, *Over the Top*.

As the second film of the two-picture deal with Cannon and Warner Bros. this felt like the product of an executives brain-storming session. But *Over the Top* was announced by Cannon in 1984 and while Stallone went off and busted-blocks with *Rambo: First Blood Part II* and *Rocky IV*, Golem and Globus pitched the idea around, looking for backers, until the deal with Warner Bros. was struck. Warner Bros. were a lot more hopeful and interested in the potential of *Cobra*, but took the two-picture deal anyway.

The concept for *Over the Top* came from a story written by Gary Conway in 1979 and rejigged later by David Engelbach. Originally called *Meet Me Halfway* it told the story of a truck driver trying to reconnect with his estranged son whilst also pursuing his talent for arm-wrestling. When Cannon Pictures greenlit the idea, they recruited Stirling Silliphant to come up with a screenplay for a gritty trucker-film that had *Miami Vice*'s Don Johnson attached to star in. Silliphant had worked with the Cannon pair before on several Charles Bronson scripts plus he had also written *The Towering Inferno* and the third film in the *Dirty Harry* series, *The Enforcer*. Although he ran Cannon Films with his cousin Yoram Globus, the Israel-born Menahem Golan had plenty of directing credits. Many had been in the Israeli movie industry but he had tried his hand at helming western movies, including *The Delta Force* with Chuck Norris the year before. He wanted to direct his arm-wrestling fable but now he also wanted a proven movie star to help guarantee its success. The $10 million dollar fee (some reports said 12) that he offered Stallone was the highest salary that had ever been paid to an actor up to that point and it proved impossible for Stallone to resist. But he had reservations about the script and worked with Silliphant to create a new screenplay, now called *Over The Top*. The new story saw blue-collar truck driver Lincoln Hawk, go to pick up his son Michael (an excellent David Mendenhall) from the Military Academy he attends. Michael's mother (played by Susan Blakely who was a co-star of Stallone's in his biggest pre-*Rocky* film, *The Lords of Flatbush*) is suffering from heart disease and she wants him and his father to reconnect after being distant for over a decade. What follows is a curious blend of father/son melodrama and sports film. Hawk arm-wrestles for extra cash at truck-stops along his route but is heading to the World Championships in Las Vegas where he hopes to win enough dough to support his son, although the disapproving and wealthy grandfather (played pitch-perfectly by veteran Robert Loggia) is not a happy bunny about Hawk's plan.

If *Cobra* can loosely be considered *Rambo*-lite then Lincoln Hawk is a trucking *Rocky*. He has a heart of gold, wants to earn money with nobility but put him in a sporting contest and he has the guts to go all the way. Filming commenced in early June in 1986 and lasted nine weeks on location in California and Las Vegas. When the production was announced, a real life arm-wrestling competition was conceived by the producers and global tournaments led the qualifiers to a final week of competition in Las Vegas. Golan filmed the Las Vegas matches and used the footage in the film. The day after the real final took place, Stallone and the crew began filming their scenes at the venue with many of the supporters staying in town a few more days to be extras in the audience of the movie. Some of the actual world champion arm-wrestlers were also asked to stick around but many of them were not used for the match-ups with Stallone's character as most of them were so huge it was deemed a step too far to convince audiences that Lincoln Hawk could beat them. The final 15 minutes of the movie shamelessly becomes a *Rocky*-clone, complete with a montage of arm-wrestling set to music by Italian composer Giorgio Moroder, although it sounds like a carbon copy of Vince DiCola's electronic score for *Rocky IV*. Again, like *Rocky IV*, a soundtrack album was put together with tracks from Kenny Loggins, Sammy Hagar and Frank Stallone got one on there too. The result was like the finished film however, it was neither one thing nor another and ended up mired in middle of the road sentimentality, sprinkled with some pseudo-tough guy posturing. It's an enjoyable if unessential 93 minutes where Stallone gives perhaps the sweetest performance of his career. As Hawk tries to wear down his sons' protective walls he is gentle, warm and witty so when it comes to the arm-wrestling sequences it can feel a little jarring compared to the family-bonding. Perhaps with such a huge paycheck for *Over the Top*, Stallone felt less able to kick up a fuss over the lacklustre overall finished product.

By the time it was released in February of 1987 it was already considered past its sell-by date and the title of the movie opened the door to many film critics' negative review headlines. Stallone had to sit and watch it grind to just $16 million dollars by the end of its run, meaning a loss of nearly $10 million dollars. To make matters worse, for the rest of the year he witnessed his soon-to-be-ex wife appear in the second biggest global hit of 1987, *Beverly Hills Cop II* (behind only *Fatal Attraction)* and his new nemesis Arnold Schwarzenegger hit big with his latest, *Predator.*

Over The Top ended the year in 66th place after Stallone had claimed two of the top three places in the global box office just two years earlier. The realities of the fragile movie business were hitting home again and hitting hard. So he was forced to do what had saved him more than once before. He had to go back to one of his trusted characters and take them on a new adventure.

RAMBO III - 1988

THE FIRST WAS FOR HIMSELF. THE SECOND WAS FOR HIS COUNTRY. THIS TIME IT'S FOR HIS FRIEND.

Starring - Sylvester Stallone, Richard Crenna
Written by - Sylvester Stallone and Sheldon Lettich
Original Score by - Jerry Goldsmith
Directed by - Peter MacDonald

And so we come to the peak of Stallone as a superstar. This is the film that was talked about as much before it was released as it was after. This is the film that saw many national newspapers produce center-page spreads about how the film's production was bordering on insanity, Stallone's demands were out of control and the film was doomed to bankrupt the studios behind it. This is the film that was at the time, the most expensive movie ever made.

Rambo III was always going to materialise. The massive box office and cultural impact of *Rambo: First Blood Part II* was never going to be ignored and the next film was being discussed at the premier of Rambo adventure number 2. What was quickly established was that despite Stallone's undoubted influence over much of the direction of George P. Cosmatos on *Rambo: First Blood Part II,* he still didn't want to be overwhelmed with the scale of making *Rambo III* as writer, star and director. He was happy to script and obviously he had to star, but they needed another director. Australian Russell Mulcahy had graduated from making music videos for acts such as AC/DC, Culture Club, The Sex Pistols and Paul McCartney. He directed the music video for The Buggles' hit *Video Killed The Radio Star* which was the first music video ever played on MTV and he also made Elton John's *I'm Still Standing* video in which he made a quick cameo appearance. His first feature film was *Razorback* which became a cult hit in Australia despite its poor box office returns. But in 1985 he had helmed the science-fiction, time-jumping, Queen- soundtracked hit *Highlander* and his handling of complicated stunts and large numbers of extras in the Scotland-set scenes, got him noticed by Carolco Pictures' Vajna and Kassar and he was offered the gig to direct *Rambo III*.

A script by Harry Kleiner, who had previously written *The Fantastic Journey* in 1966 and *Bullitt* two years later and more recently the

Arnie action vehicle *Red Heat,* was read but rejected by Stallone. Soon after, Stallone sat with Vietnam veteran turned writer Sheldon Lettich to thrash out their story. After effectively righting the wrongs of the American part of the Vietnam War in the last film, the pair looked for where they could send their hero next. Choosing to highlight what they thought were injustices in the world they focused on the Afghanistan / Soviet war. The conflict had started at the end of 1979 and was still raging nearly a decade later as the Soviet Union and the Afghan military battled the Islamist militant group the Afghan Mujahideen, for the country's governance. After facing the Russians in the second film, the writing duo felt they were still the big bad guys in American cinema-goers minds. Their plot would see John Rambo trying to live a simple, peaceful life at a Buddhist monastery in Thailand, until his only friend in the world, Colonel Samuel Trautman (Richard Crenna's last appearance in the role) visits him and asks him to help with an upcoming secret mission to Afghanistan. Rambo says no thanks but when Trautman is captured during the mission, it's down to Rambo to try and find him, rescue him and get back home after killing anyone who looked bad. .

With the director signed up, pre-production quickly began with shooting locations considered in Morocco, Italy, Utah and the directors' native Australia. Mexico was initially chosen and, in a first indication that things might go off the rails, $5 million dollars was spent building extravagant sets that were later dismantled and binned as the makers decided that the location wouldn't convince as rural Afghanistan.

Aside from interiors that would be filmed in Arizona and the Thailand-set opening, production was moved to Israel. One of the big location sets to be (re)constructed was the main Soviet stronghold that Rambo would rescue Trautman from. Production designer Bill Kenney (who had also worked on the second *Rambo* and the fourth *Rocky*) was tasked to create a large fort that looked like it had been originally built by Afghans but then updated by its new Soviet occupants. He employed a crew of 80 local labourers and craftspeople who worked round the clock for 6 weeks to finish in time for filming.

Stallone himself went through a form of construction to make his physique bigger than it was in the previous film. Although only 5 feet 10, he piled on more muscle to weigh 180 pounds, 15 pounds more than in *Rambo: First Blood Part II*. The hard work and modern gym that had to be behind the cameras at all times did produce a remarkable final look on screen; he was never this muscular before and he never would be again. The rest of the cast was chosen well in advance to allow everyone time to acclimatise to what was going to be more than three months in the harsh conditions on location. French actor Marc de Jong was hired for the role of the main bad guy, Soviet Colonel Alexei Zaysen, in what was essentially a carbon copy of Steven Berkoff's villain in *Rambo: First Blood Part II*. Jong had previously found some recognition in Steven Spielberg's *Empire of the Sun* although French cinema was where he spent his busy career. (Tragically, the actor died ten years later when he slipped and fell to his death after trying to climb up the building where he lived when he couldn't find his front door key.) Dialect coach Yonny Lucas was drafted in to make sure there was authenticity with both the Russian and Pashtu accents. The majority of Afghans in the film were played by Israelis while the Soviets were a mixture of American, English and French.

Filming commenced in the second half of 1987 while Stallone's divorce from second wife Brigitte Nielsen was hitting the tabloids. The official story was Stallone was divorcing her but Nielsen insisted it was her doing and that Stallone's eccentric mother Jaqueline had actually been one of the main causes of the split. The paparazzi followed Stallone to the Israel-based production to get gossip on the celebrity parting but accidentally stumbled on a war within the movie-war. After just 2 weeks of filming, Stallone suddenly sacked senior members of the production crew. Ric Waite had been his Director of Photography on *Cobra,* but he was ordered to leave and the DoP from *Over the Top*, David Gurfinkel, was flown in. It didn't end there when an assistant director and the main camera crew were also given their marching orders. Things reached their peak when the director was fired too. Russell Mulcahy and Stallone had been at logger-heads since they both touched down in Israel with Stallone insisting that his casting of the Russian soldiers hadn't been up to much. He also insinuated that Mulcahy wasn't up to the task of such a big production in general but instead of taking up the reins of director himself, in came Peter MacDonald. The 48-year old had directed second-unit helicopter sequences on *Rambo: First Blood Part II* but had never been the main director on anything previously, let alone what was now the most expensive movie ever at more than $60 million dollars. (He did go on to direct again in TV but only four more features including *Mo' Money* and *The Neverending Story III*, but nothing on this scale).

Eventually, shooting wrapped and editing got underway. Jerry Goldsmith was asked to produce his third score for a Rambo film and he used the Hungarian State Opera Orchestra to mix the familiar themes with some new cues for the new setting. Bill Medley recorded a new version of *He Ain't Heavy, He's My Brother* to play over the end credits and the film got its world premier on May the 25th 1988. Its first week on release saw it enter the U.S. Box Office charts at number 2, behind another sequel *Crocodile Dundee II*. In the final charts for the US in 1988, *Rambo III* finished in 17th place, between *Scrooged* and *Bull Durham* but overseas it still proved popular and eventually hit a global tally of over $180 million dollars.

Critic-wise however, it was dead in the water before it even opened in cinemas. The damaging pre-publicity and the general anti-Stallone media at the time meant it had to fight the tide to get any traction with audiences. It was also the year that *Die Hard* changed concepts of male action heroes and the Russia-bating of *Rambo III* was seen as very out of step. In the gap between the release of *Rambo: First Blood Part II* and now *Rambo III*, Mikhail Gorbachev had come to power in Russia and was already starting to dismantle the old Soviet Union and make efforts to repair communications and relations with the American government. The depiction of evil Russia on screen seemed tone deaf when compared to the palpable sense of relief and hope that was spreading around the world. The top six films of the year in 1988 demonstrated that the public wanted to have fun, laugh and feel better about themselves right now, they didn't want to feel angry and betrayed like they did two years before. The top six were *Who Framed Roger Rabbit, Coming to America, Good Morning Vietnam, Big, Crocodile Dundee II* and number 6 was *Three Men and A Baby*. Tom Cruise's *Cocktail* and the romantic comedy *Moonstruck* were next, showing a distinct lack of desire to see carnage on the silver screen. The only action film in the top twenty was indeed Bruce Willis' superstar-making turn as Officer John McClane in *Die Hard*.

Rambo would not put on his headband and go to war again for two decades, such was the fallout of *Rambo III*. The studios were pleased to see that they had still made a profit on *Rambo III* but the bad blood currently circling the character meant that the tentatively-planned *Rambo IV* was removed from the agenda of studio meetings. But that left Stallone in a state of limbo as the journalistic ill-feeling towards the character meant he caught the flak too. He had become the target of social debate and his image was now the go-to example of toxic masculinity in a world where while Sigourney Weaver had broken new ground for women in popular cinema with her "Get away from her, you bitch!" killer line and performance in *Aliens* in 1986. It wouldn't be long before Linda Hamilton would push the movement further as a muscular, armed Sarah Conner in *Terminator 2: Judgement Day*.

It left Stallone in movie prison where the line between actor and character was so blurred in the media coverage, that he felt he was trapped and unable to break out. Perhaps that mindset was behind his decision-making for his next pair of film roles where he escaped from jail. Twice.

1989 - LOCK UP, TANGO AND CASH

That *Lock Up* turned out to be a fairly good movie is more luck than judgement as the film had probably the most scattershot production of all Stallone's 80's output. American producer Lawrence Gordon was one of the most familiar faces around Hollywood. As ambitious as you can be, he forced his way into the business at American International Pictures and eventually formed his own production company to forge various deals with various studios. As producer he had helped shepherd to the screen hits such as Burt Reynolds' *Hooper*, Eddie Murphy's film debut *48 Hrs* and Schwarzeneggers' biggest hit at that point, *Predator*. He'd also been instrumental in convincing studio bosses that Bruce Willis could carry *Die Hard* and make it a hit. As 1988 became 1989, Stallone found himself with a gap in his schedule and as soon as Gordon found out, he pitched him a prison drama and showed Stallone what was apparently an awful script. But by utilizing his gift of smoothing over the cracks after decades of schmoozing around Hollywood, Gordon still managed to get Stallone to commit to the movie as the star felt it was a project that he could flex some acting muscles in, instead of just his actual ones.

Die Hard co-writer Jeb Stuart was swiftly employed to write a fresh script that so far came down to a simple premise of a guy escaping from a prison. But what Stuart and Gordon didn't have was time, as the window for Stallone's involvement was small: he was set to start filming a new action comedy with Patrick Swayze called *Tango & Cash* in June. Things progressed as if a finished screenplay was available as director John Flynn was then hired. The year before he had made an intriguing drama with James Woods and Brian Dennehy (Sheriff Teasle in *First Blood*) called *Best Seller* and a quick phone call between Woods and pal Stallone cemented Flynn's credentials to direct. The newly employed director was immediately off to scout locations and to mainly find the prison itself where most of the film would be set, and filmed. Meanwhile, Lawrence Gordon booked a hotel room in New York where he locked writer Jeb Stuart, and now also Henry Rosenbaum and Richard Smith in together, with orders not to come out until they had a better script finished in record time. With an unnegotiable finish date in May, Flynn found and liked East Jersey State Prison in Rahway, New Jersey and Stallone and crew arrived to start filming on the 6th of February. From that day until the last, the shoot involved pages of story and dialogue being written the day before a scene had to be shot. Many days during the production, Flynn and Gordon had to pacify their star, the prison and their film crew for hours at a time while they waited for new pages to arrive on set. Every actor involved (including Donald Sutherland as the vicious warden and Tom Sizemore in his first big role) had to accept the conditions and were encouraged to alter dialogue and offer story suggestions as the production rolled-on.

The prison itself was very much in use at the time of filming and many inmates were used as background extras. Many of the real guards also took up the offer of the standard $93 dollars Screen Actors Guild daily rate, to stay in their uniform on camera. Flynn had been a young assistant director under John Sturgess in 1963 for the classic wartime prison drama *The Great Escape* and hoped to bring that flavour to *Lock Up* but the haphazard nature of the filming, especially in the first month, meant that everyone was pretty much making it up as they went along.

The story that was outlined (but not in detail) on day one was of everyman mechanic Frank Leone who was finishing out a prison sentence in a low-security facility (for an audience-friendly crime of defence) when he is forcibly taken to a maximum-security stockade and increasingly harassed and mistreated by the guards. Warden Drumgoole (Sutherland) eventually explains how Leone had escaped from his prison five years ago and now he wanted revenge for the damage it had done to his career. The rest of the drama see's Leone bond with a group of fellow inmates who fix up an old car in the prison workshop, play American football against some of the meaner inmates and learn a few life lessons along the way. It eventually reaches a fairly tense climax where Leone gets Drumgoole to confess to his misdoings and then Leone can be released to his waiting girlfriend.

As with all Stallone films up to this point, an injection of *Rocky* was called upon and in this case it was via Bill Conti who scored the movie and he and Stallone crafted a very *Rocky*-like music montage for the American Football in the mud sequence. Sutherland chews the scenery and everyone around him as the villain of the piece and there are a couple of surprising plot twists along the way although there's never any doubt of where the story will end up. One of the inmates that Stallones' Leone befriends is known as Eclipse in the film due his formidable size. He's played charmingly by former NFL pro Frank McRae who was 6 foot 6 inches but this was the fourth time McRae had played a man-mountain with a heart of gold opposite Stallone. He'd been in both of Stallone's first two *Rocky* follow-ups, *Paradise Alley* and *F.I.S.T.* and then he played the foreman of the meat-packing plant who has to fire Rocky in *Rocky II*. He also appeared in producer Gordon's *48Hrs* and had a comfortable working relationship with both. In *48Hrs* (and its 1990 sequel) he played the cliched shouty, angry police captain which he then parodied twice in both *Last Action Hero* and *Loaded Weapon 1*.

But despite the pandemonium behind the scenes, *Lock Up* emerged as an above average prison drama. It sits as one of Stallone's most unheralded movies with good performances all round and deserves a bit more recognition than it gets, regardless of the backstage panic. But, perhaps due to the nature of the production, it seemed distributor TriStar Pictures lost faith in the film and didn't want to use much of their money in pre-publicity. As a result, *Lock Up* snuck into cinemas on August the 4th 1989, the same day that Steven Sodebergh's *Sex, Lies and Videotape* was ushering in the new wave of low-budget, independent cinema. It was a busy summer at the box office anyway with *Lethal Weapon 2*, *Ghostbusters 2*, *Licence to Kill*, *The Abyss*, *Indiana Jones and the Last Crusade* and *Batman* all pulling in the crowds alongside soon-to-be-classic smaller films like *Dead Poets Society* and *When Harry Met Sally*.

Lock Up had a similar sense that Stallone's three previous films (*Rambo III*, *Cobra* and *Over the Top*) all had which was that they instantly felt out of date in some way. Like those three before it, *Lock Up* is absolutely fine with a lot going for it but when there was ingenuity, originality and some well-crafted sequels also being released, it seemed like a star-vehicle from a bygone age where not enough love and care had been put into its soul. On a budget of $24 million dollars, it returned just over $22 million to the studio. But

Stallone had no time to wallow as he was being fitted for sharp suits and memorizing unusually witty dialogue for his next project. *Tango & Cash* became another chaotic production and while Stallone was guilty of causing some of it he also found himself caught in a firestorm between producers and directors.

Peter Guber and Jon Peters were self-made movie moguls. Both had worked their way up through the ranks at some of the biggest movie studios and been on the periphery of some notable moments in movie history such as *Midnight Express, Shampoo, Caddyshack* and *A Star Is Born* (Peters was romantically involved with Barbara Streisand as that film was made) but as friends in the business (and when they were both financially able to) they began their own production company in the 80's called The Guber-Peters Entertainment Company (GPC). As a formidable duo, they ushered some of the biggest films of the eighties into cinemas such as *Flashdance, Rain Man* and *Batman* but they were also considered smart creatives who often came up with movie ideas and one such idea centered on taking two, top cops and putting them in prison. They sat with writer Randy Feldman and explained their concept and he went off and came back with a script called *The Set Up*. Stallone liked the premise and the chance to do something a bit lighter while also adhering to his action-hero credentials. Patrick Swayze had taken a significant step up in his career (after early roles in *The Outsiders* and *Red Dawn*) in 1987 with his iconic imagery and keeping Baby out of the corner in *Dirty Dancing*. He signed on as co-star with Stallone and production was slated to start in June of 1989. But just a few weeks after taking on the film, Swayze pulled out in favour of *Roadhouse* (and also *Ghost*) and immediately the production was threatening to stall.

The list of possible replacements was as long as could be and included Bruce Willis, Michael Keaton, Mel Gibson and Harrison Ford. But GPC and Stallone all honed in on Kurt Russell. Russell had been acting on screens since he was 12 when he was on a decade-long contract to Walt Disney Pictures. His breakthrough into adult roles came in 1979 when he played the King of Rock and Roll in the biopic *Elvis (*after actually sharing the screen with Elvis himself as a child in *It Happened At The World's Fair* in 1963*)*. His action credentials were solid with quality eighties hits like *Escape from New York, The Thing* and *Big Trouble in Little China* (where he also demonstrated the comedic talent that would be needed in *Tango & Cash*) and the pair felt they could happily share the screen together.

Feldman's script had blossomed into a comedic, action-buddy movie where both stars would have their moments to shine. Smart-suited Lieutenant Raymond Tango (Stallone) and slovenly Lieutenant Gabriel Cash (Russell) are considered the best detectives in the Los Angeles Police Department, but when a criminal kingpin Yves Perret (legendary screen character actor Jack Palance) decides they are hindering his business, he sets the duo up and they are arrested and sent to prison. After breaking out of jail, the pair hunt down Perret and clear their name. Wanting to move away from his minimal-dialogue action roles, Stallone would be playing a clean cut, impeccably dressed, glasses-wearing supercop with one eye on the stock market and a hugely inflated opinion of himself. Russell's Gabriel Cash was to be just as confident but without the personal grooming. Trying to emulate the mix of action and comedy that had been so successful in *Beverly Hills Cop* and *Lethal Weapon,* Feldman had now punched-up the screenplay with quick one-liners, fast dialogue between the stars and the chance for both actors to subtly poke fun at their star image. Or in the case of the opening scene, not so subtle: After stopping some bad guys in a truck (by copying a stunt Stallone had enjoyed in the Jackie Chan 1985 film *Police Story*) a local state trooper teases Ray Tango by comparing him to Rambo. In reply, Tango says "Rambo, is a pussy."

Russian director Andrei Konchalovsky was hired to steer the ship although after a long career in the Soviet film industry he had only recently turned his hand to American cinema and it was only his medium-hit *Runaway Train* (starring Eric Robers and Jon Voight in 1985) that had shown any propensity towards action. But on June the 12th 1989, *Tango & Cash* commenced filming in Mansfield, Ohio where the prison scenes were scheduled to film at the Mansfield Reformatory facility which was recognisable to movie-fans in its previous role as the jail where the prisoners spent their lives in *The Shawshank Redemption*.

Before production got underway and into the first few weeks of filming, the troubles between Konchalovsky and producer John Peters began. Long delays became commonplace as the pair locked horns over the tone of the movie. While Konchalovsky (and Stallone) thought they were making an action-comedy, Peters was increasingly adamant that it should be campier and more goofy. Filming continued, but very slowly and the on-set disagreements continued. It should be pointed out that plenty of reports suggested that Stallone was the voice of reason on *Tango & Cash*. He took it upon himself to act as mediator between director and producer although he firmly believed the director's approach was the better of the two. That's not to say he didn't throw his considerable weight around as well: original director of photography Donald Peterman, frustrated and fed-up, walked away from the film after four months of work, which included six weeks of pre-production. He was replaced by Barry Sonnenfeld (who went on to direct the *Addams Family* movies and the *Men in Black* trilogy) but clashed with Stallone over his methods of lighting the film. Stallone had him fired after just 7 days and replaced with a third DoP in the form of Donald E Thorin, who had already worked with Stallone that year on *Lock Up*. But there were bigger firings after three months of principal photography. The clashes between Peters and Konchalovsky had got to the point where the pair only communicated through a third-party and despite Stallone's best efforts it came to a head when Peters publicly fired the director. A new director was quickly sought but Stallone sat in the chair to keep things moving and also his *Rambo III* replacement-director Peter Macdonald (who was working as second unit director and executive producer on *Tango & Cash*) stepped up into the big seat until Albert Magnoli arrived. Magnoli was primarily a music video director but had led the Prince music-film, *Purple Rain*. The Italian arrived at a point in filming where most of the prison scenes and interiors had been completed and what was left was the action sequences and grand finale.

Although scheduled to wrap in August, filming came to an end a month later. But after reviewing an early edit of the film, Magnoli called everyone back to work for additional reshoots that finally ended in mid-October, just eight weeks before the premier of *Tango & Cash* was due. The issues and quarrels didn't end when the cameras stopped shooting, however. English film editor Stuart Baird found himself being pulled in all directions as version after version of the film was rejected by either the producers, the director(s) or the MPAA. The film classification board was instantly concerned they would have similar issues with the violence that they had seen on *Cobra* and demanded most of the blood be removed and lingering shots of deaths also be taken out. Baird had hits like *Superman* and *Lethal Weapon* on his resume and was extremely well-respected but he still found himself trying to fit square pegs into round holes. Just after filming had finished though, The Guber-Peters Entertainment Company was being dissolved as the pair went to run Columbia Pictures for Sony. This coincided with (or was because of) Warner Bros. removing them both from being a part of the editing process two days before. This then resulted in a long, drawn out lawsuit to determine if Warner Bros. or Sony owned the rights to Guber-Peters Entertainment, which was never fully resolved. But Warner Bros. knew they had to get the film ready for its December release or it would have no chance of success as January was considered a "dead-time" for new releases.

Baird drafted in Hubert de La Bouillerie to help with the immense re-editing process that was required. Up to that point the Frenchman's main credits as editor were *The Witches of Eastwick* in 1987 and the following years' *Police Academy 5: Assignment Miami Beach*. Musically, Warner Bros. had so wanted to keep the *Beverly Hills Cop*-feel to the movie that they got that film's composer, Harold Faltermeyer, to basically repeat his work again. To the point that the main theme of *Tango & Cash* could be considered as *Axel F Version 2*. As the re-editing drama dragged on, Faltermeyer was being asked to repeatedly look at the new versions and adjust his score accordingly. In the end, with the constant delays involved, he had to hand over the scoring of the movie's finale to Gary Chang, but Faltermeyer got the sole screen credit.

Finally, after going two months past its end date and $20 million dollars over its initial budget, *Tango & Cash* was released on

December the 22nd 1989, the same day as Steven Spielberg's sentimental drama *Always*. It was in the previous week that both *Driving Miss Daisy* and *Born on the Fourth of July* had been released and gathered instant awards chatter. *Tango & Cash* received awards, but not ones they wanted. The annual Golden Raspberry Awards gave the film three of its not-coveted trophies for Worst Actor (Stallone), Worst Supporting Actress (Kurt Russell for the scene where he appears in drag) and Worst Screenplay. But financially it was quietly successful. It wasn't a blockbuster by any means but it made a $10 million dollar profit domestically on its $54 million dollar final cost and worldwide it reached $120 million in total. While it wasn't critically welcomed when it hit cinema's it has since gone on to have a bit of a life of its own and despite its many, many flaws it has become a fan favourite. Even up until 2019, Stallone was being asked about a potential sequel. He announced he had drafted a *Tango & Cash 2* but couldn't yet get the backing and crucially, get Kurt Russell to commit.

The movie is something of a mess and there's little denying that but there's so much energy, charm and fun along the way that it's hard to resist. The two leads work extremely well together and manage to slip in a number of self-effacing in-jokes into the script, long before it became fashionable. Aside from the Rambo-jibe in the opening scene, there's also: 1) Cash revealing his birthday is August the 16th which is the date Elvis Presley died. 2) When asked if he was late because he stopped for coffee and a danish pastry, Tango replies "I hate Danish," in reference to his recent divorce from Brigitte Nielsen. 3) Tango's call sign on the police dispatch is '20 William 12' which is the same call sign used by Riggs and Murtaugh in *Lethal Weapon*, which Kurt Russell was close to starring in. And there are many more.

Throughout the movie, Stallone seems happy to share the spotlight with Russell 50/50 and it's their verbal sparring that saves the film from itself. The action scenes are fine but the final sequence where they storm the bad guys hideout in a quarry while driving a souped-up RV, is as ridiculous and confusing as it sounds and was clearly directed by a different person from what came before it. And with so many off-screen issues and changes in important personnel, the finished product can't help but struggle to maintain focus and a consistent tone. Much like the Will Smith and Martin Lawrence hit *Bad Boys* would do six years later, in the middle of *Tango & Cash* the main plot is forgotten about for a long time. As in *Bad Boys*, the action-storyline makes way for a family comedy as Teri Hatcher appears as Ray Tango's sister and her attraction to Cash creates some fun antagonism between the two cops. In fact, the action beats sometimes feel irritating as you want to get back to the bickering and squabbling between Stallone and Russell.

Overall though, it was put into the Stallone directory under the file name "made money but didn't really have an impact". It's fondly remembered by the generation that it was released for and stands as a testament to late-eighties action comedy. But, it was now four years and five movies since he had had a bona-fide global smash hit. *Rocky IV* was the last time he'd seen queues around the block to buy tickets for a film of his, so he felt he had to go back into that well again. But he was to find out that even the deepest wells have to run dry at some point.

ROCKY V (1990)

GO FOR IT

Starring - Sylvester Stallone, Talia Shire, Burt Young, Tommy Morrison, Sage Stallone
Written by - Sylvester Stallone
Original Score by - Bill Conti
Directed by - John G Avilsden

Five years is a long time in *Rocky*-land but it was like a lifetime in the world of cinema. 1985's *Rocky IV* had been so monumental at the box office that following it was always destined to be a tricky step to take. The step was made easier when he was offered more than $15 million dollars by a hungry studio, so it was always going to happen. As with all four films up to this point, Stallone had been mulling over the next chapter as soon as he had finished the previous one. But much as he knew he could convince the studio's to fund more Rocky sequels at this point, he had his integrity and he also had other career goals. So, if he was going to put on the hat and leather jacket and hit the streets of Philadelphia again, it would be on his terms and after accepting that Rocky shouldn't die at the end of *Rocky III*, he was determined that *Rocky V* would see his creation finally lose the ultimate fight of life. The first scene he put pen to paper on was a rewrite of the death he had outlined for *Rocky III*. The movie would end with just Adrian and Rocky, after the final fight, where he dies in his wife's arms. Adrian would then give a speech to reporters at a memorial service at the famous steps and his statue would be the last thing we ever see. And to make this death more realistic, he would have Rocky diagnosed with brain damage at the beginning of the film due to the punishment he had received from Ivan Drago in *Rocky IV*.

After a difficult few years at the box office where he'd had hits but nothing had really buried itself into the public consciousness, he felt the best topic to explore in *Rocky V* would be what happens if you have had everything but then it all gets taken away from you again. After the excess and stylisation of *Rocky's III* and *IV*, Stallone also wanted Rocky's story to end where it started. He wanted to take him back to basics, without the big houses, fancy cars and expensive clothes. Rocky's story should come full circle and come to a close back in Philadelphia and he provisionally gave it the ominous title *Rocky: The Final Bell.*

Following the franchise's tradition, the next film would begin immediately after the events of *Rocky IV,* but that presented writer Stallone with a creative conundrum. His new story required Rocky Jr. to be a teenager but in *Rocky IV* he was nine years old when he was played by actor Rocky Krakoff. Stallone had no option but to rely on some audience goodwill and in the new film, when Rocky, Adrian and Paulie arrive back on U.S. soil after the *Rocky IV* fight in Moscow, Rocky Jr. has miraculously aged an extra 4 or 5 years.

In casting Rocky Jr, the announcement that he would be played by Stallone's eldest son Sage, raised some eyebrows and more than a few accusations of nepotism. Although Sage was studying acting and had clearly indicated to his father that he wanted to pursue the profession, he hadn't done any film work up to that point. To appease the studios, Dad-Stallone auditioned a number of young actors but it was evident it would be 13-year old Sage from very early on in the development process.

While the studios had to accept an untried actor in one of the main roles, Stallone had to accept the studio's demand that Rocky should not die. With the salary he was being paid plus the pressure to not kill-off a golden goose, he relented and agreed Rocky would be left to (possibly) fight another day but the brain damage diagnosis would remain a plot-line. The final draft of the screenplay picks up immediately after *Rocky IV* ends, with Rocky showing worrying signs of illness and disorientation in the locker room after beating Ivan Drago. Tests would reveal the medical situation and that another fight could kill him so he is forced to retire from the ring. That news was coupled with his accountants stealing all his money meaning he and Adrian (Talia Shire) and Paulie (Burt Young) and Robert 'Rocky Jnr' Balboa (Sage Stallone) would be forced to move back into the poorer streets of Philly and the Balboa's best source of income would be Rocky running Mickey's old gym while Adrian goes back to shifts at the pet shop. Soon enough a homeless young fighter called Tommy Gunn (played by real life, undefeated heavyweight boxer Tommy Morrison) arrives at the gym and wants to be trained by Rocky and after some persuasion, he does. The pair bond and start to find some success but it means Rocky isn't giving his son the attention he needs and wants. When unscrupulous promoter George Duke (Richard Gant playing the role clearly based on divisive, real life boxing promoter Don King) turns Tommy's head and makes him rich and a world champion, the relationship between Tommy and Rocky sours. Manipulated and demanding respect from Rocky, the film climaxes with a street-fight between the pair which Rocky wins to his son's delight.

Stallone's overriding wish for this film to feel like the first two in the series was helped by the fact that the original *Rocky* director, John G Avilsden would return. Cinematographer James Crabe had helped fashion the look of *Rocky* but he had passed away in 1989 so Steven Poster, who had recently directed Madonna's *Like a Prayer* music video, was hired. Filming began on the 15th of January 1990 in Philadelphia and was to last six weeks. So much of the location shoot was done in residential, public areas meaning there were always thousands of fans to marshall whilst trying to get the scenes in the can.

Talia Shire had an exhausting couple of months as she was also shooting *The Godfather Part III* for her brother, the director Francis Ford Coppola. It meant she often had to fly across the country or to

Italy to reprise her other most famous screen character Connie Corleone, the sister of Michael Corleone (Al Pacino). While there was no work for Carl Weathers, Mr T. or Dolph Lundgren on *Rocky V*, Stallone had written a moment near the end where Rocky envisages his mentor Mickey in front of his eyes. Burgess Meredith had been nominated for a Best Supporting Actor Academy Award in 1977 for *Rocky* and now 82, returned to the character he last played seven years prior in *Rocky III*. Meredith's two days of work was supposed to be used during the final fight as Rocky lay dazed and almost unconscious in the street but with some reshoots, it was moved to earlier in the film as a dream sequence when Rocky is at his lowest ebb.

As filming progressed and finish dates loomed, the director, the cinematographer and the star also reached their lowest ebb. Avildsen and Stallone wanted Poster to reproduce the low-budget, natural lighting look of *Rocky* but Poster (and the studio) wanted it more polished, believing that the fans wouldn't accept reverting back to a cheaper style after the sheen of *Rocky IV*. The daily battles between director and cinematographer led to Poster quitting and walking off the project. The delays to filming also affected the director's patience. When filming eventually wrapped, John G Avildsen had little to do with the required reshoots and the editing process. Michael N Knue and Stallone worked on the edit together with Avildsen offering his thoughts and popping in when he could.

With the November 16th premier date looming and the first public screenings due on the 8th, Stallone was still deep into editing when an offer presented itself that he couldn't turn down despite the time constraints he was under. A conversation with Elton John led to the British singer offering to contribute an end title song for the film.

John and songwriters Alan Menkin and Tim Rice plus producer Phil Ramone collaborated quickly to create *Measure of a Man*. But with Elton John in England, they were forced to record with a full, 70-piece orchestra in the U.S. and then fly with the elaborate backing track to the U.K. to get the singer to add his voice. On the last day of October, the finished song was delivered to the editing suite where it was laid over a montage of black and white images from all five films that would run under the final credits. Also, it was the second Rocky film in a row that didn't really feature its most recognisable piece of music. Bill Conti returned to scoring duty and re-used a lot of the original movies' themes but *Gonna Fly Now* is notably low-key. It plays during the post-fight celebrations as all the plot threads are sewn up but it's certainly not front and center. In the final street-fight sequence however, Conti nicely combined his brassy, gladiatorial trademark sound with Snap's *Keep it Up*, which was one of a number of tracks on the contemporary, urban soundtrack. Gone was the power rock and pop of *Rocky III* and *Rocky IV* and in came the likes of MC Hammer, Rob Base and Joey B Ellis. Frank Stallone's Take *You Back* returned to a *Rocky* soundtrack but with that distinctive 90's feel layered on top. For the first time on a *Rocky* album, there was none of the orchestral score at all. The Capitol Records release instead chose to try and maximise chart sales by using the phrase 'music from and inspired by the film' which meant no Bill Conti at all and his *Rocky V* work remains unreleased to this day.

When the film itself finally opened, it did ok. It made back its $40 million budget in the US and worldwide it went on to finish its run at $120 million dollars. It was a profit but it wasn't in the same ballpark as its predecessors and therefore it was deemed a failure. In the US box office charts for 1990, it finished outside the top 30 and remains the lowest grossing film of the Rocky series. The top earners of the year were *Ghost, Pretty Woman* and *Home Alone* (which was the film that kept *Rocky V* off the top of the charts in its opening week). The reviews were mostly positive but fairly tame and there was a sense of disinterest which seemed to mirror the audience response. To have Rocky not fight in a ring at the end of the movie made cinema-goers feel cheated out of what they'd expected. It's clear why Stallone wanted to do something different but that decision proved to be part of its downfall. Some of the enjoyment of the Rocky movies is that at some point, it becomes clear that we are heading towards a boxing match. The training and motivational scenes are part of the build up and they increase the audience's anticipation but as *Rocky V* continues, there's no indication that we are going to get that climax and even during the punch-up in the street, you are still hoping there will be a real boxing match afterwards. The realisation that there won't be is deflating.

On the production side, that battle between cinematographer and director became evident when the film was released as the movie has that unmistakable 90's sheen to it which makes the attempts to emulate its roots in 1970's movie-making, unconvincing. Performance wise, it's hard to find much fault actually as Sage Stallone more than holds his own and his father said that the experience of working so closely with Sage brought them emotionally together after being estranged for a number of years due to his divorce from Sage's mother, Sasha.

Tommy Morrison managed to disprove a long held belief of Stallone, which was that he'd always said it was easier to teach an actor to box rather than the other way round but Morrison bucked that trend. He was never too shy to ask for help with his performance from other cast members and constantly had drama coaches Richard and Leslie Brander on hand for advice and late-night rehearsals. Morrison was a fifth generation boxer from Arkansas and he would often say he was a distant relative of John Wayne (hence his real-life boxing nickname of The Duke) but that was never proven. Following filming, he went on to win the real WBO Heavyweight title against George Foreman in 1993 but after stints in prison, addiction issues and failed comebacks, he tragically died of cardiac arrest from complications brought on by HIV, the virus that causes AIDS, in 2013 aged just 44.

Talia Shire probably gives her best Adrian in *Rocky V* as she has to be the voice of reason for an increasingly distracted Rocky while trying to protect him after his diagnosis. Burt Young moves Paulie further away from the abusive drunk he was in the original and he's now the unreliable but decent best friend to Rocky and supportive uncle to Robert. And for Stallone, he does everything he can to pitch his turn halfway between the Oscar nominated performance of 1976 and the movie-star version of the character we saw in *Rocky IV*. It was a tightrope act that was destined to confuse an audience who had expectations of *Rocky IV: Part 2* but got a nineties-infused love letter to late-seventies cinema. It's by no means a creative failure but following the boombastic high of that Christmas Day battle in Moscow, coming back to chilly Philly and not letting Rocky put on the boxing gloves was a letdown.

Also it didn't help that his future Planet Hollywood partners had a very good year: *Die Hard 2: Die Harder* was a big hit and meant that Officer John McClane was now the centre of a franchise, while Arnie had both *Kindergarten Cop* and *Total Recall* to celebrate. Even new tough-guy on the block Steven Seagal did better with his two films (*Hard to Kill* and *Marked for Death*) both outdoing *Rocky V*. For balance, 1990 also saw *Goodfellas* released and that only made $33 million dollars and has since gone on to be considered one of the greatest movies ever made. But, perhaps the most clear indication of how the studio and star viewed *Rocky V* is the fact that he didn't play Rocky Balboa again for 16 years.

So, Stallone was now at the point where both Rocky and Rambo were not guarantees anymore. Their last instalments had both proven profitable but it was felt that both characters needed to rest and to work out how they could fit into a contemporary world. Whether it was the times that had changed or the audience, both characters were in danger of destroying their own legacy unless they were put into hibernation and recalibrated. *Rocky V*'s lower than expected box-office did however push the franchise over the one billion dollar mark meaning it became the fourth film series to do so after James Bond, Star Wars and Indiana Jones. The problem was that everyone had banked on it doing far better, so the usual clamour for the next sequel didn't come and Stallone himself was running low on plot ideas and enthusiasm.

Regardless, the career had to move forward. For the last five years he'd made eight movies and all of them were a variation on his tough-guy image. Maybe this painful rejection of *Rocky V* was a signal for him to try and really change his tune. Many lesser cinema stars would insist that what they did before would (and must) work again, but Stallone was always trying to open up his image and have his range extended and accepted. So with the disaster of trying to be funny in *Rhinestone* in 1984 still fresh in the mind, he signed up to do two comedies.

1991 - 1992 OSCAR, STOP! OR MY MOM WILL SHOOT

This double comedy flop was an infamous moment in the bumpy career of Sylvester Stallone. The knives had been out for him on and off since he began and they had been sharpened over the perceived *Rambo III* fiasco. But after his once-impenetrable boxer also showed signs of decay with *Rocky V*, his best bet was probably to try and fly under the radar for a bit. Maybe return to the safety of a big budget action film alongside a bankable co-star or maybe some extended cameos in more prestigious fare to remind everyone that he was an actor first and a superstar second. Two comedy films was not the path of least resistance, so let's tackle *Oscar* first.

In the meetings beforehand, everything about *Oscar* may well have sounded positive. Stallone's character was an Italian American, the film would be marshalled by one of the great comedy directors and the star would be surrounded by a glut of established comedic talent. The source material had proven successful as a play and then a French film and this version wasn't going to try and reinvent the wheel.

The original stage version had been written by Claude Magnier and then turned into a movie in 1967 about a wealthy French industrialist struggling to handle a pregnant daughter, a business in crisis and various other calamities across the course of a single day. An American version was written by Michael Barrie and Jim Mulholland where the French tycoon was changed to a mob boss in Depression-era New York. Director John Landis loved the script and wanted to add it to his impressive comedic legacy. He was already Hollywood's most sought after comedy director after his hugely influential hits such as *Animal House, The Blues Brothers, An American Werewolf in London, Trading Places* and *Three Amigos*. Not to mention his watershed collaboration with the 'King of Pop' Michael Jackson which had produced the greatest pop music video of all time, *Thriller*. So with his unparalleled experience and knowhow, he went in search of the right lead actor and contacted his first choice: Mr Al Pacino. Pacino was very interested although his comedic history was chequered to say the least as his first stab at the genre in 1982's *Author, Author* had received almost universal derision. But with *Oscar* he felt he could slip into a distorted and exaggerated version of his Michael Corleone from *The Godfather* quite easily. The $2 million dollar paycheck would help grease the wheels of the deal as well. But, with pre-production starting to move up a gear, he then opted to upgrade to a $3 million dollar offer from Warren Beatty to join his big budget gangster/comic book movie *Dick Tracy*. Pacino didn't leave without offering an alternative however and he suggested his friend Stallone, since he had the requisite heritage and his name would attract financial backers even more than the name Pacino could. With the haunting memory of *Rhinestone* always in his mind, Stallone knew that a return to out and out comedy would require an excellent end product to counteract the inevitable backlash that he would receive just by announcing the project. But the signs would still be good pre-release as most in the industry knew that he did have a self-deprecating sense of humour and he was finally going to get to share screen time with Kirk Douglas. After the strong-willed legend had walked off *First Blood*, he was happy to be in the opening scene of this film as Stallone's character's dying father. And the rest of the cast list had enough pedigree to make any nervous leading man a bit more confident. Around Stallone there would be veteran comedy actors Don Ameche (*Trading Places*), Tim Curry (*Rocky Horror Picture Show*), Peter Reigart (*Animal House*) and Harry Shearer (*This is Spinal Tap*). Plenty of reliable character talent like Kurtwood Smith (who had worked with Stallone in Thailand in *Rambo III*) and Chaz Palminteri who was straight out of the New York gangsters' look-book. Also there was *Dallas* star Linda Grey who was a long-time friend of Stallone and also a young Italian actress called Marisa Tomei who would be playing his manipulative daughter. Tomei would make such an impression during filming that when Landis invited fellow filmmaker Jonathan Lynn onto the set, he noticed her and cast her in his upcoming comedy with Joe Pesci, *My Cousin Vinny*, for which Tomei would win the Best Supporting Actress Academy Award.

Stallone plays Angelo "Snaps" Provolone and the screwball comedy of errors and misinformation is set mainly in his character's New York mansion. Landis and production designer Bill Kenney created a huge, two-story set, over 13,000 square feet, that had running water and electricity so it could operate like a real home. Filming began in September 1990 with an April 1991 release date ahead but production was delayed when a massive fire at the Universal backlot in Los Angeles where they were filming wrecked most of the main set, the props and many of the period cars that had been rented for the shoot. Using the publicity and continuity photographs that had already been taken, the production crew worked around the clock to rebuild and remake everything that had been destroyed in the blaze. It also meant production was moved to Florida at the Disney/MGM Studios there and Universal Florida also. Filming resumed and despite the disruption it still managed to wrap principle photography on the 17th of December. Upon release in April 1991 though, it was attacked by many critics to the point that it almost seemed personal. There were some positive reviews however and that's not a surprise because *Oscar* is an enjoyable, pacey comedy with Stallone playing up to his stereotype and he is the centre of every storyline. Everyone around him is working at a high level too and Landis keeps the mix of wordplay, slapstick and farce going throughout. A version of this with Al Pacino in the lead would have been very different. But, it had cost $35 million dollars to make and in the end it made back just over $23 million in total. For the record it sits at number 3,514 in the all-time US box office charts. Since it was originally released it has come to be reassessed slightly and the general consensus is that the film and performances were perfectly good but the problem was the image. Audiences at that time were just not prepared to accept him in anything that wasn't action orientated, which perhaps means that following this with another comedy wasn't the best of ideas.

But between *Oscar* and *Stop! Or My Mom Will Shoot,* came a business venture that brought together an unlikely trio and temporarily overshadowed their day jobs. *Planet Hollywood* was the brainchild of investors, entrepreneurs, restaurateurs and film producers Keith Barish and Robert Earl. Earl from Middlesex in England and Los Angeles born Barish conjured up a lavish plan to use 80's movie star power to force a global chain of restaurants into success. The polished burger joints would prey on the evergrowing celebrity culture and offer patrons the illusion of being within the elite of Hollywood. With his experience of Hard Rock Cafe and Medieval themed eateries, Earl sat and listened to the producer of films like *Sophie's Choice* and *The Running Man* about a tinseltown-themed chain with actual tinseltown stars at the forefront. Famous actors running restaurants was nothing new but the likes of Robert DeNiro's *Tribeca Grill* (which had opened in New York the year before) kept the celebrity status of their owner a discreet fact rather than making it the main selling-point. Grasping the concept immediately, the pair set about writing a wishlist of their preferred talent and three names were clearly ahead of the rest: Stallone, Schwarzenegger and Willis. Barish approached Schwarzenegger first after they had struck up a good working relationship on *The Running Man*. Then came Willis with Stallone only being approached once the other two had already committed. The offer that the action heroes accepted was a variable combination of appearance fees, investment opportunities and company stock ownership and the megawatt trio all saw the potential. By promoting *Planet Hollywood* at every available opportunity, they would be increasing their own chances of remuneration when the glammed-up burgers and fries started selling. Bruce Willis' then wife Demi Moore was not yet the biggest female star in the world, but *Ghost* in 1990 had pushed her into the limelight and she became star investor number four. By having the stars financially involved beyond mere celebrity endorsement, they were self-motivated to push the brand with every chance they got. Willis offered to bring his band, The Accelerators, to perform at every new opening they could and they were just one part of the unmissable razzmatazz of the first *Planet Hollywood* unveiling on October the 22nd 1991 on fifty-seventh street in Manhattan, just a short walk from the Hard Rock Cafe there. The aesthetic was meant to attract a jeans-wearing brigade with some frivolous cash to burn rather than an upmarket clientele. Movie memorabilia lined the walls and in total the first *Planet Hollywood* cost $8 million dollars to open.

As the concept rolled out globally, Stallone and his business partners embarked on a mission to never be seen publicly without a *Planet Hollywood* cap, jacket or t-shirt on display. Schwarzenegger even named-checked the brand in *Last Action Hero*. Watch any interview with any of the three in the early nineties and more often than not, the logo will be visible on them somewhere. Las Vegas, Orlando, Minneapolis and many other U.S. locations soon felt the star-power and London, Moscow, Paris, Tel Aviv and Dubai were among the 60 *Planet Hollywood*'s that were running simultaneously around the globe at its peak. As the phenomenon grew, every celebrity wanted in on the act and a piece of the attention that came with it. *Planet Hollywood* restaurants became sought-after movie premier locations with stars in attendance being given free food and beverage in return for wearing the t-shirt and posing for strategic photos under the garish signage. In 1996, the company went public on the stock market but by the same years' end, profits were already falling. Barish and Earl opened *All Star Cafe*'s using the same methodology but with sport as its focus (Tiger Woods celebrated his 1997 Masters victory at the *All Star Cafe* in Myrtle Beach) but the bottom was already falling out of the enterprise. The novelty soon wore off as the decade came to an end and the celebrities on hand to promote *Planet Hollywood* went from A-list down the alphabet as rapidly as the increasingly inedible food was being left on unfinished plates. Barish left the company in 1999 and they first declared bankruptcy a year later. Schwarzenegger officially bailed out in 2000, Stallone did the same soon after but Willis's official involvement past 1999 has never been clarified. As of March of 2025, there are only three official *Planet Hollywood* restaurants operating (in Disney Florida, Doha and New York) and if you were to ask the movie legends about their history with the brand, they'd develop a sudden case of business amnesia. But while the move into restauranteering was still in a positive state, Stallone had a movie career to continue to negotiate. He may have been signing official documents to go into partnership with Arnold Schwarzenegger in *Planet Hollywood*, but it soon became evident that they had not buried their cinematic rivalry.

In recent years, Schwarzenegger has publicly admitted how he tricked Stallone into making *Stop! Or My Mom Will Shoot* which is for many, the lowest point of Sylvester Stallone's professional output. In the real or not so real battle between the two men, this is the only example of where Stallone tried to imitate Arnie and not the other way around. 1991 would prove to be the biggest professional year of the Austrian's life as it was the year *Terminator 2: Judgement Day* wowed audiences, soaked up colossal amounts of money and introduced ground-breaking special effects into the industry thanks to writer and director James Cameron. But in the three years leading up to it, he had cleverly mixed his staple of adult-action movies with carefully judged comedies. He followed *Predator* and *The Running Man* with *Twins* and he then followed *Total Recall* with *Kindergarten Cop*. Both *Twins* and *Kindergarten Cop* used audience-perception and his unmistakable image to their advantage and both were hits. *Twins* remains 5th on his list of box office successes with $216 million dollars in 1988 (and included a not-so-subtle dig at Stallone as Schwarzenegger's character stops at a poster for *Rambo III on the street*, compares those muscles to his own, and laughs). Since 1985 and the *Rambo II* and *Rocky IV* smashes, Stallone had not really had a bona-fide, cultural-moment, big hit movie. *Cobra, Over the Top, Lock Up, Tango and Cash*,

Rambo III and *Rocky V* had all done ok in varying degrees but none had really dominated cinemas and become cultural touchstones. Perhaps with an air of desperation and perhaps also with a stubborn self-belief, he looked again for a comedy and this time a real 'four-quadrant' comedy too. ('Four-quadrant' has become a painfully common phrase with movie studio executives. It refers to a genre film that will/should appeal to the perceived, all-four demographics of cinemagoers: Young men, young women and older men and older women). The script was written by Blake Snyder, William Osborne and William Davies and is based on the simple premise of a police detective who is trying to crack a case when his mother comes to visit and gets embroiled in the action whilst also behaving how mothers in movies are expected to behave.

Estelle Getty was a veteran performer in theatre, film and TV until her big break came later in life in the comedy series *The Golden Girls* which finished its very successful seven-year run just as she was making *Stop! Or My Mom Will Shoot*. The screenplay cried out for a male-lead who would be prepared to have his tough screen image deflated during the movie and it was sent to the offices of Arnold Schwarzenegger. Upon reading it, so the story now goes, Arnold decided it was a terrible script but instructed his team to put out the word that he was going to do it "before Stallone had a chance to say yes." This fabrication did indeed make its way back to Stallone and, as he admits himself, was one of the major reasons he agreed to the role. Director Roger Spottiswoode, like John Landis had done with *Oscar,* surrounded Stallone with trusted talent. Jo Beth Williams (best known for *Poltergeist*) played the long-suffering love interest, Roger Rees was proving his comedic talent as a recurring character on the unparalleled sitcom *Cheers* but he always gave good villain too. Character actor Martin Ferrero did what he could after already helping out on screen in *Oscar* as well. (Despite an excellent career that included memorable roles in *Miami Vice, Heat* and *Planes, Trains and Automobiles,* Ferrero would forever be remembered as the man eaten on the toilet in *Jurassic Park*). It's also worth looking out for brief, early roles for Ving Rhames (*Pulp Fiction, Mission: Impossible* franchise) and Richard Schiff (*The West Wing*).

Stallone's character Sergeant Joseph Bomowski is straight out of the most average American sitcom. He dresses in GAP, wants a simple life and is infantilized by every woman he knows. Of course it ends with his mother helping to solve the case and get the bad guy while everyone learns to love each other a bit better. It's not especially funny but it's not unforgivably bad either. It contains an image that Stallone himself wishes could be struck from all memory when, in a dream sequence, his character is seen holding a gun while wearing an adult-sized nappy/diaper. But, Stallone's comedic performance here is a vast improvement on his *Rhinestone* work. He is relaxed and subtle for the most part and he is doing exactly what the film demands of him. Alan Silvestri's jaunty score reminds you that it's lightweight stuff here and despite its complete predictability, it's an inoffensive watch. If you go into it expecting a very family-friendly, early-nineties comedy in the vein of *Three Men and a Baby*, you'll have a pleasant 87 minutes half-asleep on the sofa on a Sunday afternoon. Some more astute critics noted that it probably had a better chance of working for Stallone than *Rhinestone* and *Oscar* because it seemed like it should be more within his wheelhouse as there was a fair amount of action wedged between the comedic scenes, but the execution of it overall was lacklustre. Its reported $45 million dollar budget meant that it lost money in the US by taking in a meagre $28 million but globally it made back its investment with a worldwide gross of just over $70 million dollars. Like *Rambo*

III and *Oscar*, reports of it being a disastrous financial flop were actually unfounded but unfortunately that bit went unreported which meant it was ticked off as another Stallone bomb. In the years since, it is often the butt of a joke from the star himself and he teases that if his kids had been naughty, he would force them to watch it.

The two-headed comedy experiment that was *Oscar* and *Stop! Or My Mom Will Shoot* was seen at the time as the end of Stallone's career. It caused numerous retrospective articles in publications that had more than a whiff of "do you remember when Stallone was good?" He knew that trying to go against the image he had been pigeonholed into was unlikely to end well, yet he had tried anyway. He was being paid handsomely regardless of the outcome so financially he never had to worry for his future or his family's, but when you've been top dog for a number of years it must be very painful to see others sitting on your throne. And in the case of Arnold duping him into a film, it meant that his biggest box-office competition was now laughing at him. But if this phase of the Stallone / Schwarzenegger rivalry saw a big win for the former Mr Universe, then karma was about to even up the score again. The very next year, Arnie would very publicly fall back to earth and never fully regain his former glories while Stallone would confound the critics and naysayers by producing two modern classics, neither of which involved characters he'd played before.

1993 - CLIFFHANGER, DEMOLITION MAN

Seven years prior, *Rocky IV* had been a monster of a success but since then a new Stallone movie had become increasingly disappointing. While most had turned a decent profit, none had had the cultural footprint that the title of "biggest movie star in the world" would suggest. His once reliable *Rocky* and *Rambo* were now on indefinite hold and the studio's focus had been turned towards Tom Cruise, Bruce Willis, Harrison Ford, Mel Gibson and yes, Arnold Schwarzenegger. The first two years of the nineties had seen Arnie take Stallone's mantle as king of the muscle bound movie. 1990 had brought *Total Recall* and in 1991 he had the biggest film on the planet in *Terminator 2: Judgement Day*. 1993 was expected to follow suit as the high-concept and high-budget *Last Action Hero* was surely going to cement the Austrian's position. Rumours were also spreading that Steven Spielberg was outdoing himself in production of two very different titles but no one yet knew how *Schindler's List* and *Jurassic Park* would turn out. Harrison Ford was making *The Fugitive,* Robin Williams was creating *Mrs Doubtfire* and Tom Cruise was deep into *The Firm*. It seemed 1993 was all sewn up before it began, leaving the likes of Sylvester Stallone scratching his head and wondering what to do next. The offers coming in were either versions of what he had done before or nonexistent. But then two opportunities would come from unexpected sources that would see him take back his hard won crown. One was caused by Sting and the other by John Candy.

Carolco Pictures had been loyal to Stallone and in 1990 they wanted to get him to sign for something lighter. After three *Rambo* movies, *Escape to Victory* and *Lock Up,* they had a good working relationship so when they approached him about a John Hughes comedy with John Candy co-starring, he showed interest despite his track record with that genre. The film was about two feuding neighbours and would be called *Bartholomew vs. Neff.* Both stars agreed and principle photography would have started in the summer of 1991 but the film, like so many do, fell apart. Eager to still work with Stallone, Carolco then came up with a few new options, but both were back in the comfort of the action genre. The first was a long-gestating project called *Isobar* which would have seen Stallone battle a monster onboard a runaway train. It was to partner him with Kim Basinger but disagreements over script changes saw that film fall by the wayside too. What was left was another option called *Gale Force.* David Chappe's script had started a bidding war throughout the mid to late eighties. Carolco had eventually stumped up half a million dollars with a bonus of another $200 thousand dollars to Chappe if the film ever reached a cinema screen. Finnish director Renny Harlin was already on board having made the fourth *Nightmare on Elm Street* film in 1988 but then scoring big with *Die Hard 2: Die Harder* in 1990. Chappe's *Gale Force* story was about an ex-Navy SEAL battling modern pirates at a coastal town during a hurricane. Over the next year, a huge $4 million dollars was spent on rewrites until the whole idea was deemed too expensive and written off. But Harlin and Stallone then had their attention turned towards another outdoors, battle-with-nature adventure story called *Cliffhanger.* Free-climber John Long had written a novella called *Rogue's Babylon* which had then been the inspiration for screenwriter Michael France to create an action script (although this fact was only discovered later when proof of John Long's story connection to Michael Franks script led to a $400 thousand dollar payout and a screen credit of 'Based on a premise by John Long'). Franks was paid half a million dollars for his work by Carolco and once they had the screenplay to themselves, Stallone was allowed to put his stamp on it. The story saw Mountain Rescue ranger Gabe Walker (Stallone) and his team reluctantly getting embroiled with highly trained armed thieves who have stolen millions from the U.S. Treasury but have lost the cases of money all over the Rocky Mountains. The budget was a massive $70 million dollars as Harlin and Stallone wanted to film on location as much as possible and had added ambitious action sequences and set-pieces that they were unwilling to compromise on, including a shocking opening scene and the most expensive aerial stunt ever performed.

But before getting to those harsh locations, casting needed to be finalised. Christopher Walken was locked in as the main villain Eric Qualen with John Lithgow joining as his second in command. Michael Rooker would play Walker's best friend Hal Tucker with Janine Turner picked to play the love interest who had to be adept at doing action as much as everyone else. Ralph Waite joined as the elder statesman of the Rescue Rangers team and his casting was also used to manipulate the audience's emotions when he was killed off during the movie, as he was easily best known as the patriarch figure of the long-running TV drama, *The Waltons*. British actors Craig Fairbrass and Caroline Woodhall joined Leon Robinson in rounding out the senior villains with veteran Paul Winfield taking on the role of US Treasury Agent Walter Wright whose main function in the film seemed to be to provide the audience with regular recaps of where we were in the plot. Mountain ranges in

Spain, Austria, New Zealand, France and Germany were all scouted but Cortina in Italy was eventually chosen for the main location shoot with Cinecitta Studios in Rome getting used plus some extra filming was to take place in Durango in Colorado. As cast and crew made their way to Italy, news broke that Christopher Walken had dropped out. Harlin briefly reconsidered his original choice for the main bad guy, David Bowie, but realised he already had the ideal replacement on the plane, and so John Lithgow was upgraded from secondary villain to the main antagonist.

The original opening to *Cliffhanger* had been designed to show Gabe Walker's affinity with his environment by rescuing a rare bird from a mountain top, but Harlin immediately told Stallone he wanted to replace that with a shock to the system that would tell the audience that this is not the kind of film they expected. Initially reluctant to have Stallone as his main lead due to the baggage of his previous roles that he brought with him, Harlin convinced him to be shown failing in the opening scene. Harlin's intention was to make it clear to the audience early on that even though Stallone was the hero, he wasn't infallible. It resulted in one of the great openings of any action movie. After some majestic sweeping shots of the mountains we find Hal (Rooker) and his girlfriend Sarah (Michelle Joyner) having to cut short a rock climb due to Hal's twisted knee. Gabe has gone to help with what should be a straightforward rescue but a harness breaks and despite Gabe climbing along a rope to try and rescue Sarah (and indeed telling her that she's "not gonna die") she slips out of Gabe's grasp and plummets thousands of feet, screaming her way to her death. A lot of the filming for the scene was done for real over an abyss in Italy with actress Joyner supported by invisible safety wires. Close-ups and green screen work was done on the Rome soundstage but when edited together it had the desired effect and some critics said the opening was so powerful, the rest of the film could never surpass it. But they also had a million dollar aerial sequence up their sleeve too. The high-altitude robbery was to involve the thieves escaping with the money from one plane to another via zipline, mid-flight. Stuntman Simon Crane won plenty of plaudits for doing it for real as both planes travelled at 150 miles per hour at an altitude of 15 thousand feet and since it cost $1 million dollars, it was only done once. It remains in the Guinness Book of Records as the costliest aerial stunt of its kind in movie history. Although the crew was producing the goods, the same couldn't be said for Carolco Pictures. Their financing of the movie began to stutter and twice in Italy production had to be shut down because the crew had not been paid. TriStar Pictures had put up half the budget but Carolco had to get a huge $40 million dollar loan from Credit Lyonnais Bank Nederland to keep the film alive. Stallone himself put some of his own salary (reportedly $2 million of it) back into the production as well. (Carolco's financial woes meant that despite the success of *Cliffhanger*, they made very little profit after repaying all their creditors).

Production wrapped and editing began while composer Trevor Jones created the memorable score with the National Philharmonic Orchestra. The South African had previously written for plenty of big films including *Tango & Cash* director Andrei Konchalovsky's earlier film *Runaway Train* and also the fantasy adventures *Time Bandits, Labyrinth* and *The Dark Crystal*. The previous year he had composed for the sweeping drama *The Last of the Mohicans* with a similar soundscape and ambition to his work for *Cliffhanger*. Months before the premiere, *Cliffhanger* garnered global buzz when the first trailer appeared in cinemas. It was unlike anything else that was being previewed in multiplexes and made a huge impact on the films' positive, pre-release word of mouth. Jones and the producers used only images of the movie with no dialogue at all and the music wasn't your standard action beat; a combination of motifs from *Ride of the Valkyries* by Wagner and Mozart's *Requiem* led to the climax of *Oh Fortuna* from *Carmina Burana* by Carl Orff as just two words - 'Hang On' - propelled towards the audience. The only information given was the movies' title and the stars' surname and it still stands today as one of the finest examples of movie-trailer expertise. Perhaps influenced by the European-based shoot and director, the excellent final score for the movie itself also leaned into the expansive operatic bent of the trailer.

Released on May the 28th in the United States it was an immediate hit making over $20 million dollars in its opening weekend. It went to number one in all the major global territories and spent an extraordinary 11 weeks in the number one spot in Japan. It finally grossed $225 million worldwide, making it the 7th biggest hit of the year. And that was in the unique year in which Spielberg's *Jurassic Park* ate up most of the competition. It's a film that stands as strong now as it did when audiences were wowed by it in 1993. The opening scene is brilliantly conceived and serves to do exactly what Harlin had intended it to. From then on, it is relentless and relentlessly entertaining. Stallone perfectly plays the reluctant hero (it does have similarities to the themes of *Die Hard* and was nicknamed 'Die Hard on a Mountain' by several journalists) who doesn't have any training in combat or weapons and relies on his wits, improvisation and unique knowledge of the terrain. Harlin juggles the action superbly and just about manages to keep things on the right side of ridiculous. Lithgow has since said it is one of his favourite films and watching him as Qualen, it's impossible to think of anyone else in that role, even Christopher Walken. Michael

Rooker, Janine Turner and the rest of the supporting cast throw themselves wholeheartedly into their roles and the film deservedly sits as one of the best of Stallone's career. And talking of his career, after a number of years without a hit and with plenty of whispering in the shadows that he was all washed up, the sense of satisfaction mixed with relief was palpable. It was a major moment for him as he'd now starred in a critical and commercial hit with a brand new character for the first time since *First Blood* over ten years before. To make it even better, a month after *Cliffhanger* was released Schwarzenegger premiered *Last Action Hero* to much fanfare but little success. It grossed only $137 million which was way below expectations (and the stars' predictions) for the $85 million dollar production and it was considered by all involved as a flop. He would bounce back the next year with *True Lies* but he never had a huge solo success after that again.

While he was on the pre-release promotional tour for *Cliffhanger*, he was also hard at work on his next film which was to be unlike anything he'd done before (In the official "Making of.." TV special for *Cliffhanger*, he talks to the camera about the snowy movie while dressed in the complete *Demolition Man* cop uniform, which was rather confusing for viewers). It was going to involve action and stunts but it was set in the future, which was something he'd experienced only once when he played Joe 'Machine Gun' Viterbo in the Roger Corman produced *Death Race 2000*, the year before *Rocky* hit. Since he'd become a star, sci-fi was a genre he'd avoided in favour of contemporary, present day stories. At various points, his name had been considered for roles in *Star Wars* and *The Terminator* but he'd never found the right project or the right project had never found him. Until 1993.

College graduate Peter Lenkov arrived in Hollywood as an aspiring writer but with nothing on his resume so far. Driving around in a beaten up old car he would listen to the only tape he had in his beatbox on the back seat. Sting had written a song called *Demolition Man* in 1980 which had been recorded and released as a single by Grace Jones, but Sting's band The Police also recorded their version for their 1981 album *Ghost in the Machine*, and it got stuck in his head. Combining his appreciation of the new wave of cop films like *Lethal Weapon* with the never-ending myth of Walt Disney's cryogenically frozen body being in the news again in the late 80's, his mind got to work on a new story. His initial pitch saw a frozen cop and a frozen bad guy, thawed out and fighting to the death in a future where crime is a thing of the past. Lenkov's story was dark in tone with a hint of *Blade Runner* and ended with the hero living out the rest of his life with his now, much older wife. Lenkov also suggested Mickey Rourke as the star. Despite Warner Bros. not fully grasping the concept, they bought the script from Lenkov and added it to the thousands of other unmade screenplays they owned. That was until Ohio born screenwriter Daniel Waters took a look at it and asked if he could have a go at a rewrite. Waters had made his name with the dark comedy *Heathers* in 1989 and gone on to co-write the Bruce Willis off-the-charts-insane vanity project *Hudson Hawk* and crucially *Batman Returns* the year before. The Lenkov original script was a straight-up action flick, but Waters thought there was potential for a lot of fish-out-of-the-water comedy with the basic premise of a violent cop and criminal being transported into a serene and peaceful environment. The new version of the story he settled on was of supervillain Simon Phoenix and supercop Sergeant John 'Demolition Man' Spartan, who are both woken up in 2032 after being cryogenically frozen in the 90's.

They continue their brutal cat and mouse chase but in a post earthquake-ravaged Los Angeles where fighting, sex, swearing and even salt have been eradicated from society. Far from being an adult thriller, Waters saw this as a comic-book movie that put action and laughs on an equal footing. 33-year old Italian-born Canadian Marco Brambilla was brought in as director, with a recommendation from David Fincher (who had just completed *Alien 3*). Brambilla was a contemporary artist who had turned his skills towards visually impressive commercials on television, which had been the path to big screen directing for Fincher and Tony Scott previously. Warner Bros. felt he could bring some of his artistic flair to the project and he and Waters got to work on more rewrites and more ideas. They added Robert Reneau to their writers room as his movie credentials included the Carl Weathers' solo project *Action Jackson*. The trio's latest screenplay began with the two leads being awoken in 2032, but another writer Fred Dekker (whose efforts went uncredited in the final film) wrote a prologue set in the nineties to show the pair in their normal environment so that when they do get the the future, the differences are more evident. Dekker was quoted as saying, "If you don't show Kansas, Oz isn't all that special."

Producer Joel Silver had already been lobbying some lead actors for the main roles and had approached Steven Seagal and Jean-Claude Van Damme as the hero and villain respectively. Silver had already been to talk to Stallone but he'd initially rejected the film. But when Seagal and Van Damme both said no, and with the latest rewrites adding a lot more comedy, Stallone was now intrigued. He suggested Jackie Chan as his opposite number but Chan declined as he did not want to play the bad guy. Like Stallone, Wesley Snipes had already said no to the film when Silver approached him with it.

But both Joel Silver and Marco Brambilla went to visit Snipes on the set of *Rising Sun* (co-starring Sean Connery) and their passion for *Demolition Man* won him over and he agreed to be Simon Phoenix. Quick-talking stand-up comedian Denis Leary was given the role of the underground rebel leader Edgar Friendly and was asked to rewrite most of his dialogue to suit his rapid-fire approach. Veteran stage and television actor Nigel Hawthorne was very hesitant about joining the film as the machiavellian Raymond Cocteau (who is secretly orchestrating the bad deeds of Simon Phoenix despite being considered the saviour of humanity). He didn't want to be in a Hollywood blockbuster but he was trying to get the lead part in the upcoming *The Madness of King George* and the potential studio wanted to see how he could hold the attention on the silver screen (Hawthorne went on to win the Academy Award for Best Actor for the role). He was also convinced by the producers that his role was very Shakespearean and his long-standing love for the playwright's work helped persuade him. The female-sidekick part of Lenina Huxley went to Lori Petty, whose star was on the rise with prominent roles in *Point Break* and *A League of Their Own*. With a budget of $45 million dollars, the film went into production on the 12th of February 1993.

The 2032 of *Demolition Man* is set in the fictional new-state of San Angeles, which was built after an earthquake that wiped out the old L.A. and surrounding area. To achieve the required look, filming took place in the most futuristic locations that 1990's Los Angeles had to offer. To reinforce John Spartan's nickname, the script called for the initial 1996-set opening scene to end with a building being demolished. Warner Bros. saw marketing potential and partnered with MTV to create a competition called the "Demolition Man Jam" where the eventual winners were invited to join Stallone and

Snipes to watch the blowing-up of Belknap Hardware and Manufacturing Company in Louisville in Kentucky. It wasn't the only full-size structure that the production raised to the ground as L.A. officials approved the use of explosives on a large demolition for the first time in thirty years on their Los Angeles Department of Water and Power building. But more than just buildings blew-up in the first few weeks of filming as Lori Petty and Stallone didn't get along from the start. Joel Silver made the decision early on that a change needed to be made, and citing the age-old public excuse of "creative differences" and after just three days of work, Petty was fired. 29-year-old Sandra Bullock had been working on TV and some smaller films such as *Love Potion Number 9* and *The Vanishing* and was one of a number of actresses who had already auditioned for an upcoming action film called *Speed*. Her comedic talent was evident and she stepped in to replace Petty within 24 hours. In other supporting roles, comedian Rob Schneider was cast as a member of the SAPD who is as shocked at Spartan's behavior as his colleagues (he would pretty much repeat that role opposite Stallone in *Judge Dredd* two years later) which included young actor Benjamin Bratt (who would work with Sandra Bullock again when she was an established movie star in *Miss Congeniality* in 2000). There was also Bob Gunton as the disapproving Chief George Earle (who was a year away from his most memorable role as Warden Norton in *The Shawshank Redemption*) to round out the main cast. While there were no further cast changes, the weather was not quite so agreeable. Rain caused frequent set damage that caused delays and Stallone significantly strained his arm in training which also shut production down for 10 more days. The planned 72-day shoot eventually ran to 112 days which meant many of the production crew had to be replaced as they had commitments to other jobs that couldn't wait.

The budget had also spiralled and went from $45 million up to nearly $80 million by the time they wrapped but some of that cost was offset by some very un-subtle product placement. Midway through the film, the conniving Cocteau invites Spartan and Huxley to a fancy dinner. The joke being that he invites them to fast-food chain Taco Bell, which have now become the only top-class restaurants in the tranquil world of 2032 San Angeles. As Warner Bros began to think about global audiences, they realised Taco Bell was not a well-known brand outside of the United States. So for Europe and much of the rest of the world, dialogue was re-dubbed and signage was digitally changed to Pizza Hut. Both companies were owned by PepsiCo at the time anyway. Having said that, the dubbing wasn't particularly well done with actors clearly mouthing one restaurant name while the voice is saying the other and in the background of some shots Taco Bell logos are still clearly visible in the non-US release. There were also several scenes between John Spartan and his now grown-up daughter filmed, but that plot line was entirely removed as test audiences felt a bit squeamish about the hero's daughter being of similar age to his new love interest and in general their storyline was deemed overly sentimental and at odds with the rest of the movie.

The film went straight to number one at the box office when it was released on the 8th of October 1993. Its $14.5 million dollar opening was the biggest start for a film in October ever and it went on to make $160 million worldwide. While that wasn't in the top ten for the year (it was 12th in-between Clint Eastwood's *In the Line of Fire* and Jamaican bobsleigh comedy *Cool Runnings*) it was considered both a commercial and critical success. *Demolition Man* garnered some of the best reviews of Stallone's career with plenty of genuine (and rare) praise for his comedy work. The difference in box office between *Demolition Man* and Arnie's *Last Action Hero* was only $20 million dollars, but the reaction couldn't have been more different. Schwarzenegger's movie came across as smug and self-indulgent while *Demolition Man* was having fun with the audience and its big star was in on the joke. At one point, Snipe's bad guy steals a machine gun from a museum dummy with the comment, "Sorry Rambo, I need to borrow this." In *Last Action Hero*, Schwarzenegger's character goes into a video store where there is a big, cardboard advert for *Terminator 2* starring Sylvester Stallone. That gag (like many in *Last Action Hero*) was heavy-handed and clumsy but Stallone's jokes at the expense of Arnie fared much better: While Spartan and Huxley are driving, it is explained to Spartan that The Schwarzenegger Memorial Library was built as a legacy to former President Schwarzenegger. His response is - "Somebody put me back in the fridge." The underlying message that runs throughout the action and comedy of *Demolition Man* is that if you remove everything that could possibly hurt or offend someone in society, are you really living at all? A societal debate that is raging more now than it was then. The pop music of everyday life in 2032 is old radio jingles and people are instantly fined if they swear in any way. One of the funniest scenes involves Spartan and Huxley "having sex". While Spartan is expecting the traditional method, Huxley puts some technical headgear on him and proceeds to have the 2032 version which involves thoughts-only and zero physical contact. And there is that puzzle that has yet to be resolved: toilet paper has been replaced by three seashells in every bathroom. Sandra Bullock's character is the link between the grubby past and the pristine future. Bullocks' Lenina Huxley is obsessed with the 90's that she has heard about (on her office wall is the *Lethal Weapon 3* poster, a film also produced by Joel Silver). She finds Spartan's violent nature, potty mouth and carnal desires fascinating rather than intolerable. And while none of the film's creators ever claimed to be pushing a political agenda or commenting on an increasingly divisive America, the film is even more reflective of 21st century planet earth now, than it was when it was made. Another way that it warrants new viewings is the same way that *Back to the Future Part II* is revisited. That 1989 sequel and *Demolition Man* enjoyed dropping in a plethora of ideas and inventions that are now being assessed for their predictive accuracy. In 1993, *Demolition Man* imagined that by the 2030's we would all be in driverless cars, be able to call up all sorts of information on a personal device, have our household lights controllable by voice, hold conversations from miles away via a video screen and there would be an increasing divide in society between those who wanted a grounded, hands-on life and those who felt that a sanitized, naive existence where there was no possible chance of ever being offended, was the better way to live. Fortunately though, we still use real toilet paper.

One of the big changes to the Lenkov script is the sense that this is a comic-book film. *Demolition Man* was released the year after *Batman Returns* and two years before the 2nd and 3rd sequels to 1989's *Batman (Batman Forever* and *Batman & Robin)* but they share a visual theme. The tone is very similar as is the set design and while composer Elliot Goldenthal produced a memorable score, there are definite vibes of Danny Elfman's *Batman* themes. The costumes are designed by Bob Ringwood and are intentionally striking with the SAPD uniforms in particular having a very comic-book friendly feel. Despite *Demolition Man* having no origins in graphic novels, DC Comics did produce a limited series which was written by Gary Cohn, with the artwork coming from Rod Whigham and Kevin Maguire. John Spartan's look is always somewhere at a Comic-Con.

So, like *Cliffhanger* earlier in the year, *Demolition Man* was a sizable box office hit and critics were universal in their praise too. It was very unusual for Stallone after nearly two decades of battling negative print reviews, whether justifiable or not. He was now happy with his partner Jennifer Flavin for five years and his career was back on track, with the added bonus of getting some credit for his work. Also for the first time, he wasn't feeling the need or feeling the pressure to return to either Rocky or Rambo as he was being offered seemingly good scripts on original projects with positive prospects. And after successfully sharing starring duties with Wesley Snipes he was willing to do it again, but this time with Sharon Stone.

1994 - 1995 - THE SPECIALIST, JUDGE DREDD, ASSASSINS

In 1984 a short-lived but copious book series called *The Specialist* was published by author John Cutter. In the space of two years, eleven books were released where mercenary Jack Sullivan would get embroiled in various revenge missions, usually helping a love-interest to get some payback. John Cutter was actually the pen-name of Texas-born John Shirley who was at the forefront of cyberpunk novels and short-stories whilst also being prolific in horror, fantasy and westerns, not to mention a music career that saw him co-write two albums with *Blue Oyster Cult.* His series with the umbrella title of *The Specialist* was one of a number of lone-wolf thrillers that were part of a long-standing attempt to find something that would challenge Ian Fleming's lucrative Bond novels which were guaranteed money-earners at the box-office. The ideal pitch would be a strong male lead character with plenty of potential for action but in a contemporary setting so filming could take place at real locations instead of having to build expensive period or fantasy worlds. Jason Bourne and Jack Reacher were years away and a *Mission: Impossible* movie pitch was only just arriving on Tom Cruise's desk.

The Specialist books were popular reads, but they didn't instantly spark studio interest until they inspired a screenplay by Alexandra Seros. The native Californian was studying acting at UCLA where she also showed a talent for writing and gained a Masters Degree in Dramatic Arts: Film History and Criticism. Wisely realising that her acting dream couldn't be her only avenue for income, she produced short stories and screenplays that she hoped to sell. Two of her scripts garnered interest: one was called Point of No Return (internationally, the film was called *The Assassin*) which was an adaptation of *La Femme Nikita*, the French action hit for Luc Besson in 1990. The American remake would star Bridget Fonda and Gabriel Byrne and proved a modest hit in 1993. Her other work was *The Specialist* which she had written long before *Point of No Return*. She had changed the lead character into a bomb-expert who uses impressive devices to dispatch bad guys, so as to distinguish *The Specialist* from the glut of gun-carrying heroes of the time. Selling the script in 1990, Mario Van Peebles was looking at directing and possibly starring. When he dropped out it was offered to Steven Seagal in late 1992 but after he had hit big with *Under Siege* that summer, he suddenly demanded a nine million dollar fee which producer Jerry Weintraub was not prepared to accept. Weintraub still believed in the movie and before his option to make it ran out he got some serious interest from Warren Beatty. At the time, the star was on precarious ground as a bankable commodity. His infamous box-office disaster *Ishtar* with Dustin Hoffman in 1987, was still being mentioned as a shorthand for misguided, expensive flops. But he'd given himself a lifeline with *Dick Tracy* in 1990 and then *Bugsy* the year after and while neither film set the box-office alight, neither were they considered catastrophes. The idea of *The Specialist* appealed to Beatty as he smelled a potential franchise that could run and run but what Beatty was unaware of was that he was being used as bait to lure Sylvester Stallone.

Cliffhanger and *Demolition Man* had put him back in the game as a marketable commodity and Weintraub wanted him for the thriller. Stallone was looking at many projects as he now had the cache back to pick and choose his next option. With a March 1994 start date for production immoveable, Weintraub had to play hardball and gave Stallone a 15-minute window to sign on for *The Specialist* or Warren Beatty was going to be given the role. Another tempting carrot that was hung in front of him was that up and coming music video turned feature director, David Fincher was apparently lined-up. After committing to *The Specialist* and championing Fincher as his director, Stallone was eventually overruled as Weintraub and his associates couldn't get past the disappointing reception to *Alien 3* in 1992 which was Fincher's only movie as director at that point. Fincher was told he wasn't going to direct *The Specialist* and he went off and found *Seven*, the next year.

But with the main star secured, Stallone was allowed to start script rewrites alongside New York born screenwriter Akiva Goldsmith (although Goldsmith's contribution went uncredited). The lead character was now called Ray Quick and even though Stallone had been happy with Alexandra Seros writing him as a lonely, melancholic character the forces of big business soon put pressure on Goldsmith to make it much more traditional action fare. Other influences over the ever-changing drafts included the recent success of steamy, erotic thrillers for the big screen which was initiated by *Basic Instinct* in 1992. The film made an international star of Sharon Stone and she was in more bedroom-based movie action the year after in *Sliver*. She initially tried avoiding *The Specialist* but after she had committed to it, the script suddenly had nudity and gratuitous sex forced into it despite Stone's reticence.

The plot was now almost unrecognisable from the original novels and the screenplay that Seros had sold. Ray Quick is a hitman for hire who uses cleverly designed bombs to eradicate his targets. He gets involved with Stone and tries to help her get revenge on the criminals that killed her parents whilst Quick is also having an ongoing battle with a former colleague from the armed forces who has become the gangsters' amoral head of security. James Woods was cast as the high-energy security chief that wants his own payback on Quick and it's reported that some of his most flamboyant scenes were cut out as they were overshadowing the more understated work of the two leads. Eric Roberts was cast as the gangster and again, a lot of his dialogue was shredded in the final film so as not to distract from the Stallone and Stone show. Stone's reluctance for the project saw her clash with Woods on set several times although the pair would reunite the next year to great success on Martin Scorsese's *Casino* for which Stone would receive an Oscar nomination. Two thirds of the way through *The Specialist* there is a confrontation in a hotel lobby between Stone and Woods characters which could easily have been a deleted scene from *Casino*. But that interaction comes just after the infamous shower scene where Stallone and Stone have sex in extravagant fashion. It's over the top and totally unnecessary and explains why both actors felt the need to finish a bottle of vodka beforehand to get through it.

Filming in Miami and Tennessee ended in early May and Peruvian director Luis Llosa set off to the editing room to make sense of the footage he'd shot. Llosa had made the decent hit *Sniper* with Tom Berenger the year before but this was his first taste of having to accommodate a demanding producer, an ever changing script and huge stars who also had their own visions of what the film should be. But he did have a couple of things on his side, including the music. As if signaling the intent for *The Specialist* to become an ongoing series of movies in the vein of 007, they hired John Barry to write the score. Barry's last Bond score had been in 1987 with *The Living Daylights* but he'd never been busier with *Dances with Wolves* in 1990 followed by *Chaplin* and *Indecent Proposal* among others. But he went above and beyond with his work on *The Specialist* and elevated the messy thriller with his sublime orchestrations. (Another Bond connection is that in his autobiography, Roger Moore said he was offered a part in *The Specialist* but declined and later said he was grateful for that decision). But Barry's input aside, *The Specialist* is a patchy, schizophrenic film that wavers between traditional action, soft-porn and an extended episode of *Miami Vice*. James Woods more than once elevates the film with his frenetic, scenery-chewing turn (what was cut out must have been extraordinary) because Stallone and Stone are left with very poe-faced characters that border on irritatingly dull.

The Specialist was released on October the 7th and went straight to number one making a worldwide total of more than $170 million dollars so it was a solid financial success. As with so many titles on Stallone's filmography that are considered failures, it's not a bad film but it's not that good either. The positives are there to enjoy; aside from John Barry's luscious music, Cuban-American singing star Gloria Estefan scored a global hit song with *Turn the Beat Around* from the soundtrack. Also, Luis Llosa and his cinematographer Jeffrey L Kimball (who had done *Top Gun*, *Beverly Hills Cop 2* and *True Romance* before *The Specialist*) fashion some stunning visuals with the various explosions bordering on art. Also, the death-by-little-bomb gimmick is refreshing for the times and……..James Woods. Additionally in the plus column is the fact it made much more money than Schwarzenegger's latest, the man-pregnancy comedy *Junior* that was released a few weeks later. (For balance, in the summer of 1994 he had the third biggest film in the world with *True Lies*). But, the last twenty minutes are a mess, with the final action set piece hard to follow and insipid. And then there's the sex. Failing to understand that the boundary-pushing sexual acts depicted in *Basic Instinct* were intrinsic to the plot, the makers of *The Specialist* can't justify their inclusion. Their intimate scenes (especially the shower scene that so troubled Stone) feel wildly awkward, gratuitous and serve absolutely no purpose in the story of *The Specialist*. In modern filmmaking, with an intimacy coordinator on-set, it makes you wonder if Stone's concerns would have led to the whole scene being scrapped. Despite the profit the film generated, the consensus was that it was underwhelming and already felt out of date, as in the second week of release it was knocked off the top of the charts by *Pulp Fiction*. Tarantino's masterpiece sent shock waves through an already concerned big budget Hollywood. It wasn't so much than an independent filmmaker had released an adult-targeted movie that featured male-rape, drug overdoses and a record 265 uses of the f-word, but it was that it had made $200 million dollars on an $8 million dollar budget. From then on, asking for $50 million plus for a standard action film became a lot harder.

While *The Specialist* had its origins in works of literature, its niche fan-base meant that the wholesale changes that it went through from book to screen went largely uncriticized. But when you transfer a beloved comic-book creation to the silver screen, you are asking for a world of opinions on the outcome. Superhero movies by 1995 were all about the caped crusader. 1992's *Batman Returns* was considered a superior film to the cultural landmark of its predecessor and *Batman Forever* was now due in the summer. Superman had been the king of the capes in the eighties but 1987's woeful *Superman IV: The Quest for Peace* killed the franchise immediately and star Christopher Reeve's interest in ever doing it again. But a decade before that, when Stallone was working on *F.I.S.T.* and *Paradise Alley* the year after *Rocky* shocked the world, a new comic was published in the U.K. In December of 1977, the United Kingdom was finally allowed to see the film that the U.S. was obsessing over, *Star Wars*, but in February of that year *2000AD* first started to find its audience in comic-book shops around the country. The weekly, science-fiction release from IPC Magazines quickly discovered that its prime attraction was the character Judge Dredd. Like all the best comic-book creations, the style and the excitement was a veil for the deeper message and its commentary on the culture of the times. Dredd exists in a dystopian future of MegaCity One, where he is a law enforcement officer who is authorised to carry out arrest, conviction, sentence and execution and his stories would satirize the state of police brutality and justice in the Britain and America of the late seventies. Created by writer John Wagner and artist Carlos Ezquerra, his popularity saw him get his very own publication in 1990. A movie version of the character was talked about since the first arrival of *2000AD* on the newsstands and in the mid-eighties the magazine ran a reader poll on who they would like to see play Dredd on the big screen and the winner was Clint Eastwood (with Ridley Scott directing). Then in 1990 a real attempt was being made to transfer Dredd to the cinema with Tim Hunter directing and Arnold Schwarzenegger in the title role. Michael de Luca and William Wisher then came up with an original story for a film and Wisher and Steven E de Souza are credited with the screenplay although at least half a dozen more have been unofficially named as contributing to the elongated script writing process. *Cliffhanger* director Renny Harlin was among the directors considered along with Peter Hewitt (*Bill and Ted's Bogus Journey*), The Coen Brothers, Richard Stanley and legendary *Superman* director Richard Donner. But none had a connection to the character like Danny Cannon, a young director from Luton in England.

Cannon had impressed with his debut feature that he'd also co-written called *The Young Americans* with Harvey Keitel. As a teenager he had created a fake movie-poster for a Dredd movie that was published in *2000AD* in 1987. His poster declared Harrison Ford was Dredd with co-stars Daryl Hannah and Christopher Walken. His enthusiasm and talent combined to win him the job but Schwarzenegger had dropped out and Stallone was now being offered $15 million to take on the role. The success of *RoboCop* in 1987 helped assure the money-men that this new helmeted character could work as well and John Wagner, the original writer of the comics, told Cannon that Stallone was actually perfect for the part. The main filming was set to take place at Shepperton Studios in Surrey in England and not just because the characters origins were in the UK but Cannon believed the technicians were better. A whopping budget of $80 million dollars was signed over and Cannon hoped that his decision to make *Judge Dredd* instead of *Die Hard with a Vengeance*, would be proven wise. With Stallone onboard, casting the rest of the film became a lot easier and the star helped by suggesting a few people he'd worked with before. Max von Sydow had been in *Escape to Victory* with him and was cast as the wise mentor figure, Chief Justice Fargo. Armand Assante had played Stallone's brother in his first directorial effort *Paradise Alley* in 1977 and he was given the bad guy gig as Rico who is Dredd's biological brother which prompted Assante to copy some of Stallone's mannerisms and speech patterns on film. Rob Schneider from *Demolition Man* was given the comedic sidekick role of Fergie in a part that had been offered to, and turned down by, Joe Pesci. With Diane Lane and Jurgen Prochnow also accepting roles, filming got underway on August the 3rd 1994 as *Clear and Present Danger* with Harrison Ford landed in cinemas.

Soon after filming really started, Cannon and Stallone found they had really different visions for the film. As a lifelong devotee of the character, Cannon imagined a dark, satirical reproduction of life in MegaCity One in the vein of *Blade Runner* while Stallone, who had no knowledge of Dredd before he was offered the part, wanted it to be more fun and comic and that it should play on his tough guy image in the way that *Demolition Man* had succeeded. Stallone demanded many rewrites as shooting progressed and he and Cannon clashed constantly. Gianni Versace had designed the Judge's uniforms for the movie production which included the infamous helmet. In the comics from the first issue, Judge Dredd never, ever removed his helmet. It was one of the reasons that the original creator approved of Stallone's casting as he had the mouth, jawline and deep voice that he had envisioned. But with a studio paying the highest salary for an actor up to that point, they were not going to allow their star to be half-seen for the whole movie. Cannon agreed to allow a scene where the helmet was removed but he wanted it to go back on soon after. He lost that battle. And when filming wrapped in November he was reportedly locked-out of the studio for the extensive re-shoots that were ordered soon after. Alan Silvestri was tasked with writing the music (after Jerry Goldsmith dropped out) and after submitting his work he was recalled for three more days of recording after new scenes were suddenly filmed and added to the movie. *Judge Dredd* was released in the U.S. on June 30th 1995 on the same day as *Apollo 13* and two weeks after *Batman*

Forever, which went on to be the highest grossing film of the year. The third Batman film made more than $330 million dollars, as did *Apollo 13* and most painfully for Danny Cannon, so did *Die Hard with a Vengeance* that summer. *Judge Dredd* finished its worldwide run on $113 million dollars and was considered a flop. The reasons for that are far more than just having Dredd take his helmet off, although that fact stirred up a lot of vocal negativity from the comic book fanbase. The first fifteen minutes of the film show Dredd in MegaCity One and declaring "I am the law!" which is fun, intriguing and visually impressive. But it soon falls into the cliched plot of Dredd being blamed for a crime he didn't commit and it then becomes a buddy movie with Stallone and Schneider right up until the inevitable good guy/bad guy punch up. If it wanted to be the new *RoboCop*, it lost its nerve in search of a lower, family-friendly rating. But like *The Specialist*, it's not terrible, it just leaves the sensation of something much better that was abandoned along the way.

So after two critical and commercial hits in *Cliffhanger* and *Demolition Man* he'd followed that with two underperformers. But he wasn't done in 1995, he had another film ready for release in October but *Assassins* was almost snuck into cinemas, such was the lack of confidence of the studio. It was a strange pre-release for a film with so much pedigree behind it; the writers of *The Matrix*, the director of *Lethal Weapon* and one of the hottest young actors opposite one of the most famous in history. The premise of *Assassins* was initially simple with an older, retiring assassin being targeted by the new kid on the block with something to prove. *The Matrix* was still five years away from changing sci-fi cinema forever but the script was written and sold to producer Joel Silver around the same time as *Assassins*. The team of Lana and Lilly Wachowski (formerly known as Larry and Andy before they both transitioned in the 2000's) were Chicago based writers who had been earning some money writing for horror comic book series like Clive Barker's *Hellraiser* and *Nightbreed*. Their breakthrough was a favourable meeting with Hollywood super-producer Joel Silver whose list of credits was the envy of Tinseltown; *Lethal Weapon, Die Hard, Roadhouse, 48 Hrs, Predator, The Last Boy Scout* and a year before, *Demolition Man*. Silver gave the Wachowski's one million dollars for their script and an order for two more scripts to be written (one was *The Matrix*). Stallone was the first choice for Silver to play the role of Robert Rath, the hitman who wants to retire from the industry although Sean Connery and Michael Douglas had also been considered. It had also been a temptation for Mel Gibson as both star and director after he had collaborated so well with Silver over the course of the three *Lethal Weapon* films up to that point. But Gibson was starting to ramp up prep on *Braveheart* and had to pull out of the project entirely to focus on what would become his crowning glory. But Gibson didn't leave *Assassins* for dead, he had already engaged his *Lethal Weapon* director Richard Donner and he was now committed to helm the new movie. Despite a hefty $15 million dollar paycheck, Silver and Donner were happy to have Stallone accept the part and for the actor, it came with the chance to play a more rounded, sympathetic character in a real world setting.

The search for the hothead young assassin who wants to kill Rath to prove his proficiency, began with a long list of names. Kevin Bacon, Johnny Depp, Woody Harrelson and Christian Slater all auditioned and were seriously considered before the filmmakers settled on Antonio Banderas. The Spanish actor had been enjoying successful collaborations with director Pedro Almodovar on more than half a dozen Spanish language movies. He made his American film debut in *Mambo Kings* in 1992 (with Stallone's *Paradise Alley* and *Judge Dredd* co-star Armand Assante) followed by supporting roles in *Philadelphia* with Tom Hanks and *Interview with a Vampire* with Tom Cruise and Brad Pitt. His intensity and unpredictability made him perfect for the role of the newly-named Miguel Bain. Julianne Moore (real name Julie Ann Smith) was just starting to find significant roles on the big screen after supporting appearances in the likes of *The Fugitive, Benny and Joon* and *Body of Evidence* alongside independent productions including *Short Cuts*. She had just finished work on her first co-starring job, opposite Hugh Grant in the family comedy *Nine Months* when she was approached to play Anna, who was a cyberhacker known as Electra, that Rath ends up protecting and falling for. With the main cast set, filming was to take place in a number of locations in the U.S. in Seattle, Washington and Oregon and also in Puerto Rico from April of 1995. But before a scene was shot, Richard Donner and Joel Silver drafted in writer Brian Helgeland to do a complete rewrite. Helgeland would go on to win an Oscar for *L.A. Confidential* and to write hits such as *A Knight's Tale, Mystic River, Man on Fire* and *Green Zone* but in 1995 he was relatively untested. The plan was to tone down the harsher edges of the violence and boost the love story. The new script was so different from the original that it enraged the Wachowski's to the point that they demanded their names be removed from the film. After considerable correspondence, the Writers Guild of America refused their request and the final writing credits were shared on screen between the Wachowski's and Helgeland.

Filming wrapped on July 24th and as editing got underway, Richard Donner approached composer Michael Kamen for the score.

Kamen had created the unique soundtracks for *Die Hard* and *Lethal Weapon* and was a trusted friend and collaborator of Donner's but when the director received Kamen's compositions he felt they were slow and dreary and not as lively as he wanted. Donner asked Kamen to have another go but Kamen was now hard at work on *Die Hard with a Vengeance* so Donner went to Mark Mancina to step in. A student of Hans Zimmer, Mancina had recently forged his own name with scores to the action hits *Speed* and *Bad Boys*. Mancina worked as fast as possible under the time constraints but in the end, Donner still used a couple of Kamen's original cues alongside Mancina's work.

Assassins was released on October the 6th 1995 and debuted at number two in the charts behind *Seven*. On its $50 million dollar budget, it returned just over $80 million which didn't cover the costs of the minimal advertising by Silver Pictures and Warner Bros. It's a curiosity that the studio hardly promoted the film despite the end product being a good, engaging thriller. Stallone is excellent as the world weary killer and for the first time, is happy to play the mentor figure. Up until his character meets Julianne Moore's Electra, Stallone plays it very subdued and subtle and many of his action hero traits have been wisely dampened down. He and his director clearly recognised that Banderas was giving it full power so the choice was made for Stallone to counter balance that energy with a calm and it works. When you include Moore's kookiness-with-a-hard-edge performance, it all combines into an interesting slant on what could have been a tired format and it was in the hands of one of the most skilled directors in the business. Like so many action thrillers, the ending doesn't quite give the pay-off punch that it should but overall *Assassins* is a pretty compelling, fun watch. Indeed, Richard Donner maintained right up until his death in

2021 that he liked the film and couldn't understand why it wasn't a bigger hit. The retiring hitman format did come back from the grave again with Keanu Reeve's instantly iconic *John Wick* but that wasn't until 2014.

Perhaps the hangover from *Judge Dredd* and *The Specialist* put audiences off seeing Stallone again quite so soon and most of the movie media coverage was about *Seven, Casino, Get Shorty* and *Leaving Las Vegas* around the time of release. But the facts and the accountants' spreadsheets didn't lie, it wasn't a hit and it meant a trilogy of releases that hadn't struck a chord with audiences in the way they had been intended. Tentative talks about sequels to 1993's *Cliffhanger* and *Demolition Man* had quickly reached a creative and financial dead end. Now seemingly without any ongoing franchise's to fall back on, Stallone was suddenly in danger of running out of chances, twenty years after *Rocky* had made him a star.

1996 - 1997 - DAYLIGHT, COP LAND

Stallone's cinematic output in the nineties was symptomatic of the changing times within the industry and society at large. *Die Hard* and *Lethal Weapon* had ushered in the next wave of acceptable action on the silver screen. The tolerance for the *Rambo*-infused central character in a popcorn blockbuster was waning and the more sensitive souls of John McClane and Martin Riggs, as portrayed by Bruce Willis and Mel Gibson, became the next big trend. Audiences now wanted fallible heroes who perhaps didn't know exactly what they were doing at all times and were driven more by love than anything else: *Die Hard*'s John McClane is just trying to save his estranged wife and Martin Riggs unstable state of mind in *Lethal Weapon* is due to the recent death of his sweetheart. *Speed*'s central duo are falling in love as they roar around Los Angeles in their unstoppable bus and after a long hiatus from the screen James Bond had returned in 1995 with a new face (Pierce Brosnan) and a new intention to not be quite so misogynist and insensitive. For Stallone's rival Arnold Schwarzenegger, he'd had his two biggest hits in the 90's already with *Terminator 2: Judgement Day* and *True Lies*, both of which required his lead character to learn to love a child or to learn how to love his wife again. Harrison Ford's motivation in *The Fugitive* is due to the grief over his murdered spouse and the *Bad Boys* action scenes play second fiddle to the domestic strife of Martin Lawrence's Marcus Burnett and his male-love of partner Mike Lowry (Will Smith). It's no surprise then that Stallone found himself in new territory and sometimes found it hard to understand where he fitted in. The result in 1996 and 1997 is that he did *Daylight* and *Cop Land* and if nothing else, these two projects showed he had range. One had a b-movie plot that would have starred Paul Newman or Steve McQueen had it been made in the 1970's and the other was what the critics had been taunting him to do ever since *Rocky*.

Daylight is an old-school disaster movie in the vein of the classics like *Towering Inferno, Airport* and *The Poseidon Adventure*. A group of mismatched innocents get trapped in an increasingly life-threatening location while a reluctant hero tries to get them to safety. Some of the innocents die and some find redemption along the way. In the case of *Daylight*, the tunnel under the Hudson River explodes and collapses at both ends so it's up to former New York City Emergency Medical Services Chief Kit Latura to find a way in, find the group of trapped souls and find a way to get them out. Directed by Rob Cohen, at first glance it seems to be a very standard action picture, but there are a few noticeable changes in the Stallone-as-hero performance. At more than one point during the film his character essentially says "I don't know what to do." and it's his love-interest played by Amy Brenneman (fresh off her role as DeNiro's amor in the exceptional *Heat*) who has to cajole him into carrying on with the rescue attempt. It's a subtle change which had already been injected into his character's self-doubt in *Cliffhanger* but it was now clearly influenced by the developing attitudes to portrayals of heroism on screen. The supporting cast includes an early role for future *Lord of the Rings* legend Viggo Mortensen and recognisable character actor Stan Shaw plays the doomed transit officer trapped with the others in the tunnel. (Shaw has history with Stallone as he played Dipper in the original *Rocky*, who is the boxer that is given Rocky Balboa's locker to use in Mickey's gym). *Daylight* is also another chance to watch Stallone and his eldest son Sage on screen together. After transferring their father and son chemistry to the screen in *Rocky V*, in *Daylight* they only share a few scenes together as Sage is one of the band of survivors that have to be saved. But this second family reunion onscreen proved to be their last. Tragically, sixteen later Sage Stallone passed away at the age of just 36. Born in May of the year that *Rocky* hit cinemas, the first child of Stallone and his first wife Sasha, was found dead at his home in Los Angeles in 2012 after not being heard from by anyone for four days. Despite splashy newspaper headlines suggesting he had taken an overdose, the coroner's report said he passed away due to coronary artery disease caused by atherosclerosis and no suspicious toxins were detected in his body apart from readily available pain remedies. Following *Rocky V* and then *Daylight*, Sage Stallone found work in low budget and sometimes experimental projects and made his directorial debut with the 2006 short film *Vic* about a down on his luck Hollywood star recounting their former glories (perhaps a dig at Dad?). His work to get *Vic* made was also one of the reasons he did not reprise his role as Rocky Junior in *Rocky Balboa* that same year.

As with many classic disaster movies, most of the drama takes place in a central location. The collapsing tunnel was almost entirely reconstructed as a whole in Rome at the Cinecitta Studios where cast and crew relocated for three months of filming. The director had originally wanted Nicolas Cage to play the lead role and had also looked at Kurt Russell, perhaps believing that Stallone's presence and resume would distract from the plot and it would become just another vehicle for the *Rambo* legend. But as he always does, Stallone threw himself mentally and physically into the project despite turning 50 on set. In media interviews around filming and the release of *Daylight* he was suggesting that this would be his final, big action movie as he was finding it harder than ever before. The impressive set-pieces in the film cleverly mixed full-size stunts on location in Italy with detailed miniature work back in Monterey, California and in the end, it's a welcome addition to the disaster movie genre. Its desire to follow the well-trodden tropes of disaster movies of old sometimes hold it back but there are terrific action-sequences and it does what it sets out to do.

Despite being paid in the region of $17 million dollars to appear, he had put up nearly $3 million dollars of his own money to get the film completed to the standard required. On a total budget of $80 million it just about doubled that investment with a worldwide total of $159 million dollars. But like *The Specialist, Judge Dredd* and *Assassins* before it, *Daylight* still wasn't judged as a hefty success. The reviews were mostly passive and dismissive but the critics were about to be woken from their Stallone-slumber by something very different and very unexpected from the action-star. In August of 1997, *Cop Land* hit theatres.

Cop Land is admired and appreciated for a number of reasons but one of the chief topics of conversation when the film is mentioned is the cast. If you're a fan of cinema and love a gritty crime thriller as much as a crowd-pleaser, the cast-list reads like a wish-list. *Cop Land* features: Sylvester Stallone, Harvey Keitel, Ray Liotta and Robert De Niro in the main roles with added support from Peter Berg, Janeane Garofalo, Robert Patrick, Michael Rapaport, Annabella Sciorra, Noah Emmerich, and Cathy Moriarty. Depending on your movie-nerd credentials you may not be familiar with every name but, it's a collection of talent that Martin Scorsese and Quentin Tarantino would assume is unachievable. Director and writer James Mangold based the film on his childhood memories of growing up in Washingtonville, New York in a development about 60 miles from New York City. He remembered that most of the residents around him and his family were either retired or serving police officers. The stress, unhealthy lifestyle and shorter life expectancy of their profession created a tribal mentality among the officers and corruption was rife. Mangold wanted to represent that unique atmosphere but upgrade the corruption he saw and combine it with a modern-western aesthetic. The result was his script *Cop Land* which saw small-town Sheriff Freddie Heflin (Stallone) caught between maintaining the face-value status-quo in the fictional town of Garrison, New Jersey by turning a blind-eye to the blatant illegality of the off-duty cops around him and the pressure from Internal Affairs investigator Lieutenant Moe Tilden (DeNiro) who senses there is corruption going on but needs Hefflin's help to prove it. Mangold said years later that he had wanted an unknown in that role originally to emphasise the characters' non-importance to the others around him, but Stallone's agent and he himself pushed to be given the chance. Mangold said no a number of times, insisting that the character was nuanced, soulful and soft and he couldn't possibly consider hiring Judge Dredd. But Stallone wore down the director by promising he wouldn't take over the picture and he would do everything that was asked of him without question and that included piling on the weight that Mangold told him was one of the non-negotiables. Stallone gained 40 pounds and wore odd, outsized shoes to give him an awkward flat-footed gait. He let his hair grow unkempt and submitted to Mangold's will to remove every trace of the movie star from his performance. Tricks and mannerisms that Stallone used in his action roles were to be stripped away and every effort was made to de-Stallone the actor.

Filming took place mostly on location in Edgewater and Fort Lee in New Jersey with the public water and electric works building doubling up as the Sheriff Hefflin's police station. Mangold deftly handles the plot that see's Michael Rappaport's young, brash cop involved in an off-duty racist shooting incident which is then covered up by Harvey Keitel's Lieutenant Ray Donovan and his allies who all remain loyal and grateful to Donovan for creating this cop-haven across the bridge from their intense day-jobs. Keitel is superb as the instigator and designer of this land of cops with intense support from Robert Patrick (the liquid metal T-1000 from *Terminator 2: Judgement Day*) John Spencer (*The Rock* and TV's *West Wing*) and Peter Berg (now also as well known as a director of *Friday Night Lights, The Kingdom* and *Deepwater Horizon*). De Niro pops in and out of the film trying to antagonise the bad cops and encourage Hefflin to take a stand until the climax of the movie sees the beleaguered Sheriff go against path of least resistance alongside Ray Liotta in his second-best career performance on film (*Goodfellas* will always be his best). Stallone's portrayal is quite astonishing. He embodies the figure of a sorrowful, resigned lawman brilliantly. And even when he does shoot a few people in the finale, it never feels like an action-star doing his thing. His scenes with Annabella Sciorra are heartbreaking as his character loves and cherishes the woman who he saved from drowning as a child but now has to watch her struggle with an abusive husband instead.

Howard Shore provides the mournful, haunting score with the London Philharmonic Orchestra and the soundtrack is filled out with a couple of Bruce Springsteen tracks, *Drive All Night* and *Stolen Car*. Mangold complained later that production company Miramax enforced an edit to the ending that was a lot more hopeful and convenient than he wanted but overall the film is as impressive and impactful as it was when it premiered at the Ziegfeld Theater in New York City on the 6th of August 1997. It's considered Stallone's best performance since the original *Rocky* and it's hard to disagree. It also left everyone who saw it with an overwhelming sensation of a parallel career that never was. Had he not found himself being paid extraordinary sums of money to maintain his physique and inject his filmmaking knowledge into tentpole action blockbusters, who knows what his CV would look like today. As Mangold insinuated in his initial hesitancy to hire Stallone, how many other studios, directors and visionaries considered him for a part in their groundbreaking work but assumed his imposing surname would overshadow their original vision and that Stallone would assert his movie-star power over the whole project? For example, here's a quick list of films that were made without him but which had Stallone attached to at some point : *The Godfather Part III, 48 Hrs, Beverly Hills Cop, Die Hard, Face/Off, Pulp Fiction, Seven* and yes, *Star Wars* and *Superman* both took long looks at having Stallone in their cast list. Of course, every well known actor has a list of near-misses like this and 99 percent of them didn't end up with a career as long and impressive as Stallone's, but *Cop Land* continues to leave that nagging feeling that the actor Sylvester Gardenzio Stallone had to take a back seat to Sylvester Stallone the icon.

Despite that exceptional cast list, everyone involved believed in the script and the film so much that the budget was kept down to an extraordinary $15 million dollars which wasn't even the salary for one Stallone in *Daylight*, that same year. It was released to wide acclaim and it earned Stallone the Best Actor award at the Stockholm International Film Festival but went on to gross a surprisingly low worldwide total of $63 million dollars. It was a chunky profit but not the kind of numbers to prompt a permanent change of direction for Stallone and it was eye-raisingly ignored by BAFTA and Oscar in their next awards shows which were dominated by James Cameron's *Titanic*. So, despite the critical high-point and a newfound standing and respect from his peers, *Cop Land* didn't herald the new age of Stallone as a serious character actor. Because next up, he was an animated ant.

1998 - 2001 - ANTZ, GET CARTER, DRIVEN

Animated films in the 21st century are huge opportunities for studios to make huge sums of money. In 2024 alone there were more than one hundred animated feature films released in global cinemas, catering to all manner of different audiences and demographics and two of those releases, *Inside Out 2* and *Moana 2*, both recorded more than a billion dollars at the box office and both those hits came from the traditional king of animated movies: Walt Disney Pictures. One of the many revenue streams for Disney now is remaking their animated films as (apparently) live-action features. This has led us to new variations of *The Lion King, Cinderella, Aladdin* and *The Jungle Book* all hitting box office gold again. The company has been the dominant force in putting animated stories into cinemas since they started the genre with their *Snow White and the Seven Dwarfs* in 1937 and then in the nineties they changed the rules of their own game with the release of *Toy Story* in 1995. The new offshoot of Disney called Pixar was tasked with pushing the boundaries of digital animation instead of the traditional hand drawn visuals. *Toy Story* looked like no animation had before but that wasn't the only ingredient that made it a phenomenon; they also employed a huge movie star to voice the main character in the form of Tom Hanks. This was another innovation in the medium and it meant that animated features could now have big names attached to it to add to the marketing potential. As with any original and successful idea in the movie industry it didn't take long for other companies to want a slice of this new profitable pie. Dreamworks was a relatively new studio on the block but it came with the heavyweight leadership of Steven Spielberg and music executive David Geffen and Jeffrey Katzenburg who had been a loyal Disney board member until deciding to branch out. Just four years after their live-action studio had been set-up they also developed Dreamworks Animation and their first project was to be *Antz*. A decade before, when Katzenburg was still at Disney, they had been working on a story idea called *Army Ants*. Now with his new friends at Dreamworks, the idea had resurfaced and they greenlit it as their debut in the cinematic animation genre. At the same time, Disney's Pixar was announcing they were prepping a similar sounding project called *A Bug's Life*. The media quickly latched on to the irresistible storyline of the disgruntled former employee taking on the might of Disney at their own game. What followed was a very public race to get their cartoon insect films into cinemas and make the most money. Dreamworks even moved their original release date of the spring of 1999 back to October of 1998 so it would directly compete with Disney's effort. Dreamworks were hoping *Antz* would appeal to a slightly more sophisticated audience as it was anticipated that *A Bug's Life* would skew more towards Disney's safe, kid-friendly crowd. The other difference that they hoped would propel *Antz* to more success was that they were designing the animated characters, the dialogue and even the plot around their star voice-cast rather than the traditional method of writing a script and then finding the voices. The basic plot would see an anxious worker ant called Z (Woody Allen) fall for Princess Bala (Sharon Stone) while also stopping a military coup by General Mandible (Gene Hackman). As if those three headliners weren't enough to tempt cinema-goers, they also had the talent of Jennifer Lopez, Dan

Aykroyd, Christopher Walken, Danny Glover and, as Corporal Weaver and Z's best friend, Sylvester Stallone. It was the first time Stallone had done pure voice work and his scenes with Woody Allen are good fun with his unmistakable sound being made the most of. Little did any of the cast realise at the time but it was just the start of a very profitable line of work for actors with a few days free on their hands. In the end, the all-powerful Disney proved its strength again with *A Bugs Life* finishing with over $360 million dollars globally and ending 5th in the 1998 worldwide charts while *Antz* finished 25th with less than half that amount.

But while *Antz* was part of something new, Stallone had turned his attention to his next live-action project which was trying to revive something old. He had decided to mark the 20th Century becoming the 21st Century by making *Get Carter*. A 1970 British crime novel written by Ted Lewis called *Jack's Return Home,* had been turned into an uncompromising thriller the following year starring Michael Caine. The *Get Carter* of 1971 centered around a London gangster who returns to his home town in the north of England to investigate his brother's suspicious death. While the film did decent business when it was released it grew in reputation over the years as Caine's performance brilliantly raises questions of morality as he brutally gets to the truth. In 1999 it was ranked 16th on the list of the best 100 British films from the British Film Institute with Total Film ranking it as the best British film of all time. A blaxploitation remake in 1972 starring Bernie Casey called *Hit Man* was the only attempt to directly reproduce the premise but Warner Bros and Franchise Pictures announced an official remake in 1997. David McKenna was tasked with creating a screenplay which would transfer the very uncompromising, unglamorous British original to the United States. McKenna had tackled tough circumstances in his writing before as a 26 year old when he sold the white supremacist drama *American History X* to New Line Cinema in 1998. Commercial and music video director Tarsem Singh was originally set to helm the production before being swiftly replaced with Samuel Bayer who had a similar CV that included Nirvana's *Smells Like Teen Spirit* music video and Robbie Williams' *Angels*. But with Stallone all but confirmed in the lead role, the New Zealand born Stephen Kay was given the task. An October the 18th start date was put in everyone's diaries as the script took shape. Early vigorous discussions between Kay and Franchise Pictures centred around the approach where the director was keen to make the picture less about revenge and more about resolution, the financiers were stressing a more traditional "Stallone-style" picture. The titular Jack Carter had now been transposed from the UK and he was an American gangster living and earning in Las Vegas who takes the train back to his home of Seattle when news of his brother's death reaches him. The twisty, violent tale would have a quality supporting cast including renowned British actress Miranda Richardson, Rachel Leigh Cook and John C McGinley. There were also two other very notable additions to the supporting roles. Ever since they had worked on the war-time prison and football adventure *Escape to Victory* in 1981, Stallone and Michael Caine had remained friends and in contact. Caine was to film one short cameo in the remake but his part was increased as shooting began and he was eventually required for two days' work. Stallone also got another friend involved and it was one who really appreciated the job. Mickey Rourke had been one of the most in-demand dramatic actors of the eighties with his acclaimed work in *9 1/2 weeks* and *Angel Heart* but after a string of disappointing projects he'd left acting to focus on boxing. As he tried to return to the profession in the mid-nineties his bad boy image was preventing him from getting cast. Stallone vouched for his friend to be a part of *Get Carter* and offered a part of his salary as collateral if Rourke proved problematic and if it cost the production some time and money. The result was that Rourke was the epitome of professional and Franchise Pictures offered him a role in their next thriller called *The Pledge* with Jack Nicholson.

Filming wrapped on the 14th of January 2000 after location work in Las Vegas, Washington and British Columbia in Canada which gave Stallone more than five months to prepare for filming his next project, *Driven*. Director Kay and Franchise Pictures continued to wrangle over the severity of the violence and the morality of Jack Carter with both Kay and Stallone wanting the harsher edges to remain. Meanwhile, Tyler Bates was given the opportunity to provide the score for his first big studio movie after already working with Kay on a low budget drama in 1997 called *The Last Time I Committed Suicide* which starred Thomas Jane and Keanu Reeves. Bates wisely chose not to reinvent the wheel and faithfully updated the iconic theme music from the original movie that had been composed by Roy Budd. The main title theme is actually called *Carter Takes A Train* which is why Stallone's Jack Carter also travels by train back to his childhood home. The rest of the soundtrack was filled with contemporary dance and electronic tracks from the likes of Moby, Mint Royale, Groove Armada and Paul Oakenfold. The film was released in October of 2000 and the reviews reflected the concerns of the director and star in the editing room. It was considered ok with some nice touches and good performances but in the end it was a bit too routine for its own good. Predictably, the UK press were vicious in their condemnation over remaking what they saw as a peerless classic. Financially it was a flop making just $20 million dollars back from its $60 million dollar budget.

While he'd been an actor for hire for the last number of years, he had always been scribbling ideas for new projects and one that he had fleshed out into a full script was based around his recently reignited love of motorsport. This obsession with engines had been sparked by his long stay in Europe when making *Judge Dredd* in 1995 and the preoccupation with all-things motorised that was around him day and night.. Car racing and Formula One in particular had grabbed his attention and he had set about writing a story that could capture that intense, high-speed world on and off the track. He worked fast and had a full draft completed by the start of 1996 but finding the financial backing for the film proved elusive. Movies about car racing were rarely a guarantee of success. James Garner's *Grand Prix* in 1967 and Steve McQueen's *Le Mans* in 1971 had both tried to transfer their petrol-headed devotion onto the silver screen but hadn't quite managed it. And both those movies had been the dreaded "passion project" for their lead actors, which often leads to a lack of clarity and poor judgement over the finished movie's accessibility for an audience. 1990's *Days of Thunder* centered around the circular tracks of NASCAR and was a financial success but that was attributed more to Tom Cruise's presence than the sport itself. But Stallone reasoned that *Rocky* had worked because the boxing was secondary to the love story so he had crafted his new tale around the personal relationships of the drivers rather than the results on the track.

As the latter half of the nineties wore on and he released *Assassins* and *Daylight* to lukewarm reception and *Cop Land* to ecstatic critics but underwhelming box office, the script he had named *Driven* was always ticking over. A chance conversation with his *Cliffhanger* director Renny Harlin uncovered a mutual love for fast cars as Harlin confessed he had been trying to get a film greenlit about the life of Brazilian Formula One star Ayton Senna, ever since Senna had been tragically killed during the 1994 San Marino Grand Prix. Stallone had also contemplated a Senna biopic before switching to a fictional film set in the world of F1. The pair decided that they could both scratch their car-film itch if they combined resources and the reteaming of the creative force behind *Cliffhanger* was enough to convince Franchise Pictures and Warner Bros. to finance *Driven*. Soon Stallone was being seen in the paddock of Formula One races all over the world and happily talking to the media about his forthcoming film. He'd been courting the drivers of the day such as Damon Hill and Jean Alesi to make guest appearances in *Driven* when it started shooting and British business tycoon Bernie Ecclestone, who was the founding father of modern F1, was also a part of the pre-production meetings.

The story outline that Stallone and Harlin had settled on was of a young racing driver who has the talent to win but needs the experience and wisdom of an older, ex-driver to push him towards greatness (2025 hit *F1: The Movie* with Brad Pitt follows the plot and beats of *Driven* almost exactly). But even with the best will and make-up in the world at 54 years of age, Stallone was always going to be the former driver who is drafted back into the world of Formula One and not the new hotshot character. 25-year old Leonardo DiCaprio was their first choice for the role of Jimmy Bly as the actor was in high demand since *Titanic* in 1997. He was initially interested but soon had to drop out when *Driven* kept getting delayed. As 1999 became 2000 the film hit a huge hole in the road when the casual chats between the filmmakers and Formula One turned into nailing down specifics for shooting. Ecclestone and his team became increasingly uncomfortable with the access that Stallone and Harlin wanted to make the movie as authentic as possible and it soon became clear that there was no solution in sight and arrangements were scrapped. With Formula One no longer a part of the project and insisting that any mention or similarity towards their brand be withdrawn from the script, the star and director turned to CART. The Championship Auto Racing Teams had been established in 1979 by a breakaway group of team owners from the United States Auto Club Championship Car division. They moved all around the world with their open-wheeled races that had a similar feel to Formula One but the bosses of CART were more than happy to allow *Driven* to piggyback on their season. (CART was starting to show signs of decline in 2000 however and after the 2003 season, it closed down operations for good). Camera crews were dispatched to many races throughout the first half of 2000 with the main bulk of filming with the actors set for between July and October in Toronto.

So now casting had to be completed and without DiCaprio, a raft of similar young actors were considered for the role of Jimmy Bly. Former model and high school football player turned actor Kip Pardue was eventually chosen after impressing the year before with his role in the ensemble sports drama *Remember the Titans* starring Denzel Washington. German actor Til Schweiger was cast as Beau Brandenburg who is the arrogant reigning champion in the film but is so clearly meant to mirror Ferrari F1 driver Michael Schumacher. The team owner Carl Henry was to be played by Rex Linn who had worked with Harlin on the mega-flop pirate movie *Cutthroat Island* in 1995 and also with both Harlin and Stallone in *Cliffhanger* as the FBI agent who is really one of the thieves, Richard Travers. But then the opportunity came up for Stallone to give that role to Burt Reynolds. One of the biggest movie stars in the world in the seventies and through to the early eighties, his career had suffered more than most when Stallone helped usher in the new breed of male lead actor. His Oscar nomination for Best Supporting Actor for his role in *Boogie Nights* in 1997 had been a high point in an otherwise grim decade for the *Smokey and the Bandit* star and he was delighted to be part of a major movie production again.

After spending $72 million dollars, the film was released in April of 2001 and was the first Stallone film since *Cop Land* to reach number one but that was where the good news ended. After the disaster of *Cutthroat Island,* the $54 million worldwide gross for *Driven* sent Harlin to movie jail and he was never given a major film again. Stallone of course did not suffer a similar fate but it was a disappointment after he'd put so much time and love into the project. *Driven* shared some of the traits that *Assassins, Daylight, Get Carter* and *The Specialist* suffered from, namely the interference of too many people trying to put their stamp on it in an attempt to make the film as commercially viable as possible. Kip Pardue has to carry the weight of the movie but he is miscast and his screen-acting inexperience means he looks twitchy and awkward. Without the requisite leading-man charisma, the emotional core we are supposed to latch onto isn't there. DiCaprio would have been a fascinating bit of casting and would have certainly elevated the role. But on the whole, the end product is predictable, cliched and ironically for a motor-racing film, it feels rushed. By trying to incorporate almost an entire season of racing into a final running time of 177 minutes, many plot lines are glossed over and character development is sudden and unconvincing. The editing is sometimes so fast that a scene that is just starting is suddenly over and dialogue is replaced with yet another montage and some pop music to try and cover over the cracks. It's not a disaster but it veers towards excruciating melodrama so often that if

Driven had been one of the cars in a Formula One Grand Prix, it probably wouldn't have found the exit of the pit lane.

The failure of *Driven* (and *Get Carter* and Antz) meant that the new millennium started in very underwhelming fashion for Stallone. To see those years of hard work trying to get the film finished and released result in *Driven* finishing 73rd on the 2001 Worldwide Box Office charts was disheartening to say the least. The two biggest films of the year were kickstarting two huge new franchises, *Harry Potter* and *Lord of the Rings,* but still Stallone was reluctant to resurrect his own pair of money-generators. *Rocky V* was now more than a decade old and *Rambo III* was further back in time than that. But he would have to bring them both back eventually as the next four films in his career would see him sink further away from feeling like a major Hollywood figure.

2002 - 2003 - D-TOX (EYE SEE YOU), AVENGING ANGELO, SHADE, SPY KIDS 3D: GAME OVER

Four films over the course of a couple of years would, to some, seem like a prolific output from a much in demand actor. And when you factor in that the four movies were very different from each other; a pseudo-horror, a mob-comedy, a noir-esque crime thriller and a family adventure, you could be forgiven for thinking Stallone was performing at the peak of his powers. But while none of these four films are awful, they do represent a sharp decline in quality and ambition with *D-Tox* being the worst offender. Perhaps the best indicator that this film is never going to get re-evaluated as a hidden masterpiece is that despite it coming under the 2002 - 2003 heading in this book, it was filmed and edited before the end of 1999. If you step back to look at the Stallone filmography timeline, there is a curious gap in his output from *Antz* in 1998 to *Get Carter* in 2000. One of the main reasons for this is that in the gap in between, he was in Canada from January until May, making *D-Tox*.

Clinton Howard Swindle was a significant figure in U.S. journalism as his work for the Dallas Morning Herald had seen him investigate and report on scandals involving housing development, banking illegalities and police brutality. He wrote several non-fiction books but he also had a fiction effort published called *Jitter Joint* which told the story of an alcoholic police detective who is sent to a remote rehab facility where his fellow patients start being murdered one by one. But a few years before that, Imagine Entertainment had announced a new film to star Stallone that would center around witness protection. Universal greenlit the film in July of 1998 with Jim Gillespie slated to direct under the new title of *D-Tox*. The Scottish director had made his Hollywood breakthrough with the teen horror of *I Know What You Did Last Summer* in 1997 and with *D-Tox* looking to be a dark slasher film with hints of 1995's *Seven* about it, he seemed an ideal choice. Gillespie looked at Mel Gibson, Bruce Willis, Nicolas Cage and John Travolta for the main role of Agent Jake Malloy who experiences a tragedy in his life which sees him hit the bottle and get sent to the facility to recover. The A-listers he approached took his meetings but were unwilling to commit due to scheduling conflicts or a reluctance to be in an R-rated killer-thriller. To Gillespie's horror, he was informed that Sylvester Stallone was interested in the project and it would quickly go into production with Stallone onboard. Gillespie had heard tales of woe from the set of *Judge Dredd* and was very resistant to having Stallone as his leading actor. (Years later, Gillespie would say how he had misjudged Stallone and had found him very easy to work with) The large ensemble cast was fleshed out with considerable talent; Tom Berenger who had been Oscar nominated for his unforgettable supporting role in *Platoon*, Robert Patrick who had seared his stare into the brains of teenagers everywhere in *Terminator 2: Judgement Day* (and had starred with Stallone in *Cop Land)*, plus singing star turned actor Kris Kristofferson and other reliable and familiar faces such as Stephen Lang, Charles S Dutton and an up and coming Jeffrey Wright. Howard Swindle had written the screenplay himself but it had been through a few additional drafts from uncredited writers such as Ron Brinkenhoff.

When filming wrapped and the movie was edited it was tested in front of audiences and it bombed spectacularly. Universal immediately ordered re-shoots and a new ending but when that also caused derision at test screenings, the studio left it in limbo. Ron Howard and his Imagine Entertainment company had originally brought the project to the table and at one point Howard was even slated to be the director, but after this series of awful test showings and with release dates being pushed further and further back, Imagine had their name and logo completely removed from the film a year later. It meant it was left on Universal's shelf and they had no idea what to do with it. Despite spending $55 million dollars on its production, the executives at Universal believed it wasn't worth the extra cost of publicity and printing thousands of copies to send out to theatres. By the turn of the century it was gathering dust in the Universal library until they managed to sell it to a relatively new independent production and distribution company called DEJ Productions who managed to get it released domestically in September of 2002 (under the different, awful title of *Eye See You*), following a limited international release in February, almost three years since it had been made. Composer John Powell had written a complete score for the film in 1999 and when that was rejected he had composed an entirely new score but that was also mostly left unused and replaced with various tracks from the likes of William Ross, Geoff Zanelli, and Nick Glennie-Smith.

In the end, it scraped together around $6 million dollars in revenue and Universal Pictures still don't include it in their back-catalogue. Watching it now you can see what they wanted to achieve but it suffered from trying to be too many genres at once and achieving none of them. The movie would love to be *Seven* and *The Silence of the Lambs* but there is such an air of seen-it-all-before bound to a thoroughly predictable narrative that you can understand why the distributors and money-men felt short changed with the outcome. The opening fifteen minutes sets up the plot mechanically and Stallone gets to do a bit of sad-face but then everyone arrives at the snowy rehab outpost and it's a bit of a chore. Stallone's miserable figure gets sidelined as we have to get to know the rest of the inmates/patients in perfunctory fashion. It's essentially Agatha Christie's *And Then There Were None* but with intended shock-gore and a mystery element that is so easy to work out it's insulting. The killer's voice is almost identical to that of Jigsaw in the *Saw* franchise that would start two years later but even then it felt dated. (the film's trailer forgot to distort the voice so the murderer's identity is pretty much given away) In general, it isn't much fun being trapped in the snow with a bunch of characters who are all morose, angry and depressed. As hard as Stallone wanted to move away from action and gunplay, he eventually has to succumb to type but in this film he does it with a permanent, tortured expression which dilutes any impact even further. If horror is your thing, you might get something from the various, bloody deaths but if it was *Seven* they were aiming for, then they were knocked for six.

The few promotional interviews for *D-Tox* that Stallone did, he was often trying to distract from the inevitable negative reception for that film by promising that his next, *Avenging Angelo*, would be a pleasure to watch. What he probably didn't realise at the time was that this new movie was going to be released only on DVD in the United States. The action comedy saw Stallone playing a mob-boss's bodyguard but when his employer gets whacked he ends up protecting his estranged daughter. Written by Will Aldis and Canadian-American voice actor and writer Steve Mackall, *Avenging Angelo* says more about where Stallone's career was at the time, than anything else. Hollywood is a fickle beast and even though he'd been the biggest movie star in the world not long ago, by 2002 he was lost. His last set of good reviews was for *Cop Land* five years before and his last real box office hit was *Demolition Man* and that was now nearly a decade in the rear view mirror. *The Specialist* and *Judge Dredd* had both been made as tentpole films with huge financial costs and both had whimpered on release and *Get Carter* and *Driven* had given more fuel to the fire of film critics who wanted to bury the Stallone brand. The apathy of everyone involved in *D-Tox* meant that it seemed like the game was up. Now Stallone had to say yes to the meagre offers he was getting and he would have to commit to projects that he would have deemed unthinkable a few years before.

Avenging Angelo's appealing qualities included playing a character who wasn't very violent and was more sympathetic and the mob-boss would be played by one of his screen heroes, the legendary Anthony Quinn (in what turned out to be his last film). The love interest and co-star of *Avenging Angelo* would be Madeleine Stowe, who also seemed to be at a similar stage of her career. After hit films like *Stakeout, The Last of the Mohicans* and *12 Monkeys,* Stowe had reached a crossroads of her own and was trying her hand at something lighter than her previous work. One of her previous films was also the thriller *Revenge* in 1990 where she played the wife of Anthony Quinn's character and now here she was, twelve years later, playing his daughter. Canadian writer Martyn Burke had co-written the 1984 spoof *Top Secret* and had directed documentaries and short films but he was given the chance to direct *Avenging Angelo* and make Stallone a romantic comedy star. It was filmed from April to June in 2021 in Ontario and Sicily but the fact it wasn't seen in the United States until 2003 tells its own story. It was released on

DVD across different months internationally throughout 2002 and 2003 but sporadically arrived in cinemas in random European and Asian countries. It had a $17 million dollar budget and it officially returned $824,597dollars, so not even one million dollars in ticket sales. A low point to say the least but there was still *Shade* ahead.

If there was some brightness in all this career-gloom, in January 2003 he made a cameo appearance in the french action thriller *Taxi 3* playing a passenger who goes for the ride of his life in the opening sequence. Since he couldn't speak French, his dialogue was dubbed by his official French-language substitute, Alain Dorval. It wasn't much, but it was something on a cinema screen for the first time in two years.

Written and directed by Damian Nieman who had befriended the greatest sleight of hand artists in the world while he was at film school, *Shade* was billed as a neo-crime thriller with high-stakes poker at its center. The main cast was quite impressive with Stuart Townsend, Gabriel Byrne, Thandiwe Newton, Jamie Foxx and Melanie Griffith all involved. Truth be told however, none of that cast was at the top of their game when they were offered a role in *Shade* and bagging Stallone wasn't the coup that it used to be either. Stallone played The Dean who was a legendary card-shark that the team wanted to get even with. The success of *Ocean's 11* in 2001 had encouraged plenty of con-artist plots on a lower budget and *Shade* was one of them. Stallone's character is talked about far more than he is actually on screen and when he is a part of the ensemble, his star-power raises the quality considerably. Unfortunately the snappy dialogue that Nieman thought he had written needed George Clooney, Brad Pitt and Matt Damon to elevate it. The cast are also burdened with overlong dialogue sequences and distracting directing and in the end it's not half as zippy and elegant as it's trying to tell you it is. It went on limited release in the U.S. in only a dozen cinemas and went straight to DVD internationally. On its modest $10 million dollar budget it didn't even make half a million in return. One bright point for Stallone aficionados was seeing Tony Burton as part of the cast. Burton is best known as Apollo Creed's trainer Duke in the first four *Rocky* films. (Little did he know that he would play Duke one more time in a couple of years).

So to recap, he'd now completed three straight-to-DVD movies in a row and one silent cameo in a French action film. But personally, he was in a good place. By the start of January 2003, his third daughter Scarlet was having her first birthday and her sisters were turning six and four. When offered a role in the third film in the *Spy Kids* franchise, his young kids gave him the thumbs up. Stallone has turned his hand to many roles on a film set, from actor, writer and director he's also been a choreographer, a producer and even sung the theme song. But it pales into comparison next to Robert Rodriguez. Making his name writing and directing the low-budget but impressive Mexico-set action films *El Mariachi* and *Desperado* starring Antonio Banderas, he moved into Hollywood territory with the Tarantino-infused *From Dusk Till Dawn* in 1996 and then the teen-horror *The Faculty* two years later. Wanting to turn his hand to something family orientated, he made *Spy Kids* in 2001 which is exactly what it sounds like but hugely enjoyable too. Its success spawned a sequel a year later and now he was to complete the trilogy. For *Spy Kids 3D: Game Over*, Rodriguez was keeping costs down by pretty much making it by himself. His credits on the production include: writer, director, producer, production designer, editor, cinematographer, composer and visual effects supervisor. Filming was to take place almost exclusively in a studio in Austin,

Texas as he wanted to experiment with green screen technology and the final film is more than 90% made with that technology rather than building expensive sets. The basic plot sees the hero kids trapped inside a computer game controlled by The Toymaker (Stallone). The part allowed him to create half a dozen alternative characters who were all part of his evil psyche. Vanity took a backseat and Stallone willfully threw himself into his pantomime villain and more than fulfilled his remit. The film wheeled out plenty of cameos to please the parents of the kids they were taking to the cinema including George Clooney, Salma Hayek, Bill Paxton, Steve Buscemi and Antonio Banderas and for film fact fans it was also the first big screen appearance of both Glen Powell and Selena Gomez. With Rodriguez keeping costs down with his methodology, the budget was a slimline $38 million which was tiny for a potential blockbuster. It meant the overall box office of $197 million gave a bigger profit margin which pleases any studio. And the studio happened to be Troublemaker Studios, which Rodriguez owned anyway. But it also meant Stallone had been in a big hit film again, although it was disposable fun. There was also one moment near the climax of *Spy Kids 3D: Game Over* that may have sparked some thoughts in his head. When one of the heroic kids is destroying The Toymaker's wicked creations, one of his henchmen says, "That kid's like Rambo."

When you consider that the last Rambo film had been fifteen years earlier, perhaps that line written in the script by Rodriguez triggered Stallone into thinking that maybe, just maybe, that character was still in the public consciousness. He'd also been a major part of a hit film for the first time in about ten years so he had a bit of extra clout in the business again. And perhaps most important of all, unlike most of his peers, contemporaries and wannabe movie stars, he was a writer. He didn't have to just wait for someone to create a good script and for a good director to capture him on film correctly, he could make it happen on his own. As a starving, homeless young man in Philadelphia he had relied on himself rather than anyone else. After snubs and rejections and trying to fit himself into projects he wasn't right for, it took the self-confidence to write what he knew and to write what he wanted to do. Another *Rambo* adventure needed a lot of thought and a good reason to exist, but there was still that other guy.

Every *Rocky* film had somehow represented a major landmark in Stallone's life and here he was in 2003 in no-man's land. Everything he thought he understood had changed and he found himself almost back where he started but in a new, changeable and unfamiliar world. Thirteen years ago he had said goodbye to Rocky but that final round of *Rocky V* had been unfulfilling. One thing that the character of Rocky Balboa had stood for from the start was the desire to go out on his own terms, to go the distance and leave the ring with his dignity intact. So maybe one throwaway line in *Rocky V* had been more significant than he thought. When Tommy Gunn had punched Rocky to the floor in the final fight and Tommy raised his hands in assumption of victory, Rocky staggered back to his feet and told him, "One more round."

ROCKY BALBOA (2006)

IT AIN'T OVER 'TILL IT'S OVER

Starring - Sylvester Stallone, Burt Young, Milo Ventimiglia,
Antonio Tarver, Geraldine Hughes
Written by - Sylvester Stallone
Original Score by - Bill Conti
Directed by - Sylvester Stallone

A second chance, a last hurrah, a victory lap - call it what you like but the realities of the movie business mean that however significant something once was, no one is going to hand you a fitting finale for nostalgia's sake alone. The odds looked stacked against *Rocky Balboa* getting off the ground; the last Rocky film had underperformed, left little imprint on movie-goers and 16 long years had passed since its release (he'd made and released five *Rocky* films within a 14-year time-span before that). The cinematic landscape had changed too, it was now flooded with escapism in far flung galaxies and wondrous fantasy worlds. The lingering aftershocks of the September 11th attacks on New York in 2001 were still being felt and the multiplexes had now become a place of sanctuary away from the realities of the unrelenting world outside the emergency exit door. In 2005, the top four films had been the latest Harry Potter, Star Wars and Chronicles of Narnia installments and the fourth biggest movie of the year was the Cruise/Spielberg version of *War of the Worlds*, although most ticket-buyers didn't recognise its allegory to 9/11. But regardless of what was going on in the cinema industry, Stallone had the nagging sensation that he hadn't said goodbye to his almost mythical character. 1990's *Rocky V* bugged him and even by 1999, he was thinking of how he could put the boxer to bed with more dignity. Initial, tentative drafts saw Rocky's son Robert away with the US Air Force and Rocky now running the gym for underprivileged Philadelphia kids. *Rocky VI* would have seen Rocky and Adrian bonding with one troubled teen and guiding him into a professional boxing career. While the tone of the new film was always intended to be much closer to the original 1976 *Rocky*, the premise for this sixth film was already too close to the *Rocky V* plot and it was quickly trashed. Since *Rocky V,* Stallone's career had gone through a rollercoaster; there were the highs of

Cliffhanger and *Demolition Man* and the lows of *Judge Dredd* and *Assassins*. On and on went the bumpy ride with another peak of *Cop Land* and another trough with *Get Carter* and *D-Tox*. When a film was received well, discussions about *Rocky VI* were easier to arrange but otherwise there was little appetite. Stallone knew he needed to find a hook for the new movie, something that would justify its existence and wouldn't ignore the fact that he was well past his 50th birthday. As is so often the case, the answer lay in history.

In 1970, American radio producer Murray Woroner set out to determine who was the greatest boxer of all time, of any era. Gathering information from hundreds of experts over many years he fed their findings into a huge NCR 315 computer and statistically, Rocky Marciano was officially considered the winner. Marciano had retired undefeated as world heavyweight champion in 1955 and while few disputed his talent, a certain Muhammed Ali took issue with the computers' decision. Threatening to sue Woroner for defamation of character, the producer suggested he and Marciano participate in a fantasy bout and let the computer decide who would win if they were both in their prime. The pair agreed and filmed for hours together in a ring, trying to capture every possible punch and scenario that a boxing match could involve. The NCR 315 trawled through data again and the results were put into cinemas where ticket-buyers could watch what the computer had determined would happen. Both boxers were unaware of the final outcome until they too watched the movie and witnessed Marciano knocking out Ali in the 13th round. It was a last triumph for Marciano who died several months after filming the simulated scenes with Ali. Six years later, a large poster depicting Rocky Marciano poised to fight adorned the wall of the dilapidated Philadelphia apartment inhabited by one Rocky Balboa. History also guided the thoughts of the writer when in 1994, 38-year old George Foreman came out of boxing retirement to face 26-year old Michael Moorer in Las Vegas. After nine rounds of Moorer out-scoring and out-punching Foreman, in the 10th round Foreman floored the younger man and became the oldest world heavyweight champion in history. Stallone reasoned that despite *Rocky V* breaking tradition with the climactic fight in the street, *Rocky VI* would have to see him go out in the manner that he started - back in the ring.

By 2004, meetings about another Rocky film had gone up a gear. Promising to keep costs low by recreating that cold, frosty Philadelphia feel from 1976, Chartoff-Winkler Productions gave Stallone the go-ahead and greenlit the film with him as director but with a slimline budget of just $24 million dollars. Stallone had actually been prepping *Rambo IV* and was expecting to make that sequel next, but the *Rocky VI* deal was signed-off first which meant Rambo would have to wait a bit longer. In drafting a new script, Stallone fleshed out the young man against old man plot quickly ('Skill vs Will', as it was taglined in the finished film) but felt stuck over the motivation for why Rocky would get back in the ring. The character had won everything that could be won and effectively beaten an entire country in *Rocky IV*, so why would he, at 59 years of age, feel the need to lace up the gloves and potentially get seriously damaged? The answer resulted in a difficult conversation with Talia Shire. After playing Adrian for five consecutive movies, Stallone told her that she would only appear in flashbacks and photographs for the new film, as Adrian's death was the only logical and powerful factor that could push Rocky into fighting again. Despite an obvious disappointment to find out she had played Rocky's one true love for the final time back in 1990, Shire publicly gave her approval for the storyline and accepted its necessity.

Fortunately, there was a place for other returning characters notably best-friend and Adrian's brother Paulie (Burt Young) and Tony Burton as Apollo's former trainer, Duke. One of many indications that the film was to align a lot closer to the 1976 original was actor Pedro Lovell. Pedro had played amateur fighter Spider Rico, who Rocky beats in a back-street boxing match in the very first scene of *Rocky*. He returned as the same character who had since fallen on hard times and who Rocky would offer food and work to at his Italian restaurant called 'Adrian's'. The plot revolved around the loneliness and anger Rocky was consumed with since the death of Adrian because of, as his character explains, "woman cancer". When a simulated boxing match on TV depicts Rocky in his prime beating the current heavyweight champion, Mason Dixon, a real fight is put into motion in Las Vegas. Meant as an exhibition bout to improve the image of Dixon, Rocky uses it as an opportunity to get rid of "the beast" inside him and start to move on without Adrian. Along the way, he reconnects with his son Robert (Milo Ventimiglia) and finds himself helping another Philadelphia resident, Marie, with her difficult life. The casting of his son Robert would be a delicate process but there was also confusion over the role of Marie.

In 1976's *Rocky,* one memorable scene sees Rocky spotting a teenage girl that he knows hanging around with less than desirable characters on a street corner. He walks the girl, Marie, home whilst offering his unique advice on life ("if you hang around with yo-yo people, you get yo-yo friends,") but when they get to her family home she responds to his sincerity with "Screw you, creepo!" and goes into her house leaving Rocky a little dejected to say the least. 13-year old actor Jodi Letizia had played her in the Oscar-winning original and she believed she would be called upon again. But when she learned that Northern Ireland's Geraldine Hughes had been cast as the grown-up Marie, she instructed a lawyer to sue the film and a lawsuit was settled out of court.

By this time, the role of Robert Balboa had also been resolved. Stallone's own son Sage had done a creditable job playing Rocky Jnr in 1990 but the real-life father and son had found their relationship become strained again in the intervening years and depending on which story you believe, the call was either never made or never answered about reprising the role for *Rocky VI*. Sometimes casting a well known actors' screen offspring requires a suspension of disbelief but in the case of Robert Balboa, the final casting choice for *Rocky VI* fit like a boxing glove. Californian Milo Ventimiglia was the son of a Vietnam veteran and was a series regular on TV's *Gilmore Girls*. He was hoping to nail down the part of Peter Petrelli in a forthcoming new superhero series called *Heroes* when he got word that his audition for *Rocky VI* had been successful. Not only did he more than resemble a younger Sylvester Stallone, but when he was born the nerves on the left side of his face had been damaged leaving him with an identical crooked mouth. It's been said that Ventimiglia looks, sounds and behaves more like Stallone's child than his actual kids. Reigning light-heavyweight world champion Antonio Tarver went through an exhaustive audition process before being entrusted to play the frustrated antagonist, Mason Dixon and filming was set to start in December of 2005 where Stallone had set a very clear schedule of what was going to be filmed first and what would be shot last. The final shooting day would be back on top of the steps to the Philadelphia Museum of Art that he had made globally famous, but it would start with the climactic fight.

Stallone wanted to film the fight first so he could soon ditch the intense training regime he'd been on for six months and focus on his performance and directorial duties for the rest of the shoot. Also, filming the fight for this Rocky film had to be done at one, certain time. To keep within the tight budget and to add realism to the Balboa v Dixon battle, Stallone and the producers had arranged to piggyback off the real middleweight rematch between Bernard Hopkins and Jermain Taylor at the Mandalay Bay Hotel and Casino in Las Vegas. They filmed crowd reaction shots as much as they were allowed and in the style of the pay-per-view HBO format that TV viewers had become accustomed to. The crew filmed the fictional pre-fight press conference just after Hopkins and Taylor had left the stage themselves and the crowd in the arena was taken by surprise when film cameras appeared and then Rocky Balboa came out from backstage to walk to the ring with his onscreen training team of Paulie, Rocky Jnr and Duke. Without any prompting from the production, the crowd rose to their feet and were chanting "Rocky, Rocky!" for the entire walk to the ring. The fight itself was choreographed to a degree but it was also left to the actors to throw real punches and follow the general outline of the 15-round fight in the script. On the final day of filming in the arena, four optional endings were captured; Rocky wins by points decision, Rocky wins by knockout, Dixon wins by points decision and Dixon wins by knockout. This gave the producers and director the option of choosing the most satisfying finale once the rest of the film was in place. (Dixon winning by points decision was eventually chosen but the Rocky winning ending is available to see as a DVD extra and on YouTube).

After the final bout was in the can, the entire production moved to Philadelphia for the remainder of the shoot. A marble headstone was sculpted for the grave of Adrian Balboa, where Rocky spends much of his time on a foldable wooden chair, talking to her carved name. A foam option was created but it was felt to be too unrealistic so a real stone version was commissioned and it still sits in Laurel Hill Cemetery to this day (although not at the exact location as portrayed in the movie). On the last day of January in 2006, Sylvester Stallone ran up the most famous steps in movie history for what seemed like the last time. Once on top, he paused and looked back down the main avenue where he'd been filmed running in 1976 and filmed running again with hundreds of kids two years later. He staged a key scene there in *Rocky III* and closed out *Rocky V* on that same spot with his real son. Cinematographer Clark Mathis stealthily captured the moment of reflection without Stallone's knowledge and that dramatic landscape is the one that is shown as the final credits roll.

Editor Sean Albertson and Stallone locked themselves away to assemble the movie and made a few calls to ensure that showing clips from the previous films was ok with the actors in them. Dolph Lundgren and Mr T were more than happy to say yes and get a little remuneration as well but Carl Weathers proved less enthusiastic and demanded thousands of dollars for a two-second clip. The producers refused and so Apollo Creed is skillfully avoided throughout the movie. Music-wise there was no decision to make as Bill Conti was as much a part of the Rocky family as anyone. He redesigned many of his existing themes (including a rousing new recording of *Gonna Fly Now*) from the previous movies and composed one new melody for the character of Marie. As he had done before, he performed all the piano parts himself with Stallone present for many of the recording sessions in the summer of 2006 at the Capitol Studios in Hollywood. Coincidentally, Frank Sinatra had recorded his jaunty hit *High Hopes* at the same studios in May of 1959 and that track was used as Rocky's walk-out music ahead of the final fight (a comical, surprise choice of song from his best friend Paulie). Natasha Bedingfield and Three Six Mafia provided additional soundtrack songs although Bedingfields' version of the Dina Warren song *Still Here* was eventually dropped from the film. Brother Frank supplied new music too but his acapella track *Take You Back* from *Rocky* was re-used in its original format.

After several test-screenings that proved positive, the newly named *Rocky Balboa* was released in the US on December the 20th 2006, rolled out globally throughout the following January and it was a hit straight away. It made back half of its budget on its opening weekend and went on to claim more than $156 million dollars which was a significant return on its $24 million dollar budget. But the money was coupled with some of the best reviews of his career. Slipping effortlessly back into the hat and coat, here was the soft-hearted, hard-fisted son of Philadelphia that had so compelled movie goers since 1976. The excess of *Rocky IV* and the confusion of *Rocky V* had been re-configured back to a simple story of love again. The conveyance of solitary sadness and furious grief after the death of Adrian is realised so effectively that the justification for Rocky fighting again feels natural. She doesn't appear in the film aside from photos and old footage, but Talia Shire is as strong a presence in *Rocky Balboa* as ever and that's a real testament to Stallone's writing. The final bout is mostly presented as if you were watching it live on TV, but it still packs a punch and is a cinematic thrill and someone was definitely cutting onions near me as he left the ring to the cheers of the crowd for the final time. Burt Young's unique portrayal as Paulie represents how Rocky could have nose-dived had he not had boxing and the love of Adrian, and Young is as good and quirky as he was when he received a Best Supporting Actor nomination for *Rocky* in 1976. Ventimiglia convincingly goes from preppy yuppie working in the big city to his dad's biggest fan by the end. Hughes, Tarver and the peripheral cast all deliver too and the film ranks a very close second to *Rocky,* as the best in the franchise. It was written, created and released with the mindset that it was the very last time Stallone would ever portray the character (*Creed* was not even a consideration) and it rang the final bell with aplomb and class.

The only question now was, could he do the same for John Rambo?

RAMBO (2008)

LIVE FOR NOTHING, OR DIE FOR SOMETHING

Starring - Sylvester Stallone, Julie Benz, Paul Schultze, Matthew Marsden, Graham McTavish
Written by - Sylvester Stallone and Art Monterastelli
Original Score by - Brian Tyler
Directed by - Sylvester Stallone

A fourth John Rambo adventure was in the works as early as 1985, even before *Rambo III* was ramping up. The global phenomenon of *Rambo: First Blood Part II* quickly led to conversations between Tri-Star Pictures and Carolco Pictures about elongating what was now a franchise, way beyond the unavoidable third film. Using the 007 methodology as a guide, Rambo was being primed for a new adventure every two or three years and when Stallone got to the point that either he didn't want to continue, or it was felt he was too old to continue, a new actor would be drafted in and so the future would be assured.

In 1986, the branding was in full flow as the animated series *Rambo: The Force of Freedom* premiered on TV on April the 14th. The cartoon was a co-production between Carolco Pictures and Ruby-Spears Enterprises, who were at the top of their game. Joe Ruby and Ken Spears had been behind *Scooby Doo, Where Are You?* when they worked for Hannah-Barbera Cartoons Inc. before setting up their own animation studio in 1973. Michael Chain wrote the series that ran for 65 episodes in total and saw the cartoon John Rambo leading a team of do gooders who are given a mission each week by Colonel Trautman. The bad guys were more often than not a part of the terrorist group S.A.V.A.G.E. (Specialist-Administrators of Vengeance, Anarchy and Global Extortion) under the evil watchful eye of General Warhawk. British-born voice performer Neil Ross stood in for Stallone after already providing voices for the *G.I. Joe* and *Transformers* cartoons. In fact, *Rambo: The Force of Freedom* bore more than a passing resemblance to *G.I. Joe* but there was plenty of need for morning cartoons on TV and the Rambo series proved successful. Jerry Goldsmith's themes and cues from the films were repurposed for the cartoon with Haim Saban and Shuki Levy receiving credit for their 'additional music' similar to their work with the music for the *Masters of the Universe* show and *The Legend of Zelda* video game. Toys were simultaneously rushed into shops by licensed manufacturer Coleco and sales rocketed as they expanded the range to include all the peripheral figures, weapons and vehicles from the cartoon and many that were created by Coleco themselves. But as 1986 rolled into 1987, there were some concerns about the nature of the child-targeted endeavour. It was a cartoon that was trying to emulate an R-rated violent movie and within each episode there was a lot of gunplay and violence but no one was ever killed or seriously injured. The independent watchdog called Action For Children's Television (ACT) took a very dim view of *Rambo: The Force of Freedom* with its confusing moral stance and pressured the broadcasters, ABC, to ditch the show. The same accusations were being levelled at live-action TV series at the same time such as *The A-Team* which had started in 1983. By 1987, inconsequential violence on TV programmes aimed predominantly at younger viewers was no longer acceptable and *The A-Team* (with Mr T. of *Rocky III* fame of course) completed its final mission around the same time that ABC did not renew its order for *Rambo: The Force of Freedom* and the toy line soon ran out of favour as well.

But while the kid-friendly Rambo experiment was over, the main attraction was getting back in action with *Rambo III* in 1988. Despite its financial success, the most expensive movie ever made at that point found itself coming under fire. Accused of outdated, simplistic politics and outrageously unrealistic depictions of war, *Rambo III* caused a re-think of the future of the Vietnam war veteran. Finding himself defending the film instead of simply promoting it, he decided to hit pause but not delete; Stallone put Rambo on the back burner. In the mid-nineties, with efforts such as *The Specialist* and *Judge Dredd* not performing the way he'd hoped, he was finding the going tough. In 1997, Carolco Pictures finally went bankrupt after years of hanging on with loans and secretive investments. Miramax was one of many production companies who picked the bones off the carcass of Carolco, and one of those bones was the rights to the Rambo franchise. Wanting to get a new Rambo film up and running as soon as possible, Miramax approached Stallone but found him unwilling to put the headband on again citing his recent choices of *D-Tox, Avenging Angelo* and *Shade* as evidence he was trying to turn his back on the all-out action roles. But none of those films made a dent at the box office and by the end of 2003 he was open to the possibility again and casually drafted a couple of ideas that included Rambo now back in the U.S. with a wife and child taking on white supremacists and another idea that had the soldier working for the U.N. and caught up in a hostage crisis in New York. But then, Richard Crenna passed away from pancreatic cancer and Stallone couldn't envisage a Rambo film without Colonel Trautman, the only other character who had appeared in all three movies so far.

In 2004, he sat down with his pen and pad of A4 paper again to try and find a way to unlock the story. He knew that a story with no real world consequences would have little impact and writing a standard action film with Rambo at its centre just wouldn't be enough for modern audiences. He approached the United Nations and Soldier of Fortune magazine and asked them to explain where the most-troubled spots in the world currently were. Whether successfully or not, *Rambo: First Blood Part II* had tried to educate the public about very real, post-war trauma and *Rambo III* had certainly shed a light on the parties involved in the struggle to control Afghanistan. *Rambo: First Blood Part II* and *Rambo III* had also pushed the character into the realms of fantasy and even by 1988, that had started to feel inappropriate. The terrorist attack on the Twin Towers of the World Trade Centre in New York on September the 11th, 2001 had also changed western audiences. The Taliban and Al Qaeda were now names that the American public feared more than any other and since *Rambo III* had been in a Middle Eastern setting, Stallone wasn't going to go there again in the current climate.

His conversations with military personnel and war veterans led him to the 60-plus years of brutal civil war in Myanmar in SouthEast Asia, known as Burma when it gained independence from the United Kingdom in 1948. Almost instantly, the country had descended into conflict between the hardline, totalitarian government's armed forces called the Tatmadaw and various underground democratic opposition groups including The Kachin Independence Army and Karen National Liberation Army. Violent clashes, terrorism and full-scale battles raged for decades. As Stallone immersed himself further in the story and the atrocities that were being committed, he recognised the potential and also a duty to highlight the situation.

Israeli born Avi Lerner had turned his cinema chain company in Tel Aviv into film producing in Los Angeles, and after setting up his own production company Millenium Films, he found himself purchasing the rights to make Rambo films after Miramax collapsed as an ongoing business. Going straight to Stallone to present his idea, he found the star already had a drafted screenplay on his desk. Lerner immediately greenlit a fourth Rambo movie in late 2005 and Stallone started to prepare seriously by hitting the gym full-time for the first time in more than a decade. But just as *Rambo IV* was about to enter pre-production, *Rocky Balboa* was agreed to by MGM meaning Stallone had to put the gloves back on before he could reload his bow. The positive reaction and success of *Rocky Balboa* however helped Lerner gather more of the $50 million budget that the new Rambo film would need while TV script writer Art Monterastelli came in to help run a critical eye over Stallone's latest draft and offer suggestions. Monterastelli had written the 2003 thriller *The Hunted* with Benicio del Toro and Tommy Lee Jones and he'd been behind the short-lived TV series spin-offs of the movies *Total Recall* and *Timecop*. As a production start date was becoming imperative, Stallone announced he was also to direct the film. It would be the first non-Rocky film he would direct since 1983's *Staying Alive* and certainly his first action movie.

Now with the director, star and screenplay in place and with a filming start date of February 2007 locked-in, casting could now properly get underway for a Rambo film with an unusual ensemble cast. The plot Stallone had finessed saw John Rambo now living in Thailand and making ends meet by catching snakes for a seedy tourist attraction and providing boat rides up river. A group of American missionaries convince Rambo to take them into Burma by boat so they can provide humanitarian care to a village inhabited by the peaceful Karen people. Initially reluctant to put the missionaries in harm's way, the only female in the group convinces Rambo to take them on his boat. After a deadly encounter with pirates on the river, Rambo delivers them to their requested spot. A few days later, the pastor of the American missionary finds Rambo back in Thailand and informs them that the missionaries have been kidnapped and asks him to take a group of mercenaries back to the spot he dropped the missionaries off, so they can go and rescue them. Despite a bumpy start to the relationship between Rambo and the soldiers for hire, it ends in a blood splattered, bullet spraying finale where the former Green Beret saves the few remaining living missionaries and slices the main villain in half.

With Richard Crenna passed away, James Brolin was briefly considered to play Colonel Trautman until it was decided to rest the character along with the only actor to have portrayed him. For the missionaries there were two main speaking roles and the only female part was of Sarah, the missionary who manages to connect to Rambo and convince him to take them on the boat. Julie Benz was cast after making her name on TV as Darla in *Buffy the Vampire Slayer* and then Rita Bennet in *Dexter*. The missionary leader needed an emotive performance as his character arc saw him go from righteous caregiver at the start to crushing a soldier's head in with a rock by the end. Like Julie Benz, Paul Schultze had found his initial success in TV as Ryan Chappelle in multiple seasons of *24* and as Father Phil Intintola in *The Sopranos*. For the team of mercenaries, casting was multinational to reflect the nature of former soldiers who now work for the highest bidder. Scottish actor Graham McTavish played the leader of the group who takes an instant dislike to the monosyllabic boat driver and Matthew Marsden played the sympathetic team member known as Schoolboy. Marsden found fame as a young actor on British television institution *Coronation Street* before turning to film with a memorable turn in another military ensemble movie, *Black Hawk Down*. Tim Kang, Rey Gallegos and Jake La Botz rounded out the over-confident group who get a first hand look at what Rambo is capable of when pushed. To find the despicable main villain of Major Pa Pee Tint, the producers found their choice while on a location scouting trip. Despite having no acting experience, Maung Maung Khin was now living in Thailand but had been a Karen rebel since 1988 and had been on the front line until very recently. His stories of the horrific nature of the government forces were very helpful to the filmmakers but Stallone and Avi Lerner sensed that since he had seen it up close, he could bring the required malevolence to the screen himself. Khin was reluctant to accept the part as he feared reprisals from the government towards his family, but he decided the risk was worth it to get the message out of what was happening in Myanmar to an otherwise unaware western world.

With the cast, budget and screenplay in place filming began in Chiang Mai in Thailand with over 550 crew members. More than half of the crew were locally sourced in Thailand and it took a mammoth effort to coordinate the action scenes that incorporated hundreds of volunteer extras and Thai and Western stunt people. Stallone was an experienced director but this was on a scale he had never encountered so he relied on his closest colleagues such as First Assistant Director William Clark and especially his cinematographer Glen MacPherson, who had recently completed more action fare such as the Bruce Willis thriller *16 Blocks* in 2006 and the Dwayne Johnson vehicle *Walking Tall*. Getting advice and tips from anyone worthy, Stallone even turned to the director of the original *First Blood* in 1982 Ted Kotcheff who ended up with a credit on the film of Technical Consultant. Wife Jenniffer and his three daughters came for an extended visit to Thailand as Sophia, Sistine and Scarlet had enjoyed their first and possibly last chance to see their father filming as Rocky Balboa two years earlier and they wanted to take the opportunity to see him in action as his other, legendary alter-ego. Despite having his family on set for more than a week, he found the filming more gruelling than even he had anticipated. He confessed that filming on the Burmese river proved harder than filming *Cliffhanger* and things got more dangerous later on; while filming scenes very close to the Burmese border, shots were fired over the heads of the cast and crew from a distance and voices warned them to move away and close down their film. Although Stallone was well-versed in punishing his body for the sake of filming it was a new and brutal experience for some of the rest of the cast. Julie Benze and Paul Schultze in particular had to be thrown around, kicked, punched and dragged many times but the end product validated the experience. While the $50 million dollar budget was enough to get the film made, it was still limited funds for a film with the ambition and scale that Stallone envisaged. The decision was made before filming began to push the envelope of the on-screen blood-letting and to make the violence as graphic as possible. This would serve two purposes as it would not only make the film more memorable but it would allow the filmmakers to realistically portray the horrors that the Myanmar government was committing. Despite heavy rains that meant regular rebuilding of the village sets and temperatures that would reach 120 degrees, principle filming was completed on time on the 4th of May 2007.

Although the budget had been stretched to breaking point, Stallone was not willing to compromise on the score for the film. The memorable themes and compositions that Jerry Goldsmith had created for the first three films were indelibly linked to the character so the remit for young Californian composer Brian Tyler was simple; use what Goldsmith created alongside new themes for a new era of Rambo. Goldsmith had died in 2004 and left music for Rambo that was on a par with Bill Conti's connection to Rocky so Tyler understood the assignment but he also felt a strong connection to the material and the previous composer. Goldsmith had composed the music for the original *Alien* and Tyler was also working on the score for *Alien vs Predator: Requiem*, Goldsmith had composed the classic *Star Trek* theme and Tyler had scored some of the *Star Trek: Enterprise* TV show a few years earlier. The musician was open about the responsibility he felt and how honored he was to work on *Rambo*, and it showed. His use of the Goldsmith compositions work seamlessly alongside his new, elegant themes and elevated the movie considerably.

Before release in January 2008 however, complications arose around the title: Originally, the working title had been *John Rambo* and had a neat synergy with 2006's *Rocky Balboa* closing that character's story. But Stallone felt he wanted the door to remain open for further Rambo films and so he removed the first name from the title on the posters. But *John Rambo* was the official title of the movie in many countries in Asia and eastern Europe as the original *First Blood* had been released as *Rambo* in 1982. So to try and avoid confusion, the full name was reinstated on the title card and posters in the necessary locations. Another issue that affected the film's cinematic release was a legal dispute in the United Kingdom, where one of the biggest cinema chains, Odeon, refused to put the movie into any of its facilities as they had unresolved issues with Sony Pictures over the financial terms for *Rambo*. Other chains such as Vue and Cineworld were more than happy to put *Rambo* on their screens but the Odeon blockade certainly damaged the box office receipts. It returned a world wide gross of just over $120 million dollars which, while not spectacular, was an encouraging result. The film of the year in 2008 was *The Dark Knight* which was the only movie to cross the one billion dollar mark but *Rambo*'s financial success was fairly remarkable for a character that had been dormant for twenty years and whose star was now 60 years old. The critics were impressed also, singling Stallone's directing out for praise but noting the intense levels of violence depicted on screen. If Stallone had wanted to up the ante for gore in a commercial film, he certainly achieved his goal. During some of the more disturbing scenes of government forces violence we watch as women are raped, children are stabbed through the chest and a baby is thrown into a burning building. To begin the film, Stallone explains the circumstances in Myanmar with documentary footage and he doesn't shy away from showing charred bodies, rotting remains, mass graves and torture. If his task was to show these atrocities to the world amidst the framework of an adult action movie, it was mission accomplished.

Rambo is not for the faint-hearted and it's all the better for it. The violence is gruesome and upsetting at many points but in the context and structure of the movie, it works. More so than ever before, Rambo is always close to boiling point and his unwillingness to escort the missionaries up the river is more to do with keeping a lid on the rage inside him, than the safety of his passengers initially. Had the story revolved around a fictional country and artificial atrocities, perhaps it would feel more like sensationalism and unnecessarily gratuitous, but Stallone deftly keeps the motivations clear and the bloody final act of Rambo using his famous knife to slice open the sadistic Major Tint (to a full-bloodied blast of the Goldsmith *Rambo* theme) feels cathartic and justified. For many, it's too much and too extreme and even the trailer had raised eyebrows; the moment of Rambo appearing slowly behind a soldier and then apparently punching the man's head off went viral until the full film was released and it was discovered that it was the editing of the trailer that had suggested the punch-decapitation but the actuality was Rambo used his machete. In both *Rambo: First Blood Part 2* and more so in *Rambo III* you could argue that the main characters are essentially the same at the end of the film as they were at the start. Action movies at that time resisted story arcs for the central roles as the belief was that it would negate any further sequels from being effective. James Bond had zero personal growth from adventure to adventure (until Daniel Craig went to the other extreme) and the same went for John Rambo. He was still angry at the end of *Rambo: First Blood Part 2* and he went off to fight another day with Colonel Trautman at the end of *Rambo III* (an alternative ending where Rambo chooses to stay in Afghanistan with the rebels was filmed and you can find it on YouTube). But here in this 21st century Rambo story, our hero does come full circle and the final sequence filmed was him coming home. We see Rambo dressed almost identically to how we first saw him in the opening of *First Blood*, arriving at a long pathway to his family's farm in Arizona. The mailbox says R. Rambo (in 2019's *Rambo: Last Blood* we discover the R stands for Reevis) and after the intensity of the previous 90 minutes, we can feel he has finally found some peace. Although Stallone insisted that he was open to more Rambo films, this ending conveyed real closure and a satisfying finale to a movie that runs a close second to *First Blood* as the best in the series.

The legacy of 2008's *Rambo* lasted well beyond the film's cinematic life; it was, unsurprisingly, banned by the government in Myanmar. Bootleg copies began circulating among the Karen people and one of the memorable lines from the film: "Live for nothing, or die for something" became an unofficial rallying cry for the rebels and Stallone described it as the proudest moment of his career. One significant underground youth movement for democracy in the country called Generation Wave, started distributing copies of the film as a recruitment tool. As some western movie critics attacked the movie for its levels of violence, overseas Burmese natives praised it for its realism and encouraged viewings of *Rambo* to educate the ill-informed. Actor Julie Benz was so moved by the experience of filming *Rambo* that she joined the U.S. Campaign for Burma saying publicly, "I can't continue my life without trying to help the situation." Sometimes, the box office isn't the most important outcome of a movie.

2010 - 2013 - THE EXPENDABLES, ZOOKEEPER, THE EXPENDABLES 2, BULLET TO THE HEAD,

The first few years of the 2010's mostly proved productive and fruitful. He would create a real buzz and a new franchise with *The Expendables*, make one of his hidden gems in *Bullet to the Head* and lend his unmistakable voice to a CGI lion. With Rocky and Rambo recently completing their critically and financially successful send-offs, it was now the first time in Stallone's career where he didn't have a franchise in his life. From *Rocky* in 1976 and also *First Blood* in 1982, he had always had a safety net. He could repair any damage done from a recent release with the next installment of either character and then look for more original opportunities again. But now he'd closed that door and he was in unchartered territory. The world of cinema was also very different from the medium he had so dominated towards the end of the twentieth century. As studios became more and more desperate to reach the wallets of family audiences (so that an average of four tickets were bought for a cinema trip rather than one or two) the releases from the major players seemed to be leaving the adults behind. The top four films in 2009 had all been designed to try and appeal to every possible demographic at the same time: *Avatar, Harry Potter and the Half Blood Prince, Ice Age: Dawn of the Dinosaurs* and *Transformers: Revenge of the Fallen*. With *The Twilight Saga: New Moon* and *Up* also finishing inside the top ten, the chances of getting a rip-roaring action extravaganza greenlit were diminishing every year.

California-born writer David Callaham had sold his first movie screenplay in 2005. *Doom* was the big-screen adaptation of the hugely successful video game and starred Dwayne Johnson, Rosamund Pike and Karl Urban. It wasn't a big hit but it was enough to get him a deal at Warner Bros. to produce more scripts and help out when other screenplays needed some fresh eyes. One of his next submissions was an idea called *Barrow,* which was about a group of mercenaries on a mission. He revised his screenplay two more times before Warner Bros. eventually bought it in 2006 and put it into their possible development pile. It was not long after that, that Stallone had been expressing an interest in doing something as part of an ensemble. His recent *Rocky* and *Rambo* finales had brought into sharp focus that he was the last man standing. All those action stars that he had paved the way for had come and gone by now and he was the only one still having big cinema releases. Bruce Willis' fourth John McCLane film in 2007 called *Live Free or Die Hard* had made money but hadn't been critically approved like the trilogy that came before it and Arnold Schwarzenegger had been embroiled in political life as Governor of California since his disappointing third turn in his most famous role in *Terminator 3: Rise of the Machines* in 2003. Steven Seagal, Jean-Claude Van Damme, Dolph Lundgren, Chuck Norris, Mel Gibson and all the other pretenders to Stallone's-throne had either disappeared into straight-to-DVD efforts or couldn't find work at all.

The idea of movies stacked with famous stars wasn't at all new and Stallone himself was a fan of the great attempts in the past such as *The Longest Day, A Bridge Too Far* and *The Magnificent Seven* and more recently the star-packed *Ocean's 11* and its sequels. As if realising that he was now morphing into the role of the keeper of the action-hero flame whilst also sensing an opportunity to revive the kind of old-school, bang-for-your-buck entertainment that he had helped create, he found the *Barrow* script and asked if he could develop it. Taking the bare bones of Callaham's idea, he expanded the mercenaries on a mission format to include a larger team, bigger action set-pieces and changed the title to *The Expendables*.

Millennium Films and Nu Films soon backed the project that Lionsgate would distribute on the proviso that the big cast would be worth the money spent on it. Understanding the potential headlines that would be generated, Stallone approached Jean-Claude Van Damme and Steven Seagal. Seagal turned his offer down saying that he'd had a bad experience with one of the film's producers Avi Lerner and Van-Damme also rejected the career-lifeline claiming the character he would be playing had no substance. Two previous co-stars also declined the opportunity: Kurt Russell's agent said his client wasn't looking to be a part of an ensemble and Wesley Snipes was keen but he was having serious problems with the Inland Revenue Service over unpaid taxes and wasn't allowed to leave the country. The Snipes role was then offered to Forest Whittaker who said yes but then withdrew due to a scheduling conflict and so it was passed on to 50 Cent, the third actor to be offered this part, but he declined as well and eventually it went to former NFL player-turned actor Terry Crews who was building an impressive career in a wide variety of projects. The main villain role of James Munroe was sent to Robert DeNiro, Al Pacino, Ben Kingsley and his *Cop Land* co-star Ray Liotta but it was accepted by Eric Roberts. Roberts (who is the brother of Julia) had played plenty of heroic roles and also bad guys in his long career, including his part in *The Specialist* more than fifteen years before and had remained friends with Stallone since then. To fill out the rest of his mercenary team, Stallone mixed a blend of the new and not so new.

For the new, he went with Jason Statham as his main co-star. Since his breakout performance in Guy Ritchie's *Lock, Stock and Two Smoking Barrels* (and its follow-up *Snatch* with Brad Pitt) Statham had built a unique career that had gone against the tide of less and less action. His *Transporter* films series and two *Crank* movies were part of a fast-growing filmography of middle-budget, high-tempo action thrillers and he hadn't even joined the *Fast and Furious* franchise at that point. Former soldier turned UFC star turned actor Randy Couture joined the team as did wrestling superstar Steve "Stone Cold" Austin, but he was to be on the bad guys squad. Martial arts legend Jet Li joined *The Expendables* after making his Hollywood debut in *Lethal Weapon 4* in 1998 and *Rocky* fans were thrilled to learn that Stallone and Dolph Lundgren would share the big screen again for the first time since *Rocky IV*. Lundgren's movie career hadn't taken off in the way it had been expected after his star-making role as Ivan Drago. His big screen He-Man in *Masters of the Universe* had tanked in 1987 and aside from sharing the hit *Universal Soldier* with Van Damme in 1992, he'd been relegated to non-cinema releases. Mickey Rourke was another star who had plenty of gratitude to show Stallone. After extending him a life-line with a role in *Get Carter* in 2000, Rourke had struggled to find starring roles again until his eye-catching, critically adored performance in *The Wrestler* in 2008. He was signed up to play the villain in *Iron Man 2* already, but managed to carve out 48 hours to film a couple of scenes for *The Expendables*.

With Stallone writing, starring and directing and with a budget of $80 million dollars, filming began in late April in Rio and other locations in Brazil. The cast and crew then moved back to the US to film in New Orleans until wrapping on the 1st of July. It was during the U.S. portion of the shoot that production nearly had to be shut-down for good. Filming one of the complicated and brutal fight scenes, Stallone was tackled to the ground by Steve Austin. As soon as he awkwardly hit the floor, Stallone knew something was wrong. He was rushed to hospital for x-rays where it was discovered he had dislocated both his shoulders and severely fractured his neck. The only course of action was spinal fusion surgery and a metal plate was permanently inserted into his neck. Since the accident in 2010, he has had seven surgeries and has publicly stated that he has never been the same since (although news of the injury wasn't made public until after the movies' release). Despite a long delay, he returned to the shoot as he had another trick up his sleeve.

While that cast list was already impressive, Stallone was also bringing out the big guns for one special extra day of filming on October the 27th in a secret church location in Los Angeles. Having seen their early feisty relationship turn into mutual respect and eventually into close friendship, Stallone and Arnold Schwarzenegger had never been seen on screen together (they nearly did for *Face/Off* but those parts eventually went to John Travolta and Nicolas Cage) and the role of the mysterious Mr Church was written for the Governor of California. Arnie's participation had to be limited due to his political office so he switched to the rival mercenary leader character called Trench and the Planet Hollywood triumvirate was finally together when Bruce Willis took on the Mr Church cameo. The one scene sees Willis's character offer the dangerous assignment job to both Stallone's team and Arnie's team. The moment quickly became the main marketing tool for the film and the chance to finally watch the biggest action stars of all time together on the big screen.

After a successful first collaboration between filmmaker and musician on *Rambo* in 2008, Brian Tyler was asked to score *The Expendables*. Tyler set about composing suitably muscular themes and added a hard rock element to re-emphasise the testosterone and posturing on display. Some of the orchestral work sounded eerily similar to his *Rambo* work but it was no coincidence and was the result of clear instruction from Stallone. But like the film itself, the music, the premise and the all-star cast wasn't the sum of its parts. *The Expendables* relies on goodwill and nostalgia from its viewers and for the mature cinema-goer, there was undoubtedly a kick from seeing all those famous screen tough guys sharing the limelight and poking fun at their images. But the dialogue isn't as sharp as it needed to be (or thought it was) and the action set pieces, while energetic and loud, were tinged with an old-fashioned vibe and strangely unengaging. Nevertheless the film was a hit and made over $260 million dollars in the year that *Toy Story 3* and *Alice in Wonderland* both made over a billion.

While pre-production had been getting started on *The Expendables*, Stallone could slip away to a sound booth and record his dialogue for *The Zookeeper*. The fantasy comedy directed by Frank Coraci was a vehicle for Kevin James who had just had his first major film hit with *Paul Blart: Mall Cop* after making his name on TV in the sitcom *The King of Queens* which ran from 1998 to 2007. The family movie would see James's character suddenly able to hear and understand the voices of all the animals in the Franklin Park Zoo in Boston. As is often the case with the bigger budgeted family movies, the voice-cast list for the animated characters was impressive. Stallone was joining Nick Nolte, Adam Sandler and Cher as the main animals with Stallone's deep tones perfectly matched to Joe the Lion. *The Zookeeper* had a similar $80 million dollar budget as *The Expendables* but made $100 million less at the box office when it was released in 2011.

Even before *The Expendables* was having its first test screenings, a sequel was already in the works. Most original films projects have to come with a potential franchise plan, should the first installment prove profitable. The first mission had done enough to convince the financial backers to up the budget to $100 million for *The Expendables 2*. Despite announcing a second film as early as August 2010, it was only officially confirmed as going ahead the following April with a release date set for August the 17th 2012. It was also quickly established that Stallone didn't want to direct the sequel and in his place would be British born Simon West who knew a thing or two about trying to steer a testosterone-infused cast through production as his first Hollywood hit as director had been the Nicolas Cage smash *Con Air*. West had recently directed Statham in *The Mechanic* and with the fellow Expendables' seal of approval, West was onboard. The director also brought his *The Mechanic* screenwriter Richard Wenk to help Stallone with the script. As with *The Expendables,* the plot of *The Expendables 2* was largely window-dressing around getting big stars to shoot big guns.

But unlike the first film, the success of *The Expendables* meant that he now had his pick of actors to add to the cast. Whether willingly or contractually, it wasn't a surprise to see most of the original's rejoining and soon enough Jason Statham, Dolph Lundgren, Terry Crews, Randy Couture and Jet Li were confirmed. But Stallone knew it wasn't enough to rest on their laurels so he put in a request for a meeting with Chuck Norris. The martial arts master had been a friend and co-star of Bruce Lee before breaking into Hollywood with a slew of action films. His *Missing in Action* and *Delta Force* film series had been modest hits and while he found himself pigeon-holed as another Stallone-lite, he had become a cult figure and was considered an 80's legend. That was more than enough to book him a spot in an extended cameo in *The Expendables 2*. Liam Hemsworth was added to the crew as new blood and after turning a role in the first film down, Jean-Claude Van Damme was more than keen to come onboard as the new, main villain (who's character was even called Jean Vilain, just to hammer home the point). Filming was to take place mainly in Bulgaria with additional locations to be used in Hong Kong and New Orleans and production began late in September of 2011. Bulgaria was chosen as it had cheaper crews and ideal landscapes but tragedy struck when they were filming an explosion on a rubber boat and stuntman Kun Liu was killed and another was left in a critical condition (the family of Kun Liu later filed a lawsuit against the filmmakers alleging unsafe stunt conditions and the credits on the finished film contain a dedication to his memory). The production also ran afoul of the Bulgarian Environmental Protection Agency who fined them over $3 thousand dollars for breaking the law when they removed shrubs and small vegetation from the entrance to a cave with a bridge for a few key scenes.

Production continued with a vast airport set in a studio that was to be the epicentre of the final battle between The Expendables and Vilain's bad guys. After the publicity that the brief scene with Stallone, Schwarzenegger and Willis had garnered in *The Expendables*, both stars were prepared to return to the franchise for longer screen time. Through a convoluted plot device, viewers are treated to the three action icons firing weapons alongside each other and trading quips along the way: When Arnie says his customary "I'll be back," to Willis, he replies, "You've been back enough." And Arnie gets to say "Yippee Ki-Yay," before Willis can deliver his *Die Hard* catchphrase. Add-in a few Rambo references and it's all very silly but very enjoyable. And when it was released in the summer of 2012, it did better than the first film making over $300 million dollars this time. The reviews were more positive about the star-casting, the humour and the general fun to be had while the plot was as irrelevant as expected. $300 million was certainly a good return on its $100 million budget but gone were the days when these names could battle for the biggest film of the year. Had *The Expendables 2* been made and released in 1989 it would probably still be the highest grossing movie of all time but in 2012, things were extremely different. Tastes and expectations were much changed from the 1980s and the real money spinners were *The Avengers, The Dark Knight Rises, Skyfall* and *The Hobbit: An Unexpected Journey* which all crossed over the one billion dollar mark, dwarfing the income from *The Expendables 2*. But that lesser amount was still enough to guarantee *The Expendables 3* in the near future.

What wouldn't ever be guaranteed though was *Bullet to the Head 2*, despite *Bullet to the Head* being a superior, darkly comic adult thriller. Its origins were in a graphic novel by Alexis Nolent called *Du Plomb Dans La Tête* (*Lead in the Head*) and it was turned into a screenplay and renamed *Headshot* by Italian screenwriter Alessandro Camon. Two years previously, Camon had received an Oscar nomination for his original screenplay for the 2009 war drama *The Messenger* that starred Ben Foster and Woody Harrelson. The basic plot of *Headshot* was of a hitman and a cop who are forced to work together to bring down a corrupt businessman in New Orleans and Warner Bros. were excited to find Stallone was keen to play the hitman. South African filmmaker Wayne Kramer had made some notable but mid-sized hits such as *The Cooler* and *Crossing Over* and was keen to rewrite the Camon draft to inject some darker, irreverent tones. He was delighted to have a star of the stature of Stallone on board and he hired Thomas Jane to play the cop. The Baltimore actor had been hovering around stardom for years and each project was presented to him as his ticket into the A-list. He loved the script now called *Bullet to the Head* and was thrilled to be co-starring with Stallone but the producer was less than thrilled. Joel Silver had produced *The Matrix* plus every *Die Hard* and *Lethal Weapon* movie and he'd overseen *Demolition Man* and *Assassins* with Stallone, so when he wanted to recast the cop, there was little resistance from the studio. Silver was also quite open about his motivation saying that he wanted to appeal to a more global audience and having two white, American actors in the leads, wasn't going to work. So Thomas Jane was out and in his place came Sung Kang. Kang was born in Georgia in the U.S. to Korean parents and was already well known to cinema audiences from his recurring role as Han in the *Fast and Furious* franchise. While Stallone wasn't phased by the sudden change of his co-star he was increasingly concerned about the re-writes from his director. He was working with Kramer on new drafts but soon he became frustrated with the ever-darkening themes. It came to a head with Stallone and Joel Silver firing Kramer from the project with only a few weeks to go until principal photography began. But when one door closes another one opens and suddenly the stars aligned for Stallone to work with acclaimed veteran director Walter Hill.

Hill had been directing since the mid-seventies and on his list of credits included *The Warriors, 48 Hrs., Red Heat* and in 1996 the neo-Western *Last Man Standing* with Bruce Willis. Both director and star had long been admirers of each other's work and found common ground with their desire to make *Bullet to the Head* a contemporary, adult thriller with a twisted comic edge. Stallone's hitman character Jimmy Bobo became more like Stallone with each new draft of the screenplay. Hill encouraged him to play it more casually and when filming began on June the 27th 2011 in Louisiana and then New York, the pair found their stride quickly. Added to the cast was Christian Slater who hadn't been in a film that was going to have a theatrical release since *Alone in the Dark* in 2005. One of the other key additions was Hawaiian born Jason Momoa. After cutting his acting teeth on TV in a *Baywatch* spin-off show and then underwater sci-fi series *Stargate: Atlantis*, the 6 foot 4 actor was trying to break into movies and had already completed his first starring role in a reboot of the early Schwarzenegger fantasy film, *Conan The Barbarian*. He was given the role of the thoroughly nasty Keegan, the henchman of main bad guy Robert Morel (played by English actor Adewale Akinnuoye-Agbaje). Momoa's portrayal of Keegan allows for the audience to feel slightly concerned for the welfare of Stallone's Bobo because despite Bobo's tough demeanour and analogue approach to confrontation, Keegan is worse. He beats up women, kills innocents gleefully in cold blood and is thrilled to have the chance to fight Bobo with an axe in the film's climax. The preamble to the fight between Bobo and Keegan provides some of the wittiest dialogue in the movie. With axe in hand, Keegan delivers a speech designed to intimidate Bobo before they battle, to which Stallone's character replies, "Are we gonna fight or are you planning on boring me to death?".

With Walter Hill in charge you can feel the quality oozing off the screen despite the relatively low budget. It's a violent thriller where none of the characters are squeaky clean and the dry comedy (especially from Stallone) is consistently a well-timed relief from the intensity of some of the gunplay and fights. Stallone trusted Hill's advice and his performance is pitched exquisitely and should be considered one of the best of his action-catalogue. His delivery is effortless and restrained and he resists the temptations to slip into his tried and trusted mannerisms from less classy projects. When you add in the mostly-nighttime aesthetic and the pounding, blues-rock score by Steve Mazzaro you have a quality movie that makes more of itself than it has any right to. Unfortunately, the film was unfairly reviewed when it was released after having its start date moved from April 2012 to February 2013 which is a sure sign of lack of confidence from the distributors. Critically misjudged as just another macho-Stallone flick, it was financially a disaster and the lowest box office for Stallone in over 30 years. On its $55 million dollar budget, it ended its run on just over $22 million.

You win some, you lose some and he hoped to win again over the next twelve months as he and Arnie were finally going to co-star and he was going to get back into the boxing ring but this time opposite the *Raging Bull* himself, Robert DeNiro.

2013 - 2014 - ESCAPE PLAN, HOMEFRONT, GRUDGE MATCH, THE EXPENDABLES 3, REACH ME

Better late than never should be the sub-heading of this chapter. *Escape Plan, Grudge Match* and *The Expendables 3* all center on Stallone sharing the stage with a long-overdue co-star or two.

Escape Plan was released in 2013, which undoubtedly meant the on screen pairing of two of Hollywood's biggest hitters cost a lot less (and involved a lot less negotiating) than if it had been made two decades earlier. Ever since their rivalry began to grow in the 1980s, the prospect of Stallone and Schwarzenegger starring together felt like an impossible dream. There were brief flirtations with Arnie appearing in a Rambo adventure or Stallone cameoing in one of his Terminator stories but they were never more than fan-fiction fantasies. The intensity of their competition negated any possibility of the two titans joining forces. It was survival of the fittest where both wanted to be the last action hero standing. But by the mid-nineties when both careers were starting to show signs of instability and their hostility was morphing into friendship, they were tempted to point guns at each other in *Face/Off*. The original screenplay for the film was set in the future and the pair would have had great fun imitating and mocking each other's characteristics as the plot involved the two lead characters literally swapping faces. That potential movie may have been more an industry fable than actual fact but just picturing the possibility is enough to raise a smile. In the end, the lead roles went to John Travolta and Nicolas Cage and it was an instant classic. Soon enough though, life, careers and in the case of Arnie, political careers, got in the way of that pairing ever becoming a reality. But then Arnie took a day off his final months as Governor of California to appear with Stallone and Bruce Willis, in that all-too-brief highpoint of *The Expendables*. Their joint screentime was expanded further in *The Expendables 2,* but it was still really a Stallone movie that Arnie was popping in to. However, that popping in led to the conversation that if they don't do a full film together soon, they may never do it at all.

Miles Chapman was a young actor who arrived in New York and quickly realised he preferred writing plays to performing in them. That transferred to helping to script TV shows and by the time he had moved to Los Angeles, he wanted to try his hand at movie scripts. The first one he ever wrote that was made into a film was a Straight-to-DVD sequel to the Patrick Swayze classic *Roadhouse*. His sequel was called *Roadhouse 2: Last Call* in 2006 but it stoked the flames of writing more and he crafted another screenplay called *The Tomb* which centered around a security expert escaping from the most advanced prison on the planet. Summit Entertainment bought his draft and Jeff Wadlow was an early named director. Soon Wadlow's name was gone but his writer Jason Keller (who used the pen name Arnell Jesko) had made some rewrites that the studio was happy with and kept. The new versions attracted Bruce Willis to the main role of Ray Breslin with Antoine Fuqua (who had directed Denzel Washington to Oscar success in *Training Day* in 2001) in the directors chair. But that incarnation also fell by the wayside and *The Tomb* looked to be buried until Stallone read it and liked it. Summit was talking to director Mikael Hafstrom who had impressed with his Swedish teen drama *Evil* in 2003 and the horror-thriller

1408 with John Cusack and Samuel L Jackson. With a start date of April 2012 looming, writer Chapman and director Hafstrom went to visit Schwarzenegger at his office to pitch the idea of him joining the project. The Austrian had already had a conversation with Stallone about the film and he wanted to meet the pair before saying yes. The meeting was quick and Arnie was in.

Filming was divided between Austin, Texas and New Orleans where a vast indoor facility that was used by NASA to build Space Shuttles was converted into the enormous prison set for the newly-named *Escape Plan*. The supporting cast became easy to attract when the two lead surnames were mentioned. Jim Caviezel came on board as the twisted warden with footballer turned actor Vinnie Jones as his right hand man. Curtis '50 Cent' Jackson had turned down offers to be in *The Expendables* to focus on music but now he was on board as part of Breslin's (Stallone) team on the outside. Amy Ryan and Vincent D'Onofrio signed on and the extended cameo of the prison doctor went to *Jurassic Park*'s Sam Neill. The main plot remained pretty faithful to Chapman's original *The Tomb* screenplay with Ray Breslin and his team escaping from various facilities to highlight the shortcomings in security. When he takes on the job to go into a new, top secret prison, he soon finds he has been set up and getting out looks impossible. But he teams up with another inmate called Emil Rottmayer (Schwarzenegger) and the pair plan an elaborate break out from the facility. It's a good film and a well made one too, although it doesn't quite hit the bar to be called excellent. The treat is of course seeing the big guns going head to head and after a brief fight between them in the prison canteen, (which includes the line "You hit like a vegetarian!") they work together and that's the heart of the movie. There's plenty of ingenuity in the plan of escape itself and enough twists in the plot to keep the interest but it was never going to win awards for originality. Its $65 million budget was in jeopardy when it made only $20 million at the U.S. box office but internationally it was a hit and eventually totalled out at more than $135 million, which was enough to kick start the inevitable, pre-planned sequels. *Escape Plan* certainly isn't the best thing that a Stallone/Schwarzenegger team-up could ever have been but it's better to have had this, than never having had anything at all.

While he was working on *Escape Plan* he was also keeping an eye on another project as producer and writer. *Homefront* was a 2005 novel from Chuck Logan that had piqued Stallone's interest enough for him to write a screenplay for a movie that he would star in himself. When he couldn't get the project off the ground at a convenient time, he handed the main star duties over to his *The Expendables* co-star Jason Statham. Statham played Phil Broker, a retired DEA agent who lives peacefully with his daughter until a crime boss causes issues that he can't turn his back on. Stallone had considered just directing the film but again he couldn't fit it into his schedule and the reigns were handed to *Runaway Jury* director Gary Fleder. On a small $22 million budget the film grossed double that amount but isn't considered an essential addition to the Statham canon.

But before the year was out, Stallone had a gift for Christmas Day. If seeing Stallone and Schwarzenegger share the screen in an action film had been unfathomable decades before, then watching the stars of *Rocky* and *Raging Bull* in a comedy boxing movie, was deemed simply preposterous. Until it happened on December the 25th 2013. The pair had of course been seen on the big screen together in the superb *Cop Land* in 1997 but when a script that saw two ageing, retired boxers coaxed back into the ring to settle an old score, was pitched around Hollywood, getting Stallone and DeNiro to say yes felt a little optimistic. Tim Kelleher had written for a number of TV shows including *Two and a Half Men* and wrote the story and initial screenplay for *Grudge Match* which was then freshened up by Rodney Rothman whose many comedy credits included the *Late Show with David Letterman* and several other TV show pilots and even the *78th Academy Awards Show* in 2006. Peter Segal had directed plenty of comedy in film up to that point with some of his biggest hits including *Anger Management* in 2003 and *50 First Dates* the year after, both with Adam Sandler. Surprisingly, this project came to Robert DeNiro's attention first. DeNiro's first foray into comedy after his well-documented and lauded dramatic work (an extraordinary list that includes *Mean Streets, Taxi Driver, The Godfather Part II, Goodfellas, Casino* and *Heat*) was two years after *Cop Land* in 1999 when he starred opposite Billy Crystal in *Analyze This*. A year later he scored even bigger at the comedy box office with *Meet the Parents* with Ben Stiller. Sequels to both those hits and other comedic roles became interspersed with his more expected dramatic work so by the time *Grudge Match* came to him, he was more than comfortable in the genre. He was well aware that his extraordinary *Raging Bull* performance had prompted the approach for *Grudge Match* but he still had to convince Stallone that being in this comedy wouldn't tarnish his *Rocky* legacy.

Kevin Hart and Alan Arkin were also hired which would guarantee comedic talent on screen if it didn't work out with the two leads. Kim Basinger was cast as the love interest for the first time in a long time in her career and she relished the opportunity. Other supporting roles went to Jon Bernthal as DeNiro's estranged son (perfect casting) and LL Cool J as an arrogant gym owner. Despite DeNiro passing 70 and Stallone reaching 67 at the time of filming, both hit the gym with boxing trainer Bob Sale and Stallone slimmed down to 168 pounds which was his lowest weight since 1981 and he also designed the final boxing match, for which he got an onscreen choreography credit. Filming took place on location in Pennsylvania and New Orleans and although the film was supposed to release in January of 2014, it was moved to Christmas Day of 2013. On its $40 million dollar budget it didn't do well however and only recouped $45 million in total which was a bit of a surprise but also not a surprise. For cinema goers of a certain vintage the film had sentimental appeal alone but the lacklustre advertising campaign plus choosing to open the film on the same day as the excellent Scorsese/DiCaprio release *The Wolf of Wall Street*, made it a tough sell.

If you accept that *Demolition Man* isn't a comedy although it is very amusing, then *Grudge Match* is the best fully-fledged comedy of Stallone's career. Both he and DeNiro are very invested in the nuance of their characters and Peter Segal used all his experience to utilize their strengths for maximum effect. Neither of them are asked to do anything that wasn't in their wheelhouse and there is a sweet pathos that runs throughout the movie alongside the well-scripted comedic set-pieces. It's too simplistic to say that Stallone is playing a kind-of Rocky Balboa and DeNiro is playing a kind-of Jake La Motta. There are clear similarities with those two characters and plenty of onscreen subtle and not so subtle nods in their direction, but it doesn't fall into the trap of being a spoof and it stands on its own two feet. Arkin and Hart give exactly the energy and performance you hope they would and the scenes with the two stars and either Basinger and Jon Bernthal (who was also in *The Wolf of Wall Street*) nicely balance the heartwarming with the laughs. If

Bullet to the Head is his best kept secret in action cinema, then *Grudge Match* is his *Rocky* of comedy.

In mid-August of 2013, Stallone had finished work on *Grudge Match* and was back on macho duty to complete a trilogy of films for the third time in his career. *The Expendables 3* was in development as the second film was still in post-production but while Stallone was drafting story ideas he conceded how difficult a third film in a series can be. Too often in the media, the first sequel to a hit is referred to as a part of the 'franchise'. But in the movie business, the reality is that you only have a franchise if the sequel is a hit too. If discussions about a third film take place, *then* you officially have a franchise on your hands. A first sequel is ideally a continuation of the original, but part three needed to have a freshness about it. Take *Rocky III* and *Rambo III* as good examples of keeping the essence of the series intact but pushing into new territory at the same time. For the third Expendables film (which he assumed would be the last) he wanted to go out all guns blazing with a combination of in demand young talent and more of those famous surnames that went through similar career-trajectories in the 80's and 90's. Steven Seagal, Nicolas Cage and Clint Eastwood were all tentatively announced as early as 2012 but all subsequently dropped out or were not as close to making a deal as was publicized.

The screenplay was credited to Stallone plus husband and wife team Creighton Rothenberger and Katrin Benedikt who had penned the Die Hard-in-the-White-House script *Olympus Has Fallen* in 2003 and saw it finally hit the big screen with Gerard Butler in the lead role in 2013. Jackie Chan came close (yet again) to joining Stallone on screen but a combination of bad timing and Chan requiring more of a starring role, saw him withdraw from *The Expendables 3*.

One big name who was expected to come back but then backed out was Bruce Willis. Offered a total of $3 million dollars for four days' work, his agent demanded $1 million more and it caused a rift between him and Stallone and the film's producers. Stallone even took to social media to vent his frustrations publicly (although in hindsight, Willis' deteriorating medical condition may have forced his hand without Stallone and his producers knowledge). But with Willis now not returning as Mr Church, a new character called Max Drummer was created, written and accepted by a pretty decent substitute; none other than Harrison Ford (in the film, Ford's character is asked what happened to Mr Church and he replies, "He's out of the picture."). But that was just the start of the stunt casting for the third film as Mel Gibson was brought in to play the main villain Conrad Stonebanks who had been one of the founders of The Expendables team but had broken bad since leaving. Gibson was also in talks to direct but instead gave that duty to fellow Australian Patrick Hughes who's only film directing credit was the Aussie neo-western *Red Hill* in 2010. After missing out on being in the previous two films, Wesley Snipes was now out of prison and could re-team with his *Demolition Man* co-star and after working with Stallone in *Assassins* and *Spy Kids 3: Game Over*, Antonio Banderas also jumped on board to play the livewire character of Galgo, whose attempts to join the Expendables team are the funniest moments of the movie. *Cheers* and *Frasier* star Kelsey Grammer was employed for a few days work as Bonaparte, to cover some of the plot narrative that was to have been handled by the Bruce Willis character. Also back for the ride was Terry Crews, Randy Couture, Dolph Lundgren, Jet Li and of course Jason Statham who would keep up his tradition of having the last line in every movie in the series. Arnold Schwarzenegger also committed to a few days work to wrap up his character's story arc.

Before principle photography could begin in Bulgaria in August of 2013 though, Stallone had to think about the future of the franchise and bringing in some new blood. One of the first and most interesting new members of the team was Ronda Rousey. The Californian had made Mixed Martial Arts history by competing in the first all-female bout at a headline event for the Ultimate Fighting Championship (UFC) in February of 2013 and she soon became the first UFC Women's Bantamweight Champion. It was Stallone and producer Avi Lerner who approached her after conversations with UFC boss Dana White and after a couple of obligatory screen tests, she was signed-on. Adding to the real-world casting of combat sports stars was Victor Ortiz, the former WBC Welterweight boxing champion. After losing that title to Floyd Mayweather Jr. in late 2011 and suffering two further defeats after that, Ortiz was looking at other options and accepted the chance to learn on the job alongside some of the best in the business of film. Kellan Lutz had become well-known to teenage audiences for his recurring role of Emmett Cullen in the *Twilight Saga* films but Stallone was just as intrigued when he found out Lutz was a more than competent boxer and a black belt in Brazilian Jiu-Jitsu and Muay Thai. Rounding out the younger breed was Glen Powell. A 14-year old Glen Powell made his brief acting debut in *Spy Kids 3D: Game Over* with Stallone and Antonio Banderas and had been in constant, if unspectacular, work ever since. Episodic TV and minor roles in films such as *The Dark Knight Rises* had him on everyone's rising star list, but *The Expendables 3* was a big step up in his career. (his bigger step up would come in 2022 as Jake 'Hangman' Seresin in Tom Cruise's mega-hit sequel *Top Gun: Maverick*).

Filming went on until mid-October but did include a moment of almost-catastrophe in September when a truck that Statham was driving ended up in the sea after the brakes failed. Bryan Tyler was on scoring duty again and rehashed many of the themes from the first two films and things looked good ahead of the August 2024 release. That summer *The Expendables 3* upstaged everyone else at the Cannes Film Festival as every member of the huge cast rode down the Promenade de Croisette on top of a series of tanks followed by interviews with every broadcaster, TV channel, YouTuber and social media influencer that wanted one. But three weeks away from release a high-quality pirate copy of the full movie leaked out onto DVD and online. It was downloaded more than 189,000 times in the first 24 hours and it was estimated that it totalled at 2 million illegal downloads. Film distributors Lionsgate promptly filed lawsuits against ten websites with torrent download facilities (In March 2016, a California court fined all the offending websites nearly $200,000 dollars each but since most had shut down and gone offline, Lionsgate would never see that money). On official release, *The Expendables 3* out-did its two predecessors at the start and then tailed off dramatically in the US market finishing on just under $40 million dollars on its near $100 million dollar budget. But overseas it did much better, as was traditional in this franchise, and grossed $238 million in total making it possible to think about extending the franchise beyond the trilogy.

When looked at as the third film in a series, it probably ranks in the middle. The first film was pure novelty and was hamstrung by a tentative budget and simplistic plotting, while the second one had a more focussed narrative and included the fantasy-fulfillment of Stallone, Arnie and Willis in action together. This next film tried to do too much and while it crowbars in far too many in-jokes and meta references, it still doesn't distract from the very formulaic plot and pedestrian and overlong action sequences. The Stallone and Gibson face-off is a highlight but by the end of it all, it starts to feel like the final episode of a long-running sitcom where guest stars are the only trick the writers have left up their sleeves. But something that was perhaps missed by the thousands of journalists who used tired quips and age-related puns to put down the franchise in print and online, was the generosity of *The Expendables* front-man. After the surprise success of *Rocky Balboa* in 2006 and *Rambo* in 2008, Stallone had regained the power to get an $80 million dollar action picture off the ground and he used that position to offer a helping hand to many of his friends, former co-stars and past-rivals. Obviously Schwarzenegger, Willis and Ford were doing just fine but many of the others could not have needed that life-line more. Dolph Lundgren had not appeared in anything but straight-to-DVD films for a decade and the same was true of Jean-Claude Van Damme. Chuck Norris came out of semi-retirement for his cameo in *The Expendables 2* while Wesley Snipes came out of prison for *The Expendables 3*. And there was the prickly matter of Mel Gibson. The star of the hugely popular *Mad Max* and *Lethal Weapon* series and the multi-Oscar winning *Braveheart* that he also produced and directed, had fallen from grace spectacularly in 2006 with a recorded outburst of hatred and anger when he was arrested for drink driving. Allegations of spousal abuse surfaced not long after but his rehabilitation olive-branch came from Stallone and *The Expendables 3*. Stallone could have created another solo action project and left everyone else in his wake but he chose to send the lift back down and give performers that he'd either helped once before or paved the way for, a chance to shine on the big-screen again and maybe salvage a second shot at a movie career. And imagine how significant the experience would have been for up and coming actors like Glen Powell, Liam Hemsworth (in *The Expendables 2*) and Ronda Rousey (who got her role in the *Fast and Furious* franchise thanks to her *Expendables 3* casting) who could study, watch and learn from household names who had either seen their star fizzle or had kept it burning bright. It can't be a coincidence that Glen Powell is now one of the biggest draws at the movies after he immersed himself in learning from the very best; Stallone and then Tom Cruise.

But, and to paraphrase Robert DeNiro in *Heat*, there's also a flip side to that coin. Sometimes Stallone would help his friends on one of their projects and things wouldn't turn out quite so well. John Herzveld and Stallone were roommates at the University of Miami where the two shared similar ambitions to be creative talents behind and in front of the camera. The pair cobbled $1000 dollars together in 1969 to start filming a silent Western called *Horses*, that they had written. It was a silent film because they couldn't afford to add sound. The strange plot saw them play a cowboy and a native American who were hanged but are then somehow resurrected in modern day USA. The sheriff responsible for their hanging is also brought back to life and tracks them both down and shoots them dead again. The sheriff was played by Stallone's father, Frank Sr. and Stallone would later say that he felt his father had taken a little too much pleasure in shooting him. Although they sporadically filmed *Horses* between 1969 and 1971, it was never completed and never released. Fast forward to the late-80's when Stallone was now the biggest star in the world and he had given his friend a small role in *Cobra* in 1986. But that had come three years after Herzveld's feature film directorial debut with the re-teaming of *Grease* co-stars Olivia Newton-John and John Travolta in *Two of a Kind*. Herzveld had also written the screenplay but the romantic comedy was an unmitigated disaster at the box office and the star pairing never shared the screen again. Herzveld wrote and directed again in 1996 in the crime thriller *2 Days in the Valley* starring Danny Aiello and Jeff Daniels and giving a first screen role to Charlize Theron. The sub-Tarantino effort also failed, but not to be deterred he returned to writing and directing in 2001 with the Robert DeNiro and Edward Burns action thriller *15 Minutes* which again, didn't make a positive impression. But in 2014, he'd written *Reach Me* and wanted to make that his next release.

The premise of the drama was about a diverse group of people who find themselves inspired by a self-help book from an illusive author. It was an attempt to reproduce the success of the 2004 Oscar-winning drama *Crash* from filmmaker Paul Haggis where seemingly unconnected characters are drawn together as the drama reaches its conclusion. Stallone agreed to play Gerald, a newspaper editor who sends journalist Roger (Kevin Connolly) out to find the book's mysterious writer. Gerald was a bit of a departure for Stallone as he was a cerebral character prone to emotional monologues and included scenes where he could be seen on screen indulging in his real-life passion for abstract painting. And as soon as Herzveld could announce Stallone's involvement, the casting became a much smoother process. Terry Crews and Stallone had bonded through the three *Expendables* films and he took a role in *Reach Me* as did Kelsey Grammar who'd filled an important hole in *The Expendables 3*. Other former co-stars that took up the offer to join a new Stallone project included Tom Sizemore (from *Lock Up*) and Tom Berenger (from *D-Tox*). 12-year old Scarlet Stallone made her acting debut in the film and was given a small amount of dialogue to ensure it helped her towards getting her Screen Actors Guild membership card. After principal photography had started in California, one major investor pulled out forcing Herzfeld to start an online Kickstarter page for more funding. Soon they withdrew that campaign and switched to similar funding platform Indiegogo where they eventually scraped together another $175 thousand to complete the $5 million dollar budget. The film had a close to zero cinematic release and went to DVD almost instantly in November of 2014 and to date it has grossed just under $100 thousand dollars in total. *Reach Me* unfortunately comes across as a self-indulgent mess where we are expected to feel sorry for a series of characters who live rather insular, self-obsessive existences. No one is particularly bad in their roles and the direction is solid but it doesn't come close to the life-affirming impact that it thinks it does. Stallone pops in and out of the movie that steadily becomes frustrating and tedious and even though it's only 95 minutes long, it feels like much more editing was required. As ever, no one sets out to make a poor film but *Reach Me* did not reach anyone.

Stallone was now just a few years away from his landmark 70th birthday yet he was still carrying the weight of responsibility on his shoulders for big movie releases. Some he instigated himself, some he was drawn to and some he did for friendship but after nearly forty years as a Hollywood superstar, he remained a major force in the industry. It was almost unheard of and he could be forgiven for wanting to rest on his laurels. But just around the corner, someone else was going to create something magical for him and this idea would lead to an invite back to the inner circle of the Academy Awards.

CREED (2015)

YOUR LEGACY IS MORE THAN A NAME

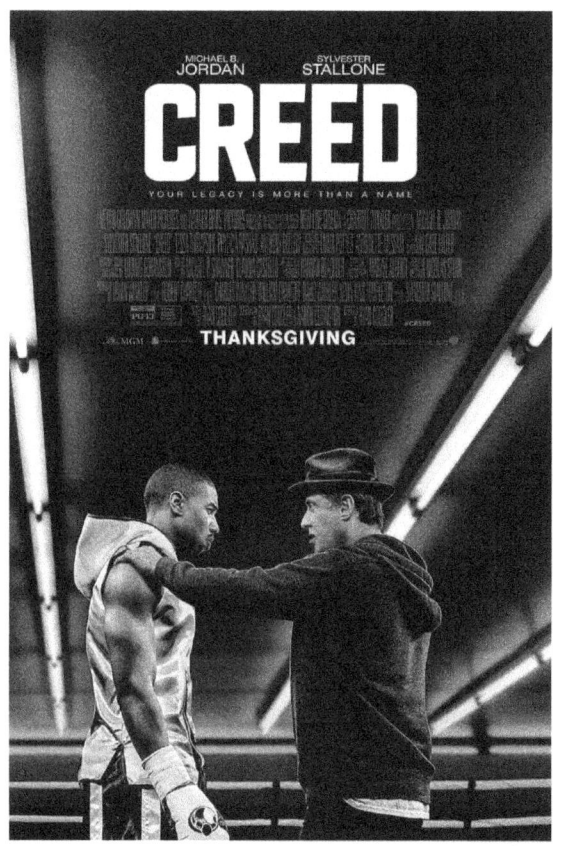

Starring - Michael B. Jordan, Sylvester Stallone, Tessa Thompson, Phylicia Rashad, Tony Bellew
Written by - Ryan Coogler, Aaron Covington, Sylvester Stallone
Original Score - Ludwig Göransson
Directed by - Ryan Coogler

The gentle strings that accompany the original *Rocky* end credits (called *Rocky's Reward*) also ended the pitch-perfect *Rocky Balboa* in 2006 and was one of many full circle moments that made the 6th and final *Rocky* story so satisfying. Stallone had now hung up his hat and coat and put to bed any lingering regrets that had haunted him since the mishandled *Rocky V*. He was now about to complete his fourth decade as an instantly recognisable superstar in cinema with all the highs and lows that that rarity entailed and as far as he was concerned both his Rocky and Rambo characters were now behind him. But unbeknownst to him a burgeoning, young cinematic partnership was fantasising about the world and the characters that inhabited the Balboa universe.

In 2013, the directorial debut of Ryan Coogler was the powerful *Fruitvale Station*. The true story depicted the final day of 22-year old Oscar Grant, who was shot and killed in 2009 by Bay Area Rapid Transit (BART) police officer Johannes Mehserle at the Fruitvale district BART station in Oakland, California. The impressive young actor playing the tragic lead role was Michael B. Jordan who had previously garnered favourable reviews for his part among the large cast of the NBC TV sports drama *Friday Night Lights* . As Coogler and Jordan bonded during production they had already discovered a mutual love of the Rocky saga. Idle conversation before a single shot had been filmed on *Fruitvale Station* quickly turned to writing notes which turned into fleshing out a story. Their basic hook was not about Rocky Balboa himself but the fascinating character of Apollo Creed. Carl Weathers larger than life portrayal of Creed had struck a chord with the duo. This coincided with MGM's wish to somehow extend the life (and money making potential) of one of their most popular properties. Coogler and friend Aaron Covington approached Stallone with an idea and the star was intrigued. He had lamented in later years that he sometimes wished he hadn't killed off the character of Apollo Creed in *Rocky IV*. He accepted that the shocking moment had worked brilliantly in terms of the film itself, but it meant that the world was denied seeing Weathers as Creed ever again and the two subsequent movies after *Rocky IV* could have explored Creed's advancing years alongside his best friend Rocky. But Coogler, Covington and Jordan had a master plan. Even in the original *Rocky*, Apollo had kids. And who was to say he hadn't fathered a few more in his heyday? What if his estranged son wanted to find out more about his late father and learn to box properly? And what if he turned to his late father's foe-turned-friend, for help?

Between the three writers, the plot of *Creed* was fleshed out. All three were keen for it to retain much of the emotion of a Rocky film but for it to feel like its own beast. This wasn't a Rocky Balboa story, this was a story that featured Rocky Balboa. Jordan hit the gym and the sparring partners and built himself up enough to convince as a heavyweight (actually light-heavyweight in this film) contender. The story would see Adonis Creed trying to forge a path as a boxer in Los Angeles, but without using his father's famous surname. Frustration and brushes with the law see him decide to find out more about what is making him so unfulfilled and angry inside. He goes to Philadelphia to seek out the first man who ever beat his father in the ring (the second man killed him, but we will get to that in *Creed II*).

After some mistrust, some doubts and some reluctance, Rocky agrees to train Adonis. Rocky is in a content if not spectacular stage in his life. He's focused on running his Italian restaurant and had all but left the fight game behind. As you would expect, the partnership bears fruit and soon Adonis is offered a shot at the title against Ricky Conlan (real-life fighter Tony Bellew from Liverpool, England who was the WBC Cruiserweight champion from 2016 to 2017). Conlan insists that Adonis uses his real name to add some punch to the ticket sales. Adonis has not only come to terms with family legacy and is helping Rocky through cancer treatment, but he has found love in Philadelphia too in the form of Bianca (Tessa Thompson) who is a talented musician with progressive hearing loss.

As you would hope, it culminates in a battle royal in the ring which was filmed at Goodison Park, the home of Everton Football Club in England. For several weeks, the film crew would run onto the pitch with multiple cameras at halftime of Everton home matches to capture large crowd shots. A ring was constructed on the pitch when matches weren't imminent, to film much of the big fight on location. It also led to more than a few weeks of bemused faces at Goodison Park when it was noticed that Rambo was sitting in the posh seats. Bill Conti didn't return to score *Creed*, but his enduring legacy was present when it was most needed. Swedish composer Ludwig Göransson had supplied the haunting music for *Fruitvale Station* and Coogler approached him again to create brand new themes for *Creed* whilst retaining the flavour of Conti's work. (The pair would work together again on *Black Panther* which would win Goransson the Oscar for Best Score. He also wrote the infectious theme for the *Star Wars* spin-off, *The Mandalorian)* But at some point worlds had to collide and aside from a pulsating training montage, the big punch the air moment musically occurs near the end of the big fight. Rocky gives Adonis the motivational talk of his life, aligning the fight in the ring with his fight against cancer. Adonis sucks in a final deep breath, stands up for the final round and the Rocky fanfare raises the roof and more than a few goosebumps on the back of your neck. It's the moment of the film and it's that moment that propelled the film towards more than $170 million dollars at the box office. It was a good year for legacy sequels as *Jurassic World* was the second biggest movie in the world behind *Star Wars - The Force Awakens*.

But aside from the box office returns that exceeded expectations, this proved to be the year that critics finally decided to invite Stallone to their elitist parties again. For the first time since *Rocky* in 1976, Stallone was part of awards season and was walking red carpets as a nominee. He won the Golden Globe for Best Supporting Actor (which you should watch the clip of on YouTube to see the sheer glee on the faces of all the superstars in the room who seem as enamored with Sly and Rocky as us mere mortals are) and he was Oscar nominated in the same category. But as the Academy Awards so often seem to, they didn't read the script. Stallone lost to Mark Rylance for his work in *Bridge of Spies* and even without a Stallone-fan hat on, that was a bit of a travesty. Rylance is a fine actor and his subtle performance in Spielberg's latest Tom Hanks collaboration was very good but all bias aside, Stallone was never better as Rocky than he was in *Creed*. The nuance and pathos of having lived Balboa's life for 40 years coupled with an actor's complete understanding of the role led to a performance of raw emotion and it seems unthinkable that Oscar didn't finally come knocking. Nominated alongside Stallone and Rylance for the award were Christain Bale for *The Big Short*, Tom Hardy for *The Revenant* and Mark Ruffalo for *Spotlight*. None of those nominees didn't deserve to be there and you could probably make a case for each of them winning but Stallone was extraordinary in *Creed*. It was an ego-free depiction of the sunset years of a fighter who once had everything and has slowly seen all that he loved vanish from his world. And now he faced his biggest fight of all against a disease ravaging his body as he tried to help the lost son of a man he felt he let down. And unless something extraordinary comes out of the woodwork in the next few years, it now seems that his *Creed* performance was his last shot at winning an Academy Award for acting.

As we now prepare to look ahead to the projects that we are yet to talk about in this book, it is just worth considering that his turn as Rocky in the first *Creed* is also his last excellent performance. Or should I rephrase that? It was the last time he was required to give an excellent performance. *Creed II* inevitably lay ahead but it didn't recapture the magic and it suffered from trying to run before it could walk (up the steps). With advancing age and without the need to work too much, you can understand why Stallone hasn't gone to dark places to produce a noteworthy performance since *Creed*. In fact it's his TV work in *Tulsa King* that is his best stuff since 2015. More on that later and perhaps we shouldn't lament what followed his work in *Creed* but be grateful we have this performance to watch and be enthralled and moved by, again and again.

2016 - 2018 - RATCHET AND CLANK, GUARDIANS OF THE GALAXY VOL 2, ANIMAL CRACKERS, ESCAPE PLAN 2: HADES

For these next few years, Stallone took a break from working on writing scripts that he would star in or direct. He had three young daughters (more on them later) and was content to take a backseat when it came to Hollywood for a while. His voice roles in *Ratchet and Clank* and *Animal Crackers* probably amounted to little more than two days' work for Stallone. His voice is so recognisable that getting someone else to try and sound like him would come across as a cheap parody, so you may as well try and get the real thing. The first one, *Ratchet and Clank* is an animated movie adaptation of a popular video game although Stallone's role, Victor Von Ion, is an original character created just for the film and so that older viewers could nudge their partners and whisper "isn't that Sylvester Stallone?". He is in good company in the cast list however as also lending their voices are Paul Giamatti, John Goodman, Bella Thorne and Rosario Dawson. Released in 2016, the film went mostly unnoticed, the reviews were poor and eventually it lost money, making only $14 million dollars against its $20 million dollar budget. *Animal Crackers* came out the following year and is based on the biscuit/cookie of the same name combined with an imaginative graphic novel by Scott Christian Sava who also directed the film. And like *Ratchet and Clank*, it's a cast list that any live-action producer would envy, including golden couple Emily Blunt and John Krasinski plus Danny DeVito and Sir Ian McKellen. Stallone's character is Bulletman who only says his name until the end of the movie (think of the character Groot who only ever says "I am Groot" in the *Guardians of the Galaxy* series). This one received more positive notices from critics but again lost its maker's money, stirring up only $14 million of its $17 million production cost.

So speaking of *Guardians of the Galaxy*, this is where Stallone enters the world of superhero films. His 1993 critical and commercial hit *Demolition Man* plays like a comic book movie in many ways and of course his controversial take on the popular character *Judge Dredd* went down poorly with devotees of those gritty comics. But his role in *Guardians of the Galaxy Vol. 2* was him stepping into a mammoth, commercial, superhero entity. The 2017 blockbuster was at the height of the powers of the Marvel Cinematic Universe. Since Robert Downey Jnr and director John Favreau propelled *Iron Man* into a huge hit in 2008, the MCU grew beyond anyone's planning. Film after film introduced characters from the Marvel backlog with a mix of wit, ambition and self-awareness. 2008 was also the year that Christopher Nolan presented the first of his exceptional Batman trilogy, with *Batman Begins*. The first *Guardians of the Galaxy* adventure was a massive hit in 2014 but it had also been a massive risk at the time. In the MCU up to that point, there had only been fairly sure-fire money-makers with two *Thor* films, two *Captain America* films, two *Iron Man* sequels and the first big team-up of *The Avengers*. (there was also *The Incredible Hulk* in 2008 with Edward Norton, but that has been largely erased from the data banks). GOTG was a very different proposition. This was sending the MCU into another galaxy with talking tree's, sarcastic raccoons and green-skinned love interests. The lead role of Peter 'Starlord' Quill was to be played by Chris Pratt who at that point was known only as being a funny, but lazy sitcom character on TV's *Parks and Recreation*. None of *The Avengers* would be turning up and it would add a much more risque sense of humour into the equation. The MCU needn't have concerned itself, it ended up as the third highest grossing film in the world in that year raking in more than $770 million dollars, more than a healthy return on the $200 million dollar investment. As Stallone knows only too well though, a hit in Hollywood means only one thing. Do it again.

Guardians of the Galaxy Vol. 2 was quickly announced and the original's writer and director James Gunn was going to be in full control of this one too. Pratt and other members of the core group would return which meant Zoe Saldana, Karen Gillan, Michael Rooker and Dave Bautista plus the voice work of Vin Diesel and Bradley Cooper. French actress Pom Klementieff was added to the group as Mantis and there was to also be a reunion of *Tango and Cash*. Kurt Russell was signed up to play the character called Ego, who is sort-of Peter Quill's father and is essentially the film's big bad guy. Stallone was asked to join the film in what is really an extended cameo as Stakar Ogord, leader of The Ravagers who are 'lovable' smugglers and thieves. The role also presented a *Cliffhanger* reunion between Stallone and Michael Rooker. Stallone's role as Ogord was hinted as becoming a recurring character in future MCU productions. But in what has been a frustrating trend for MCU films since, characters that are introduced and teased often never materialise again leaving a feeling of being slightly short-changed. There was even talk of a *Ravagers* spin-off movie or TV series but again, the MCU moved on and never made good on those half-promises. The film was released in 2017 and despite the reviews not being as overwhelmingly positive as the first film, the accountants at Marvel must have been delirious as it brought in $100 million more than Vol. 1 had made. This was pre-pandemic levels of cinema where the top grossing film of the year was *Star Wars Episode 8 - The Last Jedi* which made an eye-popping $1.3 billion dollars.

In the same year though, there was another Stallone sequel, *Escape Plan 2 : Hades*. This film is very much the *Grease 2* of the *Escape Plan* franchise. In the 80's and 90's, direct-to-DVD sequels would go ahead even though the original cast members would rarely appear. Sequelitis is a condition that doesn't often need the original stars to be involved. Just using the title of a hit plus the number 2 can often be enough for a movie studio to back a second film although they rarely produce a good movie. For example: *Jingle All The Way 2* (without Arnie), *Ace Ventura Pet Detective Jr* (zero Jim Carrey), *Basic Instinct 2* (without Michael Douglas but with a very confused but presumably well-paid Sharon Stone), *Kindergarten Cop 2* (Arnie replaced with Dolph Lungren), *Teen Wolf 2* (bye bye expensive Michael J. Fox and hello cheaper-at-the-time Jason Bateman), *Backdraft 2, Splash 2, Roadhouse* 2 and *The Great Escape 2* and my favourite when considering what happened at the end of the original film - *Titanic 2*.

Movie deals are more often than not complicated, labyrinth-like legal minefields. Deals that involve the use of an identifiable character will often have clauses in them that compel the rights holder to use the character in another movie within a certain time frame or the rights revert back to the original creators. Often there are tax breaks and bonuses for the financiers if a film produces sequels in some capacity. The lead actors may have deals where their overall pay packet is reliant on a sequel being made even before the original film is completed and released. A film sequel or original film may often be part of a larger deal between star and studio. But sometimes a deal like that, which may seem cynical at the time, can turn out to be inspired. In 1997 Bruce Willis had started work on what was described at the time as his *Jerry Maguire*. The film *Broadway Brawler* would centre on baseball and it was a project that Willis himself had willed into existence. However, a few weeks into filming the relationship between star, producer and director irrevocably broke down and the whole project was abandoned. It meant that $20 million dollars of Disney money went down the drain and Willis was soon presented with a $17 million dollar damages lawsuit as a result. Rather than face court and potentially have to pay more than that amount to Disney, Willis and the Mouse-House came to an understanding. In return for dropping the legal action, Willis would agree to star in three movies for Disney with a hugely reduced salary. Those three movies turned out to be the family comedy *The Kid* and also two of Willis' biggest hits, *Armageddon* and *The Sixth Sense*.

And sometimes a star is contractually obliged to be in a film, and all it's just a bit naff. Case in point: *Escape Plan 2 : Hades*. Directed by Steven Miller, this sequel was a straight to streaming affair. In the 80's it was damningly known as 'straight-to-video', then technological advances meant that soon became 'straight-to-DVD' and now we have 'straight-to-streaming'. The inference being that no-one involved in the film believes it is strong enough or good enough to spend the money putting it into cinema's. This sequel to the entertaining original is more centered around the new character of Shu (Huang Xiaoming) who is sent to a new prison called Hades.

Stallone is back as Ray Breslin but is on the periphery of the plot until the final third. His *Guardians of the Galaxy Vol. 2* co-star Dave Bautista is brought in as the charismatic action hero type to replace the now departed Arnold Schwarzenegger. The comparatively small budget of $20 million dollars wasn't recouped. It made only $17 million dollars on limited cinematic release in parts of Asia and Russia. I could try and review it for you but the image of the movie you probably have in your head is exactly the movie, *Escape Plan 2: Hades*. But really, the movie served as a distraction for Stallone because the final return of Rocky Balboa was imminent.

CREED II (2018)

YOU CAN'T RUN FROM YOUR PAST

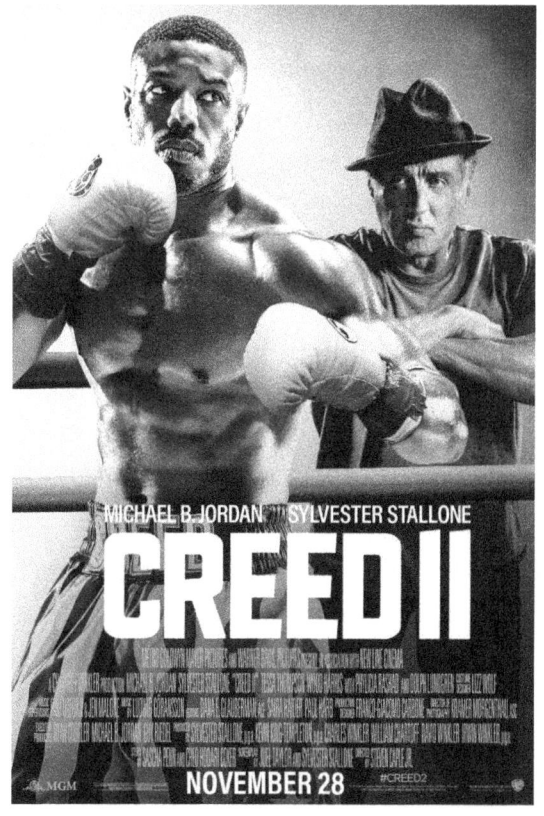

Starring - Michael B. Jordan, Sylvester Stallone, Tessa Thompson, Dolph Lundgren, Philicia Rashad
Written by - Juel Taylor, Sylvester Stallone, Sascha Penn, Cheo Hodari Coker
Original Score - Ludwig Göransson
Directed by - Steven Caple Jr.

Creed was a hit on every barometer that a film can be judged. Critically it was praised, financially it reaped millions and it was a significant part of awards season, so the follow-up wasn't just possible, it was unavoidable. On January the 5th, 2016 the first official statement of intent came from MGM and soon after that Stallone was positing the idea of Milo Ventimiglia reprising his role of Rocky's son Robert from 2006's *Rocky Balboa*. Michael B Jordan and Tessa Thompson had been keen on getting the sequel to *Creed* greenlit as soon as the first film found its audience and director Ryan Coogler was also a part of the push for *Creed II* but by the end of January of 2016 he had already pulled out of directing duties as he was taking on the vast task of putting Marvel's *Black Panther* on the big screen. The immense production was also going to include Michael B Jordan in the role of the bad guy, Killmonger, which meant *Creed II* was going to have to wait. In January of 2017, *Black Panther* commenced filming but Stallone was also hard at work on the story for *Creed II* which he was, at that point, now going to direct himself. Possible ideas for the film included a time-hopping narrative that could include Carl Weathers returning to play Apollo Creed in some capacity. One idea that stuck however was having Adonis Creed face a fighter who had some emotional connection to the Creed family. The son of Clubber Lang (Mr T) from *Rocky III* was briefly flirted with but there was really only one, glaring story idea and it virtually wrote itself; Adonis Creed fights the son of the man who killed his father. *Rocky IV*'s enduring legacy meant that the image of Dolph Lundgren as Ivan Drago was part of cinema folklore and with Stallone and Lundgren rekindling their working relationship over three Expendables movies, the option of bringing Drago back was too tempting to pass up. But while that masterplan was percolating, Stallone decided he didn't want to direct *Creed II* after all so that he could focus on his performance when filming began, as he was following-up an Oscar-nominated turn in *Creed*. Ryan Coogler suggested Steven Caple Jr after the young Cleveland-born director had impressed with his debut feature *The Land* in 2016 which centered around four Ohio teenagers pursuing their dreams of professional skateboarding. Caple jumped at the opportunity and brought in his friend from his film school days Juel Taylor who quickly went from odd jobs on various film sets to sitting with Sylvester Stallone to script *Creed II*. Once hired, Taylor and Stallone would send redrafts to each other along with additional writing help from Sascha Penn and Marvel TV show *Luke Cage* showrunner Cheo Hodari Coker, who were both also Coogler recommendations.

Word soon got out that the next *Creed* film was on the horizon and that Ivan Drago was going to be a part of it which meant the search was on to find a suitably menacing actor to play the son of the Russian fighter. Caple, Stallone, Coogler and producer Irwin Winkler looked at thousands of possible Viktor Drago's - talking to actors, athletes, bodybuilders and boxers and looked at many who lobbied for the part themselves such as UFC fighter Sage Northcutt who was one of a number who made his interest public via social media. But while searching through hundreds of training videos online, Stallone came across 6 foot 4 inch (193cm) Romanian Florian Munteanu. Munteanu had grown up in Bavaria and Munich and appeared in his first film role in 2016 in a German-Romanian movie called *Bogat*. Crucially he was also a boxer and fought under the name of Big Nasty and Stallone got in touch. The pair had a one-hour meeting on Skype and by the end of it, he was cast. Phylicia Rashad, Wood Harris and Andre Ward all returned to their roles from the first film and were joined by Russell Hornsby who was to play the boxing promoter Buddy Marcelle who pulls the big fight together. While Carl Weathers wasn't required for any new work as Apollo Creed, he was going to be a constant presence in the film and footage of his work from *Rocky* to *Rocky IV* would be recycled. While *Creed II* is clearly the second film in the *Creed* franchise, it could be argued that it is really a direct sequel to *Rocky IV*. After being beaten by Rocky in Moscow in 1985, Ivan Drago has been shunned in Russia ever since and his only focus now is ensuring his son Viktor has what it takes to be a champion in the ring. The inevitable fight between the son of Drago and the son of Apollo Creed leads to a technical victory for Adonis Creed but only after suffering a serious beating. Rocky has refused to train Adonis, fearing that another Drago would kill another Creed in the ring on his watch. After Bianca gives birth to their daughter, Adonis accepts a rematch with Viktor in Moscow. This time Rocky is back in his corner and the final bout goes the way of the titular character. While *Rocky IV* was a product of 80's excess, *Creed II* would be a much more grounded film where Ivan Drago is bitter and vengeful even after nearly 40 years since Rocky beat him. The scenes between Stallone and Lundgren would be a highlight with Drago wanting revenge while Rocky wants to leave the past in the past. Filming began in March of 2018 in Philadelphia for ten weeks with additional scenes shot in New Mexico in early June. For Michael B Jordan to creditably be able to stand toe to toe with Munteanu, he underwent a training regime more intense than for *Creed*. He gained 25 lbs and looked noticeably bigger than in the first film but Munteanu was still required to shed some weight in return. He lost 20 lbs but was still 25 lbs heavier than Jordan overall at 225 lbs in total. Milo Ventimiglia did reprise his role as Robert Balboa for the first time in 12 years, for one short scene at the end of the film where

Rocky goes to reconnect with his estranged son and finds out he is now a grandfather too. The pair had actually worked together in 2017 as Stallone had accepted a guest starring role in an episode of Ventimiglia's hit NBC TV show *This Is Us*. He played himself, offering life advice on a movie set to Justin Hartley's character Kevin Pearson, an actor who quite rightly holds Stallone in high regard.

It was during the latter weeks of filming that another bit of surprise casting became public knowledge. Ex-Mrs Stallone, Brigitte Nielsen reprised her role of Ludmilla, the now ex-wife of Ivan Drago and mother of Viktor. Nielsen was 54 and seven months pregnant when she shot her scenes but digital technology and careful filming hid the bump as she portrayed a still cold-hearted Ludmilla who has no respect for her former husband and little interest in her son. In real life, Nielsen and her former husband saw each other on set and she later described the experience of working with Stallone again as both 'amazing' and very 'professional'. As filming neared the end, Stallone posted a video of himself delivering an emotional farewell to the cast and crew after what seemed to be generally regarded as his final scene and the final time he would play the character he had created in 1970's.

Ludwig Goransson returned to score the movie although rumours had surfaced that *Rocky IV* composer Vince DiCola was going to be asked despite not having scored a film since 1986's *The Transformers: The Movie*. Two soundtrack albums would be released for *Creed II;* one featuring the orchestrations of Goransson and another that was overseen and mostly written by hip hop and pop producer Mike Will Made It (real name Michael Len Williams II). Both albums were released on November the 16th 2018, five days before the film itself went on general release. Goransson is restrained throughout the movie and only delivers subtle nods to Conti's score when Rocky is back at Adrian's grave or talking about his colourful history. The training sequences are accompanied by an urban sound aesthetic, with Mike Will Made It's productions used as the main focus. In the climatic bout however, we are treated to a full-throated blast of the Rocky fanfare and sections of Bill Conti's "Conquest" that were used for the final fights in *Rocky II* and *Rocky III*.

Costing an impressively low $50 million dollars to make, *Creed II* made $35 million on its opening weekend, outdoing the first films' opening of $29 million. It went on to gross $213 million dollars worldwide which was again, better business than *Creed* had done. (the years' top film was *Avengers: Infinity War* which grossed over $2 billion dollars, with Ryan Coogler's *Black Panther* pulling in $1.3 billion).

Creed II is a worthy follow-up to the first effort and critics were generally kind in their reviews, pointing out the rarity of a non-superhero, mid-budget film being released into cinemas. Stallone's final appearance as Rocky Balboa didn't lead to awards chatter again however and there were some criticisms of the handling of the potential of Drago's return. Aside from one conversation face-to-face at Rocky's restaurant, the rematch of Ivan and Rocky isn't as powerful as it should be. A brief fist fight between the pair at a hospital was filmed, but cut out of the final edit of the film and there is the sensation that perhaps letting the franchise plough its own path for *Creed II* would have been a wiser choice rather than forcing the Drago return into film two. It also doesn't help that by incorporating *Rocky IV* into the DNA of *Creed II*, you are opening yourself up to inevitable, unfavourable comparisons to the intensity and sheer entertainment of the 1985 film. Florian Munteanu is an imposing figure and Creed's fear of facing him is well realised but while Ivan Drago was a hissable villain in *Rocky IV,* Viktor Drago is written as a more misunderstood, sympathetic character so it becomes harder to enjoy his failure to win the final battle. And in general, if you haven't seen *Rocky IV,* watching *Creed II* could be a curiously hollow experience for the most part. Fortunately and maybe wisely, millions of film fans know and love *Rocky IV* and the pre-publicity and success of *Creed II* relied heavily on that emotional connection to the 1985 hit. *Creed II* also did what it needed to do in terms of establishing the franchise could live on after the first film and its increased profits from the original meant that *Creed III* would be a matter of when and not if.

But next for Stallone was an unexpected chance to say farewell to his other, most famous incarnation. Rocky was now fully behind him but he'd never said a definitive goodbye to John Rambo and had always left the door open. Eleven years after *Rambo* had caused carnage in Burma, we last saw him walking on home soil for the first time since 1982. So for Rambo's last stand, it was going to be back in the United States where he'd originally caused a bit of a stir.

RAMBO: LAST BLOOD (2019)

THEY DREW FIRST BLOOD, HE WILL DRAW LAST

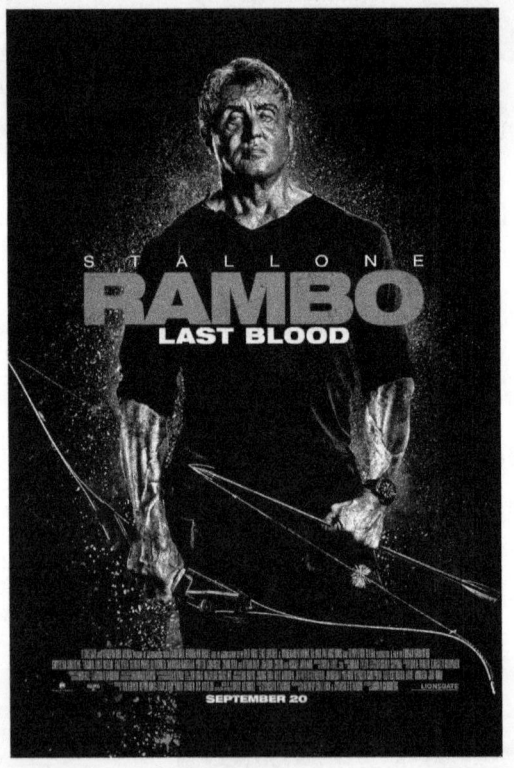

Starring - Sylvester Stallone, Paz Vega, Sergio Peris-Mencheta, Adrianna Barraza
Written by - Sylvester Stallone, Matthew Cirulnick and Dan Gordon
Original Score by - Brian Tyler
Directed by - Adrian Grunberg

Creed II was (at time of writing this book) the swansong of Rocky Balboa on the big screen. And while the movie had its positives and negatives it did give the character a few, well staged moments to say goodbye to the audience. The Rocky we see visit his estranged son and meet his grandson is the Rocky we saw in 1976 plus all the weight of what's happened since. His boxers' last real victory lap, in 2006's *Rocky Balboa*, saw him return to the role after a 16-year gap but made it look like he'd never stopped, such was the total embodiment of the role. But when it comes to the last chapter of John Rambo, the lead character in *Rambo: Last Blood* should have been given a completely different name. Of every film in this huge filmography, this is the one that boils the blood.

The well documented mis-fires like *Stop Or My Mom Will Shoot, Rhinestone* and *Paradise Alley* were just films that didn't turn out well. Good intentions were there and for various reasons and certainly not on purpose, they failed to reach their best potential. Just over 10 years before, 2008's *Rambo* had done what *Rocky Balboa* had done two years before it. It had been far better than it needed to be (or was expected to be) and while it wasn't a huge box office smash like its predecessors it had left everyone involved walking away with their heads held high. At the end of *Rambo* we see our hero returning to the United States for the first time since 1982, walking along a dirt road and past a mailbox with his surname on it as he returned to his family's farm in Arizona. It was a fitting, melancholic send-off set to the instrumental version of Jerry Goldsmith's *First Blood* theme called *It's a Long Road*. As with all things in Hollywood though, a money-making property is never really deceased when there's the slightest possibility of more income. Studio's (now more than ever) will try to resurrect any property, character or title that proved profitable at least once before. Prequel rumours began to spring up after 2008's *Rambo* with choices such as Ryan Gosling and Jason Momoa muted as portraying John Rambo back in his army days and Stallone himself wrote on social media about a 'Young Rambo' outline. Another angle for re-starting the franchise that was muted saw Rambo heading back to those chilly mountains of the Pacific Northwest from *First Blood* but this time he would be battling some almost mythical creature in a *Predator*-style hunting thriller that was to be titled *Rambo: The Savage Hunt*. Other announcements included a 2011 story from writer Sean Hood that was called *Rambo: Last Stand* which would have very much taken the character back to his cinematic roots in small town America but when Stallone got *The Expendables* up and running, Hood's ideas were binned and the writer himself said he couldn't understand whether the producers wanted a standalone Rambo movie or a movie that would pass the torch onto a younger actor somehow. 2013 saw Entertainment One and Nu Image Films declare they were creating a Rambo live-action TV series with Stallone starring, but again, follow up announcements were absent. In 2015, Stallone and the original novel's author David Morrell worked together on a script that was described as soulful and emotional but the producers wanted to use another, earlier draft that was centered around human trafficking across the border with Mexico. At the same time, Stallone expressed an interest in an origin-story for Rambo again. He found the idea of him directing a younger actor as the new recruit in the Green Berets and how John Rambo was sculpted into a killing machine, fascinating. But producer Avi Lerner and Millennium Films, Dadi Films, Templeton Media and Campbell Grobman Films held the purse strings and wanted the Mexico angle to be used.

In 2018, *Rambo V* was officially declared as a going concern and it would see Rambo confronting a Mexican drug cartel following their abduction of a young woman he had raised as his own in the last ten years, with Stallone returning as director as well. By August of that year, Stallone was out of the directors chair and in came Adrian Grunberg, who would apply his native Mexican upbringing to the film's aesthetic. Grunburg however had only directed once before with the 2012 Mel Gibson thriller *Get The Gringo* that he also wrote. He was more known as a well-established 1st Assistant Director, working on other sequels including *Wall Street: Money Never Sleeps* and *Jack Reacher: Never Go Back*.

While the plot and casting was vague from the start, filming got underway on October the 2nd 2018 (a month later than originally planned) and then wrapped in December in Bulgaria mainly, with some footage shot in Tenerife. The studio Lionsgate took a first look at it in April and ordered reshoots of some scenes for May and June of 2019. A prologue where Rambo is wearing a cowboy hat and rescues a girl in a storm by horseback in the US, was used in some versions released but omitted from the US version. It was a sign that no-one could agree on the best version of the movie.

Plot wise, the film sees the titular character at his long-deceased father's ranch in Arizona where we left him at the end of the fourth film, 11-years prior. He now runs the ranch along with his friend Maria (Adriana Barraza) and her granddaughter Gabriela (Yvette Monreal), with whom Rambo has developed a patriarchal bond. When Gabriela runs away over the border to find her real estranged father, she is kidnapped and sex-trafficked and it's left to Rambo to try and get her back. After bloody (really, really bloody) battles with various Mexican crime stereotypes, Gabriela dies and all Rambo can do is lure the bad guys to his ranch in the US, where he has constructed an elaborate series of tunnels similar to the ones used by the Viet Cong. He proceeds to hunt, maim, kill, slice, dice and chop up every bag guy and even manages to rip out the heart of the main bossman Hugo (Sergio Peris-Mencheta). Yes, he literally rips his heart out.

Yvette Monreal has the relentlessly bleak acting job of being sex trafficked, tortured and then dying in front of John Rambo while her character's grandmother, played by Adriana Barraza, is simply pushed off screen for the final act and forgotten. Paz Vega plays Carmen Delgado whose role is to patch-up Rambo after a mid-film, near-death beating and he recovers fully in 4-days by simply lying on her sofa. Vega's character is also ejected from the final act and never referred to again. Oscar Jaenada and Sergio Peris-Mencheta portray the main villains of the piece but they are criminally one-dimensional so when they get their comeuppance, you feel nothing but meh. And the final shots can't decide whether to suggest Rambo is dying or he is going to fight another day and the ambiguity feels confused and rushed. In fact, a lot of the film feels disjointed and hastened and gives no one the time to breath and to be understood. The impression is that in a bid to be an 18-certificate, R-rated film, the filmmakers got so giddy about the squeamish possibilities that they edited out the time-consuming character work and were left with a soulless series of bloody murders.

When released, the buzz was quiet. This Rambo film was deemed as a step too far in an already fragile franchise and very inessential The movie ended up 61st in the top grossing films of 2019 in the US and Canada with a total of $44 million dollars. For comparison, *Avengers: Endgame* took $858 million dollars. Technically though, its in-built global audience for anything *Rambo* saw the movie turn a slight profit by the end of its run.

It would seem ridiculous to complain about the violence in a Rambo film. *First Blood* saw one onscreen death that was indirectly caused by John Rambo. In film two, he wipes out 75 human beings in front of our eyes and in *Rambo III* that number swells to 115. The fourth instalment is counted as 254 deaths due to Rambo's actions (a lot of them due to one, huge bomb that he set off in the course of the film). In this movie, it's back down to 46. So what's so bad about that? Isn't violence and death a bad thing whatever the context? Let's exclude *First Blood* from this argument for a moment as it stands alone as a grounded thriller that raises a lot of questions about how we treat the young people we send to war. Films two, three and four however are adult-fantasy adventures. As established from film two onwards, Rambo has become the embodiment of male wish-fulfillment and after all, these are entertainment movies and they are meant to be enjoyed for the outlandish spectacles that they are. There's death, there's blood and there's moments of some gore to titillate, but by the end of each film you can feel a bit cleansed of some dark thoughts you may have had and you've enjoyed a genuine superstar doing everything they can to raise your pulse a little and make you feel like we are all on the right side of our morals really. *Rambo: Last Blood* however is a nasty, vindictive, misogynist, exploitative and borderline racist film that would have been problematic in the late 80's, but in 2019 it's almost unforgivable. To create the motivation for Rambo to go on his torture-porn spree, it's decided to create a young female character who is then killed after suffering terrible abuse both physically and sexually and so, it crosses the line in terms of what an audience can write-off as acceptable motivation for a popcorn movie.

A scene almost halfway through the film sees him confront the Mexican cartel in their own backyard. We think he is about to go "all-Rambo" on them and that's what the audience wants and what the film should want, but no. Instead, Rambo is beaten and beaten and his cheek slashed with a cross and you can barely watch his distorted face by the end of the sequence. I'm sure the filmmakers would say it's realistic for his age and to show that even John Rambo is fallible and while that would have some validity, the way it's portrayed is just miserable and leaves a bitter taste in the mouth. And the final tunnel sequence where bodies are sliced open, eyes gouged out and worse (much worse) is wince-inducing. It's trying to be a full horror movie along the lines of the *Saw* franchise and there were many moments cut before release that depicted even more unpleasantness. The most damning critic of all was David Morrell, the author of the original *First Blood* story who said he hated the film and was embarrassed to be associated with it at all.

A counter argument again would perhaps be that had this level of cruel, onscreen violence been commonplace and feasible in the 1980s, wouldn't *Rambo: First Blood Part II* have looked and felt like this? And *Rambo III* perhaps more so? Yes, there are intentional squeamish moments in Rambo films: like sewing up his own arm injury in *First Blood* which spawned a thousand ill-judged playground games and lighting gunpowder on his own torso to seal a gaping wound in *Rambo III* isn't for the faint hearted, but it's about tone. It's about the unwritten agreement between the filmmakers and the audience: we will give you a thrill and some memorable moments to talk about at work tomorrow, but we know we are a Rambo film and you as the audience need to feel the justification for what our hero is doing, otherwise we can't go on this entertainment journey. If this was indeed the film that everyone set out to make, perhaps don't call it a Rambo film and instead call it *Old Serial Killer Lures Men to his Back Garden.*

One of the glaring indications that something isn't right is Stallone himself as, unlike his delayed returns to playing Rocky, he seems to have forgotten how to exude Rambo. The character is suddenly a conversationalist and his methods of extracting information have gone from being a towering figure of intimidation to now snapping a guy's collarbone with his hands after using a knife to get under his skin. Although he promoted the film and has never suggested his displeasure with the final product, Stallone really doesn't seem to know if he is supposed to be playing his Barney Ross from *The Expendables* or an unsophisticated copy of Liam Neeson in *Taken*. Either way, Rambo has left the building. There is no punch-the-air moment and there is no sense of achievement and a wrong put right. Rambo doesn't wear his trademark bandana, there is no reference to Colonel Trautman at all and you have no sensation that the lead character has been through *First Blood, Rambo: First Blood Part II, Rambo III* and *Rambo.*

Another misstep is the end credits where a classily produced collection of moments from all those previous Rambo films only serve to remind you of how good it had been before now. It does make you wonder if Stallone could somehow squeeze out one more Rambo film himself, to wash away the memory of this one.

2018 - 2022 - BACKTRACE, ESCAPE PLAN: THE EXTRACTORS, THE SUICIDE SQUAD, SAMARITAN

When crossing over into your 70's, any movie job could be seen as a blessing for a Hollywood star. As you get older, it's very common to adjust your work and life balance in favour of those closest to you and after nearly 45 years as one of the most well known humans in the world, you could forgive Stallone for wanting to take his foot off the gas and enjoy time away from the limelight at bit more. Good quality leading man roles and even action roles are hard to come by at the best of times (unless you write them yourself) but when you are a senior citizen the choice is severely limited. Not only are you not a first or second choice to head up a big budget project but the idea of being away from your family and friends for months on end becomes virtually unjustifiable. And to make it even less appealing, the movie business has become obsessed with only regurgitating and endlessly revamping old properties and is terrified of failure with something new and original. *Star Wars* and *Marvel* films were both once impregnable but when greedy executives and ravenous shareholders demanded more income the creatives were forced to flood the market with all kinds of spin-off shows and adjacent-films and inevitably, two things resulted; Firstly, the quality dipped as quantity became more important and secondly, the anticipation built up by making an audience wait was dissipated and diluted and they ended up cheapening the legacy of when it was considered excellent. So unless you present the experienced, savvy brain of Stallone with something unique and exciting, it's unlikely he will dedicate a large portion of his later life to your film. This explains *Backtrace*, which took 12 days to make.

Only the most dedicated Stallone nut would have even heard of this addition to his filmography as it went straight to streaming and made less than half a million dollars at the box office. The Mike Maples script was directed by Brian A Miller. The Los Angeles based filmmaker was carving out a tidy career making low budget, streaming-only thrillers and had already done four Bruce Willis efforts. The declining health condition of Bruce Willis wasn't public knowledge at this point but Miller was credited as one of the reasons he could keep working despite his increasing limitations. The plot of *Backtrace* involved an amnesiac who is being chased by various interested parties to find out where the results of bank robbery were left. Matthew Modine (whose long career includes *Full Metal Jacket, Memphis Belle* and *The Dark Knight Rises*) is the lead with Stallone as the detective trying to track him down and sort things out. Even with its $6 million budget it looks as if the nine production companies involved were slowly withdrawing their financial input every day of production. There's a lot of pointing guns at each other and reciting dramatic, toe-curling dialogue but it can't be considered offensive. It's as good and as bad as a straight-to-streaming, low budget thriller could be but there is the undeniable sense of disappointment that Stallone was involved in this level of production.

It is a similar sensation watching his next release which also avoided cinemas. *Escape Plan 3: The Extractors* was announced in 2017 when the second film was released and in actual fact filming overlapped with *Escape Plan 2: Hades* so much so that it was hinted, but not confirmed, that both sequels had been made pretty much at the same time. But instead of Steven C Miller in the directors chair it was Stallone's old friend John Herzveld who could turn his hand to pretty much any aspect of movie making. Herzveld had secured small roles in *Cobra* and *Reach Me* (and also directed and wrote the latter) and had been a confidante and private sounding board for Stallone for decades. Herzveld had written the screenplay with Miles Chapman who had had the solo writing credit on *Escape Plan 2: Hades*. Returning for the third film alongside Stallone were Dave Bautista, 50 Cent and Jaime King and new cast members included Max Zhang, Malese Jow and Devon Sawa for the movie that was originally called *Escape Plan 3: Devil's Station*. Ray Breslin again has to get into a maximum security prison only so he can break out again as part of a rescue attempt and cinema-nerds would recognise a lot of the prison interiors as the State Reformatory in Mansfield, Ohio was the same real-life setting that had been used for much of the filming of *The Shawshank Redemption*. The budget from the previous film was reduced down to $3.6 million dollars and apart from a short window of cinematic release in Australia and half a dozen European countries, the film was pushed straight onto streaming platforms with virtually no advertising spend. It received slightly better reviews than *Escape Plan 2: Hades* but in total it only made back half of its budget and that spelled the end for the *Escape Plan* franchise.

It is notably a better film than its predecessor but the character of Ray Breslin has gone from tough-only-when-he-needs-to-be in the original movie to a killing machine with no remorse. Perhaps the muscle memory of making *Rambo: Last Blood* the year before was harder to shake off than they thought. And let's not dwell on the frankly inappropriate age gap between Stallone's character and his on-screen love played by Jaime King. The 33-year difference may have even stopped Roger Moore in his eighties James Bond heyday.

The working relationship between Stallone and Dave Bautista was due to continue in *The Suicide Squad* but scheduling conflicts meant the role of The Peacemaker in the final film went to John Cena (and he proved to be the highlight and got spun-off into his own adult-orientated TV show).

The Suicide Squad movie of 2021 is not to be confused with the 2016 film, *Suicide Squad*. But it really is confusing and using almost the same title for a sort-of sequel to a medium-sized DC Comic book movie hit only four years before, was asking for trouble.

DC's attempts to take on Marvel was scattershot and ill conceived throughout. The year after the all-conquering first *The Avengers* film was a mega-hit in 2012, DC tried to fight back by casting British actor Henry Cavill as Superman in *Man of Steel*. While the film did decent business, viewers were taken aback by the new Clark Kent being a bit dour, miserable and basically anti-fun. In a blatant case of trying to run before you can walk, they followed up *Man of Steel* with *Batman v Superman: Dawn of Justice* where there was suddenly a new Batman (Ben Affleck) and more sour-faced, sullen despondency. The only bright spark was Gal Gadot's first appearance as Wonder Woman. The same year, David Ayer presented us with *Suicide Squad* where a gaggle of anti-hero's do heroic things by the end of the CGI-filled story which was increasingly following the DC trend of getting closer to the edge of acceptable entertainment for families. Will Smith was being dour as Deadshot, Jaret Leto was being dour and annoying as the Joker and if it wasn't for Margot Robbie's buoyant turn as Harley Quinn then *Suicide Squad* may have been the correct term for the cinema audience, not the film. The next year they hit their high point as the fully-fledged *Wonder Woman* movie was well-received by all, but they soon drifted back to their odd creative decisions which led to 2021's *The Suicide Squad*.

A sequel to the 2016 film was always on the agenda, with the likes of Mel Gibson one of the directorial options. But when Will Smith decided he didn't want to be in it and would rather slap someone at the Oscars, the whole project was turned over to James Gunn in October of 2018. Gunn was prepping Marvels' *Guardian of the Galaxy Vol. 3* and despite being fired and then re-hired on that project, he agreed to slip *The Suicide Squad* in first. In one of those decisions that may have sounded very clever in the boardroom but became an albatross around its neck upon release, Gunn's film wasn't going to be a sequel but it would be a 'reimagining' rather than a reboot or a remake. Two characters and actors from the 2016 version would reprise their roles (Margot Robbie's Harley Quinn and Joel Kinnerman's Colonel Jack Flag) and the rest would be new. Idris Elba was essentially cast as Will Smith's replacement but in hoping that Smith may return for the expected future sequels, they gave Elba a new character of Bloodsport. While this casting news was being filtered out into the world and causing many a scratched head, one announcement made perfect sense. Gunn wanted to have a CG animal character as part of the team and created King Shark who is a man-eating, half human hybrid. Stallone was the inspiration for the character as Gunn had written the part after working with him on *Guardians of the Galaxy Vol. 2*. Although Gunn admitted he voice tested other actors for the part, he was always just delaying until he got a firm yes or no from his first choice.

The finished film premiered in the UK first on July 30th 2021 and in the U.S. the week after. But as part of the Warner Bros. strategy at the time, it was also released on streaming platform HBO Max on the same day. The drastic decision by Warner Bros' to put all its major film releases of that year onto streaming at the same time as it hit cinemas, proved catastrophic for their box office returns and many filmmakers such as Christopher Nolan went to work for other studios in disgust. With an estimated budget of $168 million dollars, *The Suicide Squad* returned just $169 million in total and has been largely forgotten although John Cena's *The Peacemaker* TV series did reach two, well-received seasons. It's a bold, distinctive film that has no issue in being confusing, off the wall and plain weird at all times. It does have its entertaining moments however with Stallone's King Shark getting plenty of funny dialogue and it's certainly better than its near-namesake of 2016.

But if *The Suicide Sqaud* and *Guardians of the Galaxy Vol 2.* saw Stallone dipping his toe into modern day superhero films with small parts, he then released his first starring role in a 21st century comic-book movie, *Samaritan*. Independent graphic novel company Mythos Comics published a small series called *Samaritan* in 2014 that was created by Bragi Schut, Marc Olivent and Renzo Podesta. The premise was a gritty, realistic take on the genre where a young kid in a tough neighborhood suspects his neighbour is secretly a superhero who was believed to have died many years before. Before producing the comics, Schut had already written the screenplay which he had sold to MGM and when they pushed forward with its production, they teamed up with the newly created Balboa Productions. Stallone's new production company had been one of many such outfits that had developed *Rambo: Last Blood* but *Samaritan* was its first real announcement (in partnership with

MGM) to make a film. Australian director James Avery was coming off his critically acclaimed but low-budget war/horror movie *Overlord* in 2018. Avery had been working on writing and directing a new version of *Flash Gordon* for 20th Century Fox but the Disney buy-out of Fox in 2019 saw that project shelved. He came on board as the director of *Samaritan* and production was scheduled to start in Atlanta in early 2020. In late February they started work but the movie was shut down on the 14th of March due to the COVID pandemic. By October, protocols were in place to allow for filming to resume and they wrapped four weeks later. Avery's composers for *Overlord*, Jed Kurzel and Kevin Kiner, also provided the score for *Samaritan* and the movie was released in August 2022, nine months later than was originally planned due to the global lockdown and its ongoing effects. Costing $100 million, it went straight to streaming on Amazon Prime Video and was decently received by critics. The film is a slow burner and Stallone's rapport with his young co-star Javon Walton is a fun watch. It eventually has to turn to CGI effects and bangs and crashes but it doesn't rely on it, to its credit. But its release in 2022 meant it was already at the tail end of the dominance of superhero movies so it got a bit lost among the glut of similarly themed releases on the ever-expanding choice of streaming services. But Balboa Productions, MGM and Amazon did announce a sequel was in development and have yet to officially say otherwise.

So by the close of 2022 his more recent output had been varied to say the least. Three of his four films from 2018 to 2022 had gone straight to streaming and his only cinematic release had seen him portrayed as a walking shark. As we get closer to the present day in his story, the streaming services would be somewhere he couldn't avoid but it also presented him with a choice: he could continue with only looking for movie scripts that may or may not be of good quality and may or may not get a theatrical release, or he could turn to television and be Sylvester Stallone properly, again.

2023 - 2025 - CREED III, GUARDIANS OF THE GALAXY VOL 3, EXPEND4BLES, SLY, ARMOR, ALARUM, TULSA KING, THE FAMILY STALLONE

If this final section was going to have a tag-line then it would probably best be described as "Sylvester Stallone is very comfortable being Sylvester Stallone". In these years from 2023 up to the present day of writing, he has allowed his own life to be presented on screen more than ever before via a documentary film and a reality TV show of his personal life. But before we get to them and his successful step into dramatic TV also, there are films to discuss. The positive is he returned, albeit briefly, to his role of Stakar Orgord in the final film of the *Guardians of the Galaxy* trilogy in the MCU. It's a cameo really but it went down very well with audiences and re-ignited some calls for a spin-off entity with his Ravagers crew but again there has never been anything official to look forward to. Released in 2023 it was another monster hit, scoring as much money as its predecessor and ending the year as the fourth biggest movie in the world in the same summer that included the double-phenomenon of *Oppenheimer* and *Barbie*.

Expend4bles (that is the official spelling, it's not a typo) came out with not nearly the fanfare of the trilogy before it and it is a bit of a curiosity. It was a commercial flop, making barely half of its $100 million dollar budget back, but it is not a creative disaster in actual fact. The problem may have been that it was a fourth *Expendables* film and the audience clamour for a fourth movie in this series was non-existent to say the least. Stallone had joined in conversations publicly of a spin-off with a female-only lead cast, called *The Expendabelles*. But when that idea fell apart, it seems some of the ideas for that movie were then combined with a desire to make a more relentless fight picture along the lines of the extraordinary Jakarta-set 2011 action thriller, *The Raid*. In came a fighting-fit Megan Fox and Asian martial arts legends Tony Jaa and Iko Uwais to join the cast that saw returning stars Dolph Lundgren, Randy Couture and front and centre, Jason Statham. Curtis '50 Cent' Jackson (a Stallone friend from the *Escape Plan* films) and veteran Andy Garcia were added as well and filming took place in London, Bulgaria and Greece in 2021, but it wasn't until 2023 that the film was finally released due to the pandemic hangover and a long editing process. Stallone is of course playing his Barney Ross character again but if this was intended as a handover of the franchise from Stallone to Statham, it isn't very subtle. Ross has a bar fight scene at the start and is involved in the opening action sequence but is then off-screen for the rest of the movie until a final, epilogue appearance. Much of the movie in between takes place on a vast tanker at sea and is like watching a video game where you have to tackle various thugs and bosses before you can move up a level. The Jackie Chan Stunt Team handled much of the stunts and fight choreography and a lot of it is unexpectedly entertaining.

Had the makers retooled it purely as a Statham-vehicle and removed connections to *The Expendables* franchise, it may have ironically kickstarted a brand new franchise. Whereas one of the criticisms of the previous trilogy of *Expendables* movies had been it sometimes felt sluggish and old-fashioned to its detriment (perhaps mirroring some of its stars), this *Expend4bles* felt very brisk and pacey and the additions of Jaa, Uwais and especially this kick-ass version of Megan Fox, had dragged the series into more contemporary surroundings. As it was though, the Expendables journey came to a stuttering halt much as the *Escape Plan* series had as well. The critics were savage, if they didn't ignore the film entirely, but you got the feeling most of them had written their withering reviews before seeing it. Unlike Rocky and Rambo, audiences had sort of enjoyed *The Expendables* idea and had forgiven a lot of the dross for the sake of nostalgia, but in the end it hadn't made much of a deep impression and the life-support machines for this franchise have now been quietly switched off. But 2023 also saw Rocky's story come to a seemingly complete close in antagonistic and unpleasant circumstances.

Creed III had already been agreed between producer Irwin Winkler and star Michael B Jordan before *Creed II* was finished and released. The star wanted it to also be his directorial debut which wasn't an issue for anyone. The 2018 conversations around a third *Creed* film included Sylvester Stallone although his final touching scenes in *Creed II* meant that having Rocky appear again would have to be carefully calibrated. Possible plot lines that were considered included having Adonis Creed fight the son of Clubber Lang from *Rocky III* but since Adonis had already battled the son of another famous Rocky opponent in *Creed II*, it was quickly dropped. Then, in April of 2021 Stallone announced he was no longer a part of *Creed III* and he would not be appearing in the film. Soon he was making public his distaste for the direction that *Creed III* was to take. He said that he didn't agree with making the film dark and that his Rocky-universe was always about hope and triumph so he could no longer be a part of the franchise. Things turned ugly when Stallone took to social media to call producer Irwin Winkler a "parasite" for ruining the legacy of Rocky. Winkler had actually purchased the rights to Rocky from Stallone in the original, 1976 deal. Since then it hadn't been a bone of contention as everyone had worked closely and harmoniously together to produce *Rocky 1-6* and the first two *Creed* films. But now, things had changed. *Creed III* went into production with actor Jonathon Majors beefing up to play a childhood friend of Adonis Creed who wants some payback in the ring, in adult life. Majors would soon be ousted from Hollywood for problematic behaviour in his personal life. He was also being set up and presented as the new big bad guy in the Marvel Cinematic Universe and he was to dominate the next phase of films, but he was quickly and unceremoniously removed from further plans after being arrested for assault on his then girlfriend in 2023.

The *Creed III* film itself is an impressive directorial debut and it did well, making $276 million dollars globally but the absence of any mention of Rocky was stark. Michael B Jordan must have felt caught between a Rocky and a hard place with Stallone and Irwin Winkler and so he chose to make this third film noticeably free of any Stallone imagery. The story credits go to Zach Baylin, Ryan Coogler and his brother Keenan Coogler. Stallone's credits are a "based on characters created by" and a contractual producer mention. It's fair to suggest that *Creed III* should have been allowed to try and stand on its own two feet and not be always reliant on the legacy of the earlier films and the finished film itself departs wildly from all previous entries with its climactic bout. Whether successful or not, director Jordan demonstrated a flair for trying something new as the fight sequence is partially played out in a heightened dream state, divorced from reality. As with subsequent *Rocky* films when Talia

Shire's ever-loyal Adrian became increasingly without agency in the plots, the same could be said for Tessa Thomspon's role as Mrs Creed. She has stuff to do with some emotion at its core but it sometimes feels added-on to ensure that Thomspon (who had become a bigger star in her own right since the first *Creed* thanks to her contribution to the Marvel Cinematic Universe, especially in *Thor: Ragnarok*) didn't feel like she was a peripheral character now. But franchises often lose interest in characters that were essential in the original films. The only possible bright light at the end of the tunnel for Stallone and his most personal of characters was in late 2023 when producer Irwin Winkler confirmed a fourth *Creed* movie was in development and Michael B Jordan, who wanted to direct again, had expressed a desire to have Stallone return.

Armor and *Alarum* are both straight to streaming films where Stallone is playing second fiddle to a male lead. *Armor,* directed by Justin Routt see's Stallone leading a gang of criminals who want the gold trapped in an armored truck that's come to an unscheduled halt on a bridge. Inside the truck is security guard James Brody played by Jason Patric, with his colleague (and son) and some gold that Stallone's band of bad boys want back. It belongs in the pantheon of low budget thrillers that were never intended to be released in cinemas and to keep these budgets low, the plot has to be based mainly around one central location and the cast numbers need to be minimal. When you can achieve this, you can afford to get Sylvester Stallone to film half a dozen scenes in a couple of days. Patric made his name in the 80's vampire cult hit *The Lost Boys*, and he was going to be the next big thing in action cinema in the 90's when he was given the unenviable job of trying to follow Keanu Reeves work in *Speed* by playing the new hero/love interest opposite Sandra Bullock in *Speed 2: Cruise Control*. Although the film did make back its production cost eventually, the awful reviews put the brakes to any hope of a *Speed 3*. The result of such a disappointment is that Patric (who is a really good actor and you should watch the 2002 crime thriller *Narc* where he stars alongside Ray Liotta) had to consign himself to smaller films and roles like this in totally predictable action flicks. While Armor isn't the worst low-cost thriller ever made, it wavers drastically from half-decent to almost awful. In some of the scenes, Stallone seems a little confused as to what the director has asked him to do but there are some bits where his experience and charisma keep things chugging along.

Alarum is directed by Michael Polish and, like *Armor*, can best be described as ok. Clint Eastwood's son Scott is the lead as a spy who is married to another spy (Willa Fitzgerald) but the pair end up trapped in a small, European town with black-clad bad guys. Small cast, one main location and again, you can get a cinematic icon to hardly break a sweat for 48 hours of work. *Alarum* wants to be akin to the 2005 hit *Mr and Mrs Smith* but despite trying to give the illusion of chemistry, the two leads are no Brad Pitt and Angelina Jolie. The director and a producer give themselves supporting cast roles which rings tiny alarm bells and when you sit down and analyse Stallone's screen time, he probably could have actually filmed it all under 36 hours. However, like *Armor*, it threatens to be entertaining more than once during its runtime and the two films share more than just the same megastar. Grindstone Entertainment Group, Convergence Media Group and Bondit Media Capital are the backers of both projects and they share an aesthetic as well; they both include some uncomfortably long pauses in dialogue and many scenes go on way too long (to save on the cost of new set-ups in new locations) and they both choose to abandon practical effects in favour of digital efforts, which may well have been a budgetary issue but the results are frequently laughable. *Armor* includes a sequence near the end in the river where the water effects are so distractingly bad you can't accept that it was their best option. Any fire or explosion is poorly realised and best of all are the gun effects. Every bullet impact looks like it was designed on a ZX Spectrum 48k from 1982 and because there are no actual blank-bullets in any of the weapons, the actors have to pretend there is recoil which is something I could do better when I used a stick as a machine gun in the 70's in my back garden. Neither *Armor* or *Alarium* are really bad movies, they have a touch of amateur about them but I hope the vacation that these films paid for was thoroughly enjoyed by the Stallone clan.

Speaking of which, let's move onto the Stallone's themselves. HIs marriage to first wife Sasha came to an end when they separated on Valentine's Day in 1985. That summer he began dating the formidable Brigitte Nielsen and six months later he was married to her. Eighteen months after that, after working together on screen in *Rocky IV* and *Cobra*, they divorced and he was single and ready to mingle again. In 1997 though, he settled down properly with model Jennifer Flavin. And despite a brief relationship break, they married and produced three daughters. Sophia, Sistine and Scarlet Stallone have dragged their legendary father into the modern world ever since they could talk. The three have been celebrities since birth by virtue of their family legacy but as they crossed into adulthood they have been forging their own paths in business, design, podcasting and acting (Scarlet Stallone has a small but recurring role in her father's TV show *Tulsa King*) among other things. But in May of 2023 the powerful women in the household had ensured that a reality series of their lives would premier on TV and be called *The Family Stallone*. It follows the rhythms, structure and production techniques of established TV shows in the genre such as *Keeping Up With the Kardashians* and *The Real Housewives of* (insert affluent town name here). The clearly staged set-ups see the family at home, at dinner and sometimes at work. The focus is more on the female side of the Stallone mansion and the patriarch is portrayed as a long-suffering mediator. But during its two seasons so far, fans of the actor and cinema do get some solid gold moments. Witness Sly visiting Arnie for an impromptu Halloween pumpkin carving competition featuring the original *Rambo* knife. Watch a birthday dinner for Stallone at a restaurant where Dolph Lundgren is among the close friends invited. And see Stallone at a street pizza parlor enjoying a slice and a chat about life and ageing with pals Al Pacino and Henry Winkler. If nothing else, please enjoy the ice-breaking eccentricity of his brother Frank who has no off-switch and is happy to play the unhinged uncle role.

But the start of their own reality show was not the only non-fiction Stallone content on the small screen as Netflix released the documentary *Sly*. It's jumping-off point was the family moving from their long-time home in Los Angeles to a new start in Florida and the natural state of reminiscence that that brings. Stallone talks his way through his beginnings, visits some of his childhood locations and runs through the struggle to bring *Rocky* to the big screen alongside new interviews with the likes of Arnold Schwarzenegger and Quentin Tarantino. It's an effective, if swift (just over 90 minutes) account of his career so far. It avoids some sensitive topics, glosses over the more sensationalist aspects of his private life and should be judged as just a good gateway to all things Stallone. It's directed by Thom Zimny who has a track record of producing short videos and concert films for Bruce Springsteen. It's hard not to shake the sensation that it barely scratches the surface of one of the most remarkable careers in Hollywood history and with the current glut of documentaries being made by the streaming services (Arnie got a three-parter!) it doesn't feel as essential as you would hope. But if that small screen slice of Stallone seemed small indeed, he had already brought his big screen aura to the box with *Tulsa King*.

American writer, producer and director Taylor Sheriden has constructed his own very profitable corner of U.S. TV. Starting out as an actor he morphed into the current king of contemporary wild west television. After writing critically praised films such as *Sicario* (and its sequel), *Hell or High Water* and *Wind River* he then created the modern western TV series *Yellowstone*, headlined by a movie star who was turning to long-running TV for the first time, Kevin Costner. The enormous popularity of the 'analogue Americans in a digital world' drama saw him write, produce and regularly direct other TV hits such as *Yellowstone* spin-offs *1883* and *1923* (starring Harrison Ford and Helen Mirren no less) plus *Mayor of Kingstown*, *Lioness* and *Landman*. And in 2022, he created, and along with showrunner Terence Winter, wrote a new comedy drama series for Paramount Plus called *Tulsa King*. It was an idea that had come from Stallone originally. He'd seen the emergence of prestige television series on streamers such as Netflix and Apple TV and wondered if his long-gestating desire to play a mobster would be better suited to the smaller screen. He'd been in and around the gangster world in *F.I.S.T.*, *Oscar* and *Avenging Angelo* and his early non-speaking roles in *Capone* and *Farewell My Lovely*. He had tried to slip into *The Godfather* as an unknown actor and then as a superstar he came close to starring in and overseeing *The Godfather Part III*. A brief, casual chat with Sheriden led to the writer completing a script for a pilot episode after just 24 hours, such was Sheriden's enthusiasm for the project and more importantly, his enthusiasm to work with Sylvester Stallone. The original gangster-out-of-water concept was titled *Kansas City King* but Stallone, Winter and Sheriden immediately started knocking down some of its harder edges. Originally, the lead role was called Tony, but obvious parallels to *The Sopranos* meant he was renamed Sal and then eventually Dwight. He was to be written as a low-level player in a crime family that had been to prison for 25 years, but that too was altered and Dwight was upgraded to the nickname of 'The General' to reflect a powerful, fearsome figure with impressive standing in the organisation before his jail time. The other injection Stallone made into the concept of the show was to increase the comedic elements. Whatever the unwarranted critical appraisal of his previous stabs at comedy, he is a naturally funny human being and any interview with him will involve self-deprecation. The absurdity of a New York mafioso stuck in the second most-populated city in Oklahoma wouldn't be glossed over and so, the newly named *Tulsa King* came to fruition.

The series centers around gangster Dwight Manfredi who is released from prison after serving a quarter of a century. During his time inside he never informed on any of his crime colleagues but despite this noble act, he isn't treated well upon his release by New York's Invernizzi crime family and is sent to Tulsa to essentially keep him out of the way. The series then follows his exploits in Tulsa as an Italian American out of his comfort zone but still using his old knowhow and methods to generate money and in the course of his actions, an unlikely group of loyal friends. The viewing figures were instantly impressive as it outdid the much-anticipated *Game of Thrones* spin-off *House of the Dragon* and was the highest rated series debut on Paramount Plus for the whole year. And it's mostly easy to see why: Stallone is having an absolute ball as Dwight who is a combination of Tony from *The Sopranos*, Ray Tango from *Tango and Cash* and Sylvester Stallone himself. Never before has his own irreverent sense of humour been transferred to his work so well. He gets to have long, witty dialogue-only scenes where he and some of his new pals discuss life, past life, the future and all manner of subjects before returning to the plot of the episode at hand, often high as a kite on marijuana. Occasionally it tries to tick a box in terms of violence, especially in the final episode of season one where unfortunately it veers towards being a bit too much like *Rambo: Last Blood*. But that aside, it is a very enjoyable if uneven TV show that is well and truly built around its star turn. He is surrounded by an impressively generous cast who all understand who the main attraction is here. In a nice casting touch, Dwight's sister in the show is played by his unrequited love interest from *Cop Land*, Annabella Sciorra. Credit must also go to other regular cast members such as Jay Will, Max Casella, Martin Starr, Garrett Hedlund, Neal McDonough, Frank Grillo and Domenick Lombardozzi. After 2 seasons and 19 episodes between 2022 and 2024, the show filmed season 3 in 2025 (with Samuel L. Jackson added to the cast list) and is expected to return for at least two more seasons or as long as the ratings and the interest of its star remain high.

Aside from his executive producer role for *Tulsa King*, his 2025 initial creative output was as a writer on the Jason Statham vehicle [A Working Man](). The story was written in collaboration with [David Ayer]() and was inspired by a series of books by [Chuck Dixon](). The idea is a very thinly veiled variation of 2008's *Taken* which changed the course of Liam Neeson's career forever. *A Working Man* was set to be a TV series but it quickly got upgraded to a feature film.

And as of now, that's all we have. A new version of *Cliffhanger* was to star Stallone as Gabe Walker again, but he soon left the project just before filming began and it has since been retooled to launch former *Downton Abbey* and *Cinderella* star Lily James as an action hero alongside former 007, Pierce Brosnan. In May of 2020, Stallone declared that a follow-up to *Demolition Man* was happening with Warner Bros. but that has yet to get any further towards reality (and finding out what those three seashells actually do). There are still those persistent rumours that another *Rambo* or *Rocky* with Stallone could be greenlit at any time but in 2027 he will hit 80 years of age. When he made *Rocky Balboa* in 2006, many critics were flabbergasted that at the age of 59 he could perform on screen in such a physically demanding role. So he is now two more decades on from that. But Harrison Ford had just turned 81 when he was leaping around in his hat and jacket one last time for *Indiana Jones and the Dial of Destiny* in 2024, so who is to say that Stallone won't produce at least one more box office number one?

CONCLUSION

I would like to think that I could come back and revise and update this book in the years to come with more exciting and extraordinary tales of Stallone films and TV. But time waits for no one, not even the most enduring film star of modern cinema. In 2026 there will certainly be some spotlight back on him as it is the 50th anniversary of *Rocky*. As someone who has well crossed the line of middle age myself, you have to marvel at what Sylvester Stallone achieved in that time and he only really got going after he was 30. As described, I discovered and became a lifelong devotee of his work as an impressionable young teenager on a family holiday thanks to the last ten minutes of *Rocky III*. I remember being aghast and wondering what had just happened as Survivors' *Eye of the Tiger* played over the end credits. Since then I have felt compelled to see what he had for me next. And as I started to want to learn more about his career I quickly realised that his career was incomparable. Despite plenty of column inches in newspapers and magazines to the contrary, in actual fact his struggle for dominance with Arnold Schwarzenegger only really lasted a couple of years. The main battle ground ended up being 1993 and Stallone convincingly claimed victory with his *Cliffhanger* and *Demolition Man* winners compared to Arnie's underwhelming *Last Action Hero*, after which the Austrian's film career never hit those dizzying heights again.

His fellow Planet Hollywood investor Bruce Willis had apparently ended Stallone's career and everyone else who considered themselves an action hero in 1987 when *Die Hard* changed the perception of masculinity on the silver screen. But Stallone was still headlining major studio releases up until the start of the 2020's, while the output of Bruce Willis became exasperatingly uninspired. But the reason for Willis's output decline in standards became clear when he had to officially retire from the business after being diagnosed with frontotemporal dementia, robbing him of his power of communication. The desperately sad end to his brilliant career meant that the last significant cinematic appearance of both Bruce Willis and Arnold Schwarzenegger could be argued was in *The Expendables 2*, thanks to you-know-who.

The aforementioned Harrison Ford is in many ways, the closest thing to Stallone. Both have been consistent, both have two iconic characters and both are still working into their 80's. But Ford's biggest successes have been similar. Aside from the *Indiana Jones* and *Star Wars* turns, think about some of his other big hits: *The Fugitive, Air Force One, Blade Runner,* the Jack Ryan movies *Patriot Games* and *Clear and Present Danger* and even his turn in *The Expendables 3* - he is still Harrison Ford. A bit grumpy, very serious about his purpose and relentless until he achieves his goal. Don't get me wrong, Ford is brilliant and one of the all-time greats, but you know what you'll get with a Harrison Ford hit. My own personal favourite is the largely forgotten 1978 World War II film, *Force 10 From Navarone*. The enjoyable boys-own adventure has an extraordinary cast - Harrison Ford, Robert Shaw (Quint from *Jaws*), James Fox (The Jackal from *Day of the Jackal*) and our very own Apollo Creed himself, Carl Weathers. Not to mention it has Bond girl Barbara Bach (Mrs Ringo Starr to you) and another Jaws in the form of the classic Bond villain played by Richard Kiel.

Sylvester Stallone's path to cinematic success has never been repeated. Actors have pushed themselves into good roles in good films and writers have had breakthroughs with scripts that mean a lot to them. But no one has the story behind the story that he had. It's a film legacy that will entertain, enthrall and excite generations to come from a writer, director, producer and actor that has been much imitated but never matched.

Legacy is a word Hollywood is embracing more than ever as it constantly tries to recapture past glories and past box office numbers. Some belated sequels work brilliantly (*Top Gun: Maverick, Bad Boys For Life, Star Wars: The Force Awakens, Blade Runner 2049* and *Mad Max: Fury Road*) and some are as poor as they were always going to be (*The Matrix: Resurrections* and *Independence Day: Resurgence*) but Stallone proved that if given full creative control, he could keep everyone happy time and time again. And the legacy of his two most famous roles continues to ripple through the industry. A movie based in the world of sports before 1976 was very different to one made after the original *Rocky* came out. An infinite number of projects tried to copy the *Rocky* magic, from *Tin Cup* and *Major League* to *Eddie the Eagle* and *Bend it Like Beckham* and from *Wimbledon* and *A League of Their Own* to *Cool Runnings* and *Friday Night Lights*, the locations and sports may be different but the methodology was always to "give me that *Rocky* feeling".

The Karate Kid (and its subsequent sequels) and the fabulously enjoyable *Cobra Kai* TV show all stemmed from a desire to create a *Rocky* for younger viewers. The original 1984 film used the same director as *Rocky* (John G. Avildsen) to get it as close in tone as possible. They even swapped soundtrack songs at the last moment with *Eye Of The Tiger* momentarily destined to be the theme for *The Karate Kid* while *You're the Best* by Joe Esposito was headed for *Rocky III*. The right decision was made thankfully. The open affection and imitation of *Rocky* in the *Karate Kid* universe is front and centre thanks to the beaten fighter at the end of original *Karate Kid*, Johnny Lawrence (William Zabka). His characters' subsequent unfulfilled promise after receiving that famous crane-kick in the face in 1984 is the central premise of Netflix's *Cobra Kai*. As played excellently by Zabka, the Lawrence character is forever referencing *Rocky* and the series creators, Josh Heald, Jon Hurwitz, Hayden Schlossberg love to put *Rocky* easter eggs in the script or on screen somehow. The most blatant homage being in the final season of *Cobra Kai* where Lawrence and the Karate Kid (now adult) himself Daniel Larusso (Ralph Macchio) go for a training run and are followed by hundreds of kids (as in *Rocky II*).

Perhaps the ultimate show of love and affection is the forthcoming movie *I Play Rocky* written by Peter Gamble and directed by Peter Farrelly who's previous credits include the run of hit comedies with his brother Bobby such as *Dumb and Dumber, Shallow Hal and There's Something About Mary,* and his solo directed Oscar winner in 2018, *Green Book*. The film will focus on those extraordinary negotiations between a penniless and homeless Stallone and the studio who wanted *Rocky* but didn't want him to star in it and then the gruelling, low budget making of the future blockbuster itself. Anthony Ippolito has been given the unenviable task of playing Sylvester Stallone in *I Play Rocky* after already portraying a young Al Pacino onscreen in the Paramount Plus limited series *The Offer*, about the remarkable process that it took to bring *The Godfather* to the big screen in the early 70's (a film that a very young Stallone tried and failed to be an extra on).

Rocky Balboa has even tread the boards in theatre. Hamburg, Prague and Broadway have staged *Rocky - The Musical*. Hamburg opened the show in 2012 which opened in New York two years later (and closed six months after that). Despite early reports that Sir Elton John was going to be involved, the new music was written by Stephen Flaherty with lyrics from Lynn Ahrens and there was a new book co-written by Thomas Meehan and Stallone to accompany it. 20 original songs featured in *Rocky - The Musical* alongside *Eye of the Tiger* and *Gonna Fly Now* (there was no room for Frank Stallone's *Take You Back* in the show or cast recording).

In 2023, the City of Philadelphia held its first 'RockyFest' where a week of Rocky-related tours, screenings, competitions and events were held and attended by hundreds of thousands of fans. Many of whom flew thousands of miles to be a part of the Rocky collective. It was so successful that it happened again in 2024 and Stallone himself was at both.

For Rambo, the ripples are possibly even bigger. The character still represents, for some the best and for many the worst of, masculinity. Did he advance the emotional maturity of half the world's population or did he set it back another couple of decades? The movie careers of not only Arnold Schwarzenegger and Bruce Willis, but also Jean-Claude Van Damme, Steven Seagal, Mel Gibson, Chuck Norris, Dwayne 'The Rock' Johnson, Jason Statham, Chris Hemsworth, Vin Diesel, Wesley Snipes and Dolph Lundgren are just some that can be traced back to the pioneering style of Stallone. The action movies that starred Nicolas Cage, Kurt Russell, Liam Neeson, Denzel Washington and Angelina Jolie plus Ellen Ripley's (Sigourney Weaver) struggles in the *Alien* films, would not have been made had Stallone not carved out the imposing, lone hero narrative so indelibly to modern audiences. The tough guys pre-*Rambo* were motivation-less and consequence-free. John Wayne, Clint Eastwood, Charles Bronson, Yul Brynner, Lee Marvin and the rest killed the bad guys and got the girl with no regret, remorse or PTSD to cloud their reasons. Good guys shot bad guys and no questions were asked. As the opening titles are still running on *First Blood*, it's clear our main character has issues they are dealing with and he does not have life all figured out. The shirtless, headbanded, gun carrying image from that legendary poster for *Rambo: First Blood Part II* adorned a million bedroom walls. Some stared at it in admiration, some stared at it for motivation, some dreamed of being him and many dreamed of dating him but the image spawned a million more fancy dress costumes, bad impressions and mis-quotes. The often shouted "Don't push me!" that accompanies a Rambo impression is never said in any of the five films.

In May of 1985, *Rambo: First Blood Part II* became part of the culture but then the following October, Schwarzenegger released his attempted carbon-copy, *Commando*. While the movie is fondly regarded and is a fun Arnie actioner, the influence is not hidden at all. He has a ridiculously good physique considering the lifestyle we are led to believe he leads, he takes his shirt off and straps a big machine gun over his shoulder whilst in combat trousers and boots and proceeds to slice through a coach-load of stuntmen with ever-increasing sizes of weaponry. In the years since, Arnie has joked how the production team of *Commando* kept checking the most recent Rambo hit to make sure their guns were bigger and their explosions were more destructive.

At some point, maybe even as you have discovered and are reading this book, a movie executive somewhere will think they have cracked the code to rebirth and restart Rocky or Rambo. Stallone himself posted script ideas for a TV series called *Rocky* in 2021. On his social media, he showed his scribbled early notes for a Rocky prequel show consisting of 10 episodes. Set in the 1960's it would see a 17-year old Robert Balboa struggling to get by in a breathless era of moon landings, civil rights movements, sexual revolutions and the cold war. The post garnered a lot of global media attention but to date, it remains just a series of handwritten ideas. The *Creed* series of films will certainly be returned to by Michael B Jordan over the course of his career, which will then always inflame the desire to see Rocky Balboa on a screen again, in some capacity. The idea of the character not being played by Sylvester Stallone seems unthinkable but it is inevitable. Billions of dollars in revenue tells us that. Will it be good? Impossible to judge but I for one, would watch it and judge for myself. They said Sean Connery could never be replaced as James Bond, after all.

Rambo though, will definitely return without Stallone. *Rambo: Last Blood* may have unsatisfactorily capped Stallone's incarnation of the Vietnam veteran, but instantly recognisable IP (Intellectual Property) is the cocaine of modern Hollywood. Reboots, remakes, reimaginings - call them what you will but a name and character and image as globally familiar as 'Rambo', was not going to be left on his porch rocking chair for long. In 2027, there is due to be a new film titled *John Rambo*. At time of writing it was to be directed by Jalmari Helander who made the 2022 Finnish movie *Sisu*, which was compared to a Rambo film upon release. Miami-born actor Noah Centineo is attached to play the titular role in his younger days during the Vietnam War. Centineo had roles in *Charlie's*

Angels and *Black Adam* and the Netflix series *To All The Boys I've Loved Before.* But perhaps his part of the military ensemble in Alex Garland's true-life Iraq war film *Warfare* in 2025 sealed the deal. If it does hit cinema screens, it is obviously the first time Rambo has been played by anyone but Stallone.

But don't anticipate it to feel like the Rambo of old. Never again will movies with such gleeful violent extravagance as *Rambo: First Blood Part II* and *Rambo III* be greenlit and released as a tentpole cinematic event. The world has moved on from pure escapism in that vein. The realities of conflict and war can no longer be ignored in favour of a few hours of entertainment on a cinema screen. The difficult questions over PTSD posed by *First Blood* are more likely to be acceptable to social media warriors who can't separate film from reality and so we shouldn't expect any guilt-free Rambo adventures in the future. The next Rambo story will have to put self-reflection and therapy front and centre. The bus loads of stunt people ready to fall down in front of one actor are gone, whether you see that as a positive or negative.

But, his two most famous characters aside, Sylvester Stallone altered the movie business and constantly rewrote the rules. His battle of wills in 1976 gave hope to thousands of writers, actors, directors and producers who previously felt they had to sell their souls for a shot at the big time. By sticking to his gut feeling and self-belief, he forged a new path that has helped allow the likes of Quentin Tarantino, Christopher Nolan and Paul Thomas Anderson to make films on their own terms. I won't name names, but actors who have 'unconventional' movie star looks are now rife on the big screen. Stallone's unique appearance made it ok to not look like everyone else in movies. Perfect physical symmetry and a crystal clear voice suddenly wasn't as important as the studio's thought it was.

And then there's the longevity. 1976 was a long time ago. *Rocky* was released before anyone had heard the name *Star Wars*. Marvel was still only a published product and the word 'franchise' was only hinted at because a sequel to *Jaws* was still two years away. As *Rocky* turns 50 in 2026, think of the legacy that its creator has built. So many times his career was deemed finished and so many times he proved them wrong. The starring roles in big box office juggernauts may be behind him now but the surname still carries heft. If TV has surpassed film as the current visual medium of choice, he's conquered that as well with *Tulsa King*. Every apparent barrier in front of him has been crossed. He's an object lesson in perseverance and hard work. It could be argued that anyone with the will could do the same, but I'd counter argue that they'd need to have the talent as well. Stallone writes, he acts, he directs and he produces. He is a creative force that doesn't have to rely on other people for his successes or failures. Yes he collaborates of course but when push comes to shove, he can retreat into his own notebook and pen and come up with something that fits him like a boxing glove.

But as he enjoys the fruits of his labours with a loving family in his twilight years, we shouldn't expect much more. He dragged himself out of poverty and now he should be allowed to rest on his opulent laurels half a century later. His three impressive daughters are forging their individual paths and despite nepotism undoubtedly playing a part, they have to battle their surname as much as they can use it. He did everything that could be done in the industry and went further. At the peak of his stardom, he was the most photographed human in the world alongside Princess Diana. The cult of paparazzi exploded as he became a phenomenon and there was nothing he could do that wasn't captured, published, recorded and dissected. While those dirty days of morality free journalism are to a certain extent behind us, he still can't walk down a single street without a phone camera recording him or being asked to put his clenched fist to a fan's jaw for a photo. But he never says no, he never turns a fan away and he always tries to give them the moment they hoped for. He understands his legendary status and what it means now and what it has meant for half a century.

I hope there's more to come as Stallone always seems to have one more punch in him. But I'm realistic and maybe the timing of this book reflects that. I'll leave the last word to an ageing, fictional boxer who is told once again that he won't be able to achieve his goal. His reply sums up the extraordinary career of Sylvester Stallone:

"It ain't over till it's over."

ABOUT THE AUTHOR

This is the first published book by Graham Clews. For the last two decades, Graham has been one of the most well known and respected broadcasters working in the English language in the Gulf region. Born and raised in Watford in England he relocated to the UAE in 2002 and has been presenting on TV for two decades. As sports anchor for Dubai One TV he has secured exclusive interviews with everyone from Tiger Woods to David Beckham and Roger Federer to Donald Trump.

Graham also hosts Abu Dhabi Sports english-language coverage of the ADNOC Pro League and other major sporting events on TV. He has also presented live TV for Sky Sports, ITV Sport and Fox Sports US including multiple live broadcasts for the Professional Darts Corporation in Dubai, China, Germany and Las Vegas.

A regular radio presenter and writer for local publications, Graham has also chaired, emceed and moderated countless events around the country. His family also have a huge legacy in TV in the UK, with BAFTA'S and other awards for acting, directing and producing on the family bookshelves.

Graham is married to Sascha and has two daughters, Katie and Emma.

www.ingramcontent.com/pod-product-compliance
Lightning Source LLC
Chambersburg PA
CBHW051645040426
42446CB00009B/991